THE TRIUMPH
OF THE SOUL

THE TRIUMPH OF THE SOUL

Cultural and Psychological Aspects of African American Music

*Edited by Ferdinand Jones
and Arthur C. Jones*

PRAEGER

Westport, Connecticut
London

Library of Congress Cataloging-in-Publication Data

The triumph of the soul : cultural and psychological aspects of African American music /
edited by Ferdinand Jones and Arthur C. Jones.
    p. cm.
   Includes bibliographical references and index.
   ISBN 0–275–95365–3 (alk. paper)
   1. Afro-Americans—Music—History and criticism. 2. Music—United
States—Psychological aspects. 3. Popular culture—United States. I. Jones, Ferdinand,
1932– II. Jones, Arthur C.
ML3556.T75   2001
780'.89'96073—dc21   00–039200

British Library Cataloguing in Publication Data is available.

Library of Congress Catalog Card Number: 00–039200
ISBN: 0–275–95365–3

First published in 2001

Praeger Publishers, 88 Post Road West, Westport, CT 06881
An imprint of Greenwood Publishing Group, Inc.
www.praeger.com

Printed in the United States of America

The paper used in this book complies with the
Permanent Paper Standard issued by the National
Information Standards Organization (Z39.48–1984).

10 9 8 7 6 5 4 3 2

We dedicate this book in gratitude to our parents, Ferdinand Taylor Jones and Esther Lillian Harris Haggie Jones. Their consistent and never-ending love for all their children grounded us in the essentials of self-confidence, guides all our relationships, and supports our attempts to honor life's callings.

Contents

Acknowledgments

Our first discussions about this project occurred when the family was gathered at the funeral of yet another beloved one of our parents' siblings, the Reverend Lois J. Anderson. The realization that we and our sisters and first cousins had become the elder generation in the family was sobering. But we all felt closer to one another, in the way that such events highlight continuity. We did not then set out to consciously transmit these feelings of relatedness to our ongoing scholarship in psychology and African American music. Looking back, though, we are aware of the natural inspiration of family connection—in its immediate and historical sense—with the passion of our research interests. We must therefore first pay tribute to the long line of forebears whose dignified day to day efforts to persevere for themselves and their children permit us today the confidence and ability to teach, to study, to consult, to sing (in Art's case) and to write books. Those visceral bonds infused this brotherly collaboration with respect and affection.

Ferd gives special thanks to Myra R. Jones for her skilled assistance and her support throughout the project. She edited chapters, made numerous constructive suggestions, and performed innumerable helpful tasks. He also thanks Katherine Cox, a dear friend, who is a steady source of information and wisdom about the jazz community. Adelbert H. Jenkins read a draft of Ferd's chapter and prompted changes that greatly improved it. The Schomburg Center for Research in Black Culture provided material and expert staff assistance to Ferd when he did research there on jazz and African American culture as a Scholar-in-Residence in 1987. Many jazz musicians and other members of the jazz community gave him information, advice, and encouragement in his ongoing investigations. He cannot thank them enough.

Art gives many thanks to Christine Chao who gave him major feedback and helpful suggestions on his chapter and provided ongoing support throughout the life of this project. His faculty colleagues Sandra Dixon, Larry Graham, Nancy Hansen, Joretta Marshall, and all the students in the Iliff School of Theology/University of Denver Joint Ph.D. Program in Religion and Psychology Colloquium in the 1996 Winter Quarter also read his chapter and provided useful feedback. Art also expresses gratitude to Vincent Hardy for his ongoing support, friendship, and informal mentoring.

Michelle Ross artfully shouldered the word processing and assembling of all the parts of the manuscript. Thank you, Michelle!

Our thanks also goes to Margaret M. Maybury at the Greenwood Publishing Group for her faith in the project and her hard work in its achievement.

Marc Crawford, professor of writing and jazz appreciation at New York University, was to author a chapter for this volume. He became ill and passed away before he could complete it. The editors are grateful for his enthusiasm for this project. Though we miss his written contribution, we benefited greatly from his support and guidance.

Working with all the chapter authors created a sense of special connection too. We were united in believing there needed to be more of these kinds of analyses of African American music than existed. We agreed on the fundamental thesis that we were all writing interpretations of different forms of the same music. The common bond of wanting to explicate the *truth* of African American reality as it can be heard in music inspired their best efforts and permeated our communications with them. We very much appreciate the opportunity to conduct our project with this distinguished group of scholars.

Introduction

Ferdinand Jones and Arthur C. Jones

"Black music then, is not an artistic creation for its own sake; rather it tells about the feelings and thinking of African people, and the kinds of mental adjustments they had to make in order to survive in an alien land."[1]

—James H. Cone

"But the ancient tones are meeting, trysting with each other in this strange land. And we know they are becoming a new tone, a new song, new colors, new dances, breaking out beyond the safe boundaries of all we have known and heard and felt and hoped and danced before. New Tone, new time."[2]

—Vincent Harding

Culture is an essential human invention because it organizes our otherwise chaotic existence into a coherent totality. Culture helps us to feel in control of our reality rather than overwhelmed by it. Specific cultures can therefore be studied to understand just how they work to maintain the psychological equilibrium of their members. The purpose of this volume is to examine African American music, one aspect of African American culture, for what it can inform us of the subjective processes that have fostered African Americans' personal stability over the course of their oppressive circumstances in North America.

Within the conception of culture, as it is being employed here, is the important observation that humans universally possess the capacity to adapt significant aspects of their environment to their own needs. Even though they may suffer adversity, they need not lose this ability.

The adaptive potential of the species, certainly observable in African Americans, is a crucial element in the individual person's sense of esteem. If you can think, perceive, or act in some ways on your own behalf, you do not feel controlled by other persons or by life's circumstances. Culture indicates the means for retaining one's self-esteem as it also determines the shape of early child-rearing that is the foundation of self-esteem. Music, a seminal cultural product, represents the resilience modes of black Americans both concretely and symbolically.

African American music also indicates the distinctive features of the cultural identity of African Americans. Over several generations of transplanted Africans and their descendants, a new musical genre evolved with varied yet interrelated components. It grew out of a synthesis of the religious, popular, and folk music of the dominant culture and the people's memories of West African music. African Americans as a cultural group are a similar blend made up of actual remnants of African language and customs, African philosophical outlooks and general sensibilities, and language, customs, and sentiments in North America that were derived from Europe. African Americans' modes of thinking, feeling, and expressing therefore represent the entirety of their experience in North America—as captives from ancient cultures making life-preserving adaptations to generations-long subjugation.

African American music, like all art forms, has the capacity to represent the entire range of human expression. Its aggregate of structures, techniques, and traditions is a unique crystallization of African plus North American values, customs, and styles.

While our focus is solely on the music that African Americans evolved, we are aware that parallel analyses can be made of other facets of black American culture. Indeed, in illuminating their respective theses, our chapter authors refer liberally and logically to such studies in sociology, philosophy, linguistics, graphic art, dance, religion, folklore, history, and literature. However, it should also be clear that music occupies an especially salient place in African American culture. Because it is so central, black music provides a uniquely fertile opportunity to understand and illuminate core features of the culture.

AFRICAN AMERICANS' COMPETENCE

The fact of African American humanity and agency asserted here has not always been accepted by American psychology. Indeed, up until the last two decades, and despite its ambition of scientific objectivity, psychology has exhibited the same distorted perceptions of black Americans that prevailed in the lay mind. Numerous theories and studies in the history of the psychology, from its earliest beginnings as a discipline at the start of the twentieth century until the Civil Rights era, supported the myth that people of African descent reacted to life's circumstances less adequately than people of European descent. Psychology's failure for so long to correct that error attests to the white supremacy myth's enormous strength. Wittingly or unconsciously, it biased psychology's earlier theorists and researchers. The potency of the white supremacy illusion is still evident in present-day "scientific" studies that unjustifiably contend that African Americans are somehow constitutionally incapable of achieving standards set by the dominant society for intellectual achievement and behavioral correctness. These mistaken conclusions endure despite psychology's increasing understanding of the complex determinants of human potentials.[3]

Academics from other disciplines, such as historians, sociologists, biologists, economists, and anthropologists, joined psychologists in doubting the fullness of African Americans' humanity, whether denying the possibility that intact African cultural behaviors could survive the capture-enslavement-transport-relocation process[4] or overlooking the power of individual memory[5] or misunderstanding the creative potential of individuals' adaptation to trauma.[6]

The weight of such scholarship was coupled with the authority of religion to authenticate the white supremacy myth, especially in the early years of the African presence in North America. Whereas science documented Africans' lower position in the hierarchy of living creatures, religion stressed their moral shortcomings. Africans were heathens who needed the guidance of "advanced" civilization.[7]

In the paradoxical judgment of some scholars, if African slaves in the brutality and comprehensiveness of the enslavement process were stripped of all that supports and nourishes the development and maintenance of a positive sense of self, then slavery was justified. Slaves required their masters to provide them with basic physical needs and moral guidance. After emancipation, other writers reasoned that ex-slaves were incapable of taking care of themselves because of generations of bondage. There was no other explanation needed then, other than their own deficiencies, for their constant poverty and hard times. If blacks remained in their socially negative circumstances for years after emancipation, it indicated to other investigators that they were *inherently* unable to rise above these circumstances. Others asked: Weren't their enslaved ancestors the least capable anyway for having been the captured rather than the avoidant or escaped Africans? Would it not be logical that African Americans are therefore descendants of an inferior class of an inferior race? Would not their self-esteem be understandably weak because of this combination of genetics, history and psychological consequences? If blacks' self-esteem was and is precarious, would not that prevent any truly independent productivity or creativity from them?[8]

Primitive, captive, broken, infantilized, undeveloped, self-hating were all the bases of African American's predilection to mental instability as well as their mental inferiority, according to the traditional academic discourse. This explained their higher incidence of social disorganization and psychological breakdown. No wonder their comparatively poor performances on measures of intelligence and academic achievement. The more generous scholars were sympathetic to the injustice of this consequential reality but nonetheless convinced of it. Others were impressed that Africans everywhere in the diaspora were intrinsically destined to be in such lamentable circumstances because they were essentially ill-equipped for the modern world.

These biased observations and spurious questions must be completely inverted in view of the enormous demonstration of creativity that is African American music. It guides us to reason in a direction very different from the race-illusioned scholars.

Since African Americans created such monumentally impressive art forms, must not their existence be evidence of their positive self-esteem? If they have formed such positive self-esteem, then it must indicate that substantial numbers of black individuals develop in supportive, loving environments. Further, it must be a fact that constructive processes were operative all along in their history in North America. Therefore, African Americans must not have been totally crushed by slavery. Their artistic creativity demonstrates so many references to West African culture that those cultural elements must possess impressively enduring qualities. They must therefore shed light on the vitality of the ancient African cultures in which they originated. And very different conclusions obviously need to be drawn about the sociology and psychology of those who were captured and traded in the Atlantic slave industry, as well as about the traders and slaveholders themselves.

A lack of understanding of the African American aspects of these psychological and cultural dynamics blunted the full appreciation for how psychologically resourceful black Americans are, as well as how much American culture is infused with African American style. The intellectual accompaniment to the Civil Rights movement was the illumination of blind spots in the academic view of African Americans. Scholarly inquiry into the psychology of African Americans was led in the last three decades by black and enlightened white psychologists.[9] However, psychologists—black and white—have been remarkably silent on the issue of African American music and its reflection of, and impact on, psychological and cultural processes. This has been true in spite of the widespread acknowledgments of the importance of oral communication among African peoples. From a variety of perspectives, it is therefore puzzling that there has been so little written about and so little research done on the subject of black music by psychologists, since the music is one of the most important manifestations of the African American oral tradition.

This all said, there *have* been scholars from several other academic disciplines who have long understood the cultural and psychological power of black music. The current volume represents one of the first attempts to bring together, under the cover of one book, insights and observations about black music by a multidisciplinary team of writers, representing the fields of psychology, ethnomusicology, anthropology, cultural studies, and music performance. We are hoping that the striking interpretive richness of these writings will encourage other scholars to explore the significant cultural and psychological dimensions of the music that black Americans continue to create, perform, and cherish. From our perspective, it is important for all of us—scholars and laypersons alike—to understand the varied ways in which this music supports, nurtures, and makes possible, again and again, the triumph of the soul. Such an understanding helps all of us to appreciate the remarkable infinite potential of the human spirit that is uncovered in an examination of the artistic creativity of people from one particular cultural tradition who are, above all else, anchored in their humanity.

We asked all our contributors to attend to a specific task. We shared with them our belief that the varied expressions of black American music—spirituals, blues, gospel, jazz, hip-hop, and other music—represents different branches of one cultural and psychological tree rather than completely separate cultural forms. We asked them, in each of their chapters, to respond to this thesis. Our contributors did in fact agree with our general frame of reference, but not without providing important and necessary commentary concerning the numerous and very specific ways in which they see each branch of the tree contributing to the health and growth of the entire tree.

We have learned a great deal from our contributors' insights and observations. Even more than we anticipated, these writings have enriched and expanded our own vision as we have continued in our attempts to understand and teach about the richly textured cultural and psychological matrix reflected in African American music. We hope that our readers will be as pleased and enlightened as we have been.

NOTES

1. J. H. Cone, *The Spirituals and the Blues: An Interpretation* (New York: Seabury, 1972, 109).

2. From a verbal accompaniment to an Ornette Coleman and Co. performance, San Francisco Jazz Festival, November 12, 1994.

3. For examples of current discussions of this issue see E. W. Gordon, "Putting Them in Their Place," *Readings: A Journal of Reviews and Commentary in Mental Health* 1 (October 1995):8–14 and "The Bell Curve Controversy," *Focus* 2 (September 1995):2–16.

4. S. Elkins, *Slavery: A Problem in American Institutional and Intellectual Life* (Chicago: University of Chicago Press, 1959).

5. G. N. Grob, *Mental Illness and American Society*, 1875–1940 (Princeton: Princeton University Press, 1983).

6. T. Thomas & S. Sillen, *Racism and Psychiatry* (New York: Brunner/Mazel, 1972).

7. J. Kovel, *White Racism: A Psychohistory* (New York: Vintage, 1971).

8. Grob, *Mental Illness*.

9. See for example, L. W. Levine, *Black Culture and Black Consciousness: Afro-American Folk Thought From Slavery to Freedom* (New York: Oxford University Press, 1977); A. H. Jenkins, *Psychology and African Americans: A Humanistic Approach* (Boston: Allyn and Bacon, 1995).

Prologue

Michael S. Harper

Effendi

The piano hums
again the clear
story of our coming,
enchained, severed,
our tongues gone,
herds the quiet
musings of ten million
years blackening the earth
with blood and our moon women,
children we loved,
the jungle swept up
in our rhapsodic song
giving back
banana leaves and
the incessant beating
of our tom-tom hearts.
We have sung a long time here
with the cross and the cotton field.
Those white faces turned
away from their mythical
beginnings are no art
but that of violence—
the kiss of death.
Somewhere on the inside

of those faces
are the real muscles
of the world;
in the ones strengthened
in experience and pain,
the ones wished for in one's lover
or in the mirror
near the eyes
that record this lost, dogged data
and is pure, new, even lovely
and is you.

1

Upon This Rock: The Foundational Influence of the Spirituals

Arthur C. Jones

The spirituals are, in essence, the religious folk songs created by the African peoples who were enslaved in North America in the seventeenth, eighteenth, and nineteenth centuries. Although it is impossible to determine when the songs first appeared, some scholars have conjectured that the most prolific period of composition was the time period beginning in the last half of the eighteenth century and continuing until the end of legalized slavery in the mid-nineteenth century.[1]

Ever since the end of official slavery, the African American community has maintained a somewhat ambivalent relationship with the spirituals tradition, in spite of the unequivocally positive impact of that tradition on the course of African American (and American) history. On the one hand, the post–Civil War world travels of the Fisk Jubilee Singers (followed by a number of other black college touring choirs) brought the unique sounds and messages of the spirituals to the attention of large international audiences.[2] Subsequently, in the first half of the twentieth century, the spirituals became part of the repertoire of such renowned concert artists as Roland Hayes, Marian Anderson, and Paul Robeson. In addition, the spirituals became an integral part of weekly worship services in African American Protestant denominational churches. All these developments reflected a widespread interest in and respect for slave songs, continuing long after the Emancipation Proclamation.[3]

On the other hand, the deeper meanings of the spirituals were often missed, even by appreciative audiences. In addition, there were doubts about the true value of the music. Moreover, there were many who felt that the spirituals reflected a shameful history that would best be forgotten. As early as 1903, the African American sociologist W. E. B. DuBois noted that the "Negro folksong . . . has been neglected, it has been, and is, half despised, and above all it has been persistently mistaken and misunderstood." DuBois saw the situation as tragic, since, in his opinion, the spirituals represented "not simply the sole American music, but . . . the most beautiful expression of human experience born this side of the seas."[4] DuBois also lamented the failure of many Americans, black and white, to appreciate the depth of meaning and history embodied in the spirituals.

The collective devaluation of the spirituals that DuBois observed has continued on some level throughout the twentieth century. For a long time, this pejorative view was balanced by the considerable respect paid to the spirituals tradition in a large number of community contexts, both within the United States and abroad.[5] In recent years, however, the situation has turned more one-sidedly negative. Interest in the spirituals, both in and outside the African American community, may have reached an all-time low.[6] Paralleling this trend is a surprisingly widespread lack of knowledge of the historical origins of these songs. For example, the spirituals are often confused with twentieth-century black gospel music. This confusion may stem in part from the strong functional and musical similarities that do in fact exist among the various historical expressions of African American sacred music. Frequently, however, the confusion reveals an ignorance of the historical contiguity of the spirituals and slavery. Among those who do understand correctly that the spirituals originated in slavery, there is often only a surface knowledge of the complex underlying history. In addition, slave songs still evoke feelings of shame and embarrassment.

In a landmark study, John Lovell, Jr., continuing the commentary begun by DuBois seventy years earlier, addressed at great length the ambivalence toward the spirituals that had persisted for several decades. He commented, for example, that those who continue to view the spirituals as "a religious cry of slavish people . . . are not well acquainted with the slaves who produced them, men and women of considerable self-respect and courage." Furthermore, Lovell noted, even so-called lovers of the spirituals "are not well acquainted with the deep underlying meanings of individual songs, and certainly not familiar with the powerful meanings of a number of songs on the same subject taken together."[7] Lovell hoped that his comprehensive study would help to correct such distortions and misunderstandings, and that the spirituals would be restored, once and for all, to their rightfully respected place in the culture.

Several scholars, from a variety of academic disciplines, have added their voices to the DuBois/Lovell legacy, hoping to correct permanently the confusions that have, enigmatically, persisted.[8] Nevertheless, Lovell's hope that, finally, the spirituals tradition would be understood and respected on a mass level has yet to be realized. Ingrained misunderstandings die very slowly. The current chapter therefore offers an opportunity to contribute to a more accurate and complete understanding of this significant part of African American culture.

What follows is a cultural profile of the spirituals within the broader context of their functional relationship with other, historically later, African American music forms. Such a profile serves two purposes: It provides a corrective view of the historical and contemporary functions of the spirituals, *and* it illuminates core cultural and psychological features of all African American music.

I will weave my discussion around three essential elements of the African (and, later, African American) cultures from which the creators of the spirituals descended. These elements are *spirit, community*, and *music*. This structural scheme will provide a framework within which the functional impact of the spirituals, historically and in recent times, can be discussed. In the section on music, I also will attempt to draw attention to the controversial issue of the extent to which the proliferation of "arranged" spirituals has compromised the cultural integrity of the music. At the end of the chapter, I will offer my views on some of the factors that have contributed to the protracted feelings of ambivalence concerning slave songs, especially within the African American community. I believe that an understanding of this issue can help us envision an enhanced role for music as a continuing source of community empowerment, particularly if that empowerment is built, in African fashion, on the shoulders of the ancestors.

SPIRIT

African Americans have always been a deeply spiritual people. This honoring of the spirits is rooted historically in the similarly prominent role of sacred belief systems in virtually all the western and central African tribal cultures from which North American slaves were captured.[9] It is therefore no accident that the first substantial body of music to be created by newly enslaved Africans in North America contained salient spiritual themes. These themes were the products of a syncretistic merging of core African religious beliefs with the distinctively Africanized Christianity that evolved gradually in the North American slave community.[10]

Understanding the African roots of the spirituals helps to dismiss the notion that the music of slavery was first and foremost a *reactive* music. There is no question that slaves employed music effectively in their attempts to transcend the psychological and spiritual horrors of inhuman bondage. However, this use of music was an improvisational employment of an already essential part of the culture. The spirituals, in other words, were not created solely for the purpose of enduring the suffering imposed by slavery. Rather, these songs were a natural extension of long-established African traditions of music created for worship and spiritual affirmation. Their use

as an aid in coping with psychological trauma was a secondary development.[11]

The theology expressed in the spirituals is in many ways a creative blend
of the best of African traditional religions and European-American Christianity. A significant piece of the African influence is the integration of
spirituality into all aspects of everyday life. Theologian Peter Paris offers
one of the best descriptions available of African spirituality: "The 'spirituality' of a people refers to the animating and integrative power that
constitutes the principal frame of meaning for individual and collective
experiences. Metaphorically, the spirituality of a people is synonymous
with the soul of a people: the integrating center of their power and meaning. In contrast with that of some peoples, however, African spirituality is
never disembodied but always integrally connected with the dynamic movement of life."[12]

Paris's definition underscores the fact that spirituality encompasses a total style and manner of experiencing oneself and the world. Paris also provides a context for understanding the fact that although there are many
differences between the religious systems of various African communities, the core features of religion and spirituality among African peoples
throughout the diaspora are remarkably similar.[13]

Typically, the "dynamic movement" of spirituality in African cultures is
facilitated by the active presence of a Supreme or High God and a host of
lesser spirits, the nature of which are detailed in the tenets of specific tribal
religions. But even when the spirits are not named or identified, the personally authentic experience of "soul" is still present. Hence, twentieth-
century African Americans are very familiar with "soul" music, which is
not specifically *religious*, in the sense of a clearly defined theology, but
definitely *spiritual*, in terms of the inner experiences generated by the music.
The emotional experience one has when listening to the singing of a rhythm
and blues song by a singer like Aretha Franklin, for example, is quite similar to what one experiences in listening to her perform gospel music. When
Aretha made the switch from gospel to rhythm and blues in the 1960s, she
retained the "soul" that has gained her the well-deserved title "Queen of
Soul."[14] While Aretha is exceptional in her communicative ability as an
artist, her tendency to perform rhythm and blues songs out of the same
deep spirit that she brings to her sacred repertoire is not at all uncommon.
In fact, in the African American experience, the "soul" is difficult to remove, even in so-called secular music. Whatever the music form, be it
rhythm and blues, jazz, rap, gospel, spirituals, or blues, black music is
consistently "soulful." The "soul" is reflected in the feelings of jubilation,
well-being, and centeredness one experiences in making, listening to, or
dancing to the music. These experiences signal the presence of a transper-
sonal spirit, even when that spirit is not named. Such experiences contribute

to a sense of personal integrity that is difficult to put into words, but indisputably real.

Among enslaved Africans in America, the presence of the spirits was not only experienced but the spirits were identified and named as well. The West African shaman Malidoma Somé writes that among his people, the Dagara, "the older you get, the more you begin to notice the spirits and ancestors everywhere."[15] Similarly, the elders in North American slave communities were acutely cognizant of the omnipresent spirits in their midst. For example, consider the poetic lyrics of one famous spiritual:

> My God is so high, you can't get over Him;
> He's so low, you can't get under Him;
> He's so wide, you can't get around him.[16]

These lyrics announce boldly that God is everywhere, that it is impossible to escape the presence and the influence of the divine.

The theology of the spirituals also mirrors the multidimensional God-concepts of many African religions, in which the will of an omnipotent "High God" is made manifest through the actions of a number of lesser spirits or deities.[17] In African religions, the people have much more intimate relationships with the lesser spirits. Typically, the High God is more powerful but also more distant from the people.

Gradually, the African gods were subsumed by the Trinity (Father, Son, Holy Ghost) of Christianity. In so doing, the creators of the spirituals formed an especially close relationship with Jesus, the most personally engaging member of the Trinity. In fact, throughout the history of African American Christianity, this experience of Jesus as one's personal friend, neighbor, mother, or father is considerably more pronounced than it is in the more abstract and relatively more intellectualized experience of Jesus in white Christianity.[18]

The intimate nature of the relationship with Jesus is expressed in countless spirituals. Consider, for example, the lyrics of one song which is still sung in many African American churches:

> I want Jesus to walk with me;
> I want Jesus to walk with me;
> All along my pilgrim journey,
> I want Jesus to walk with me.[19]

The Jesus of this song is one who lives in your home, one who possesses all the attributes of an intimate family member. This Jesus is in fact so loving that anyone who gets to know him will want desperately for others to know him as well. Another well-known spiritual expresses this wish:

Is there anybody here who loves my Jesus?
Is there anybody here who loves my Lord?
I want to know if you love my Jesus;
I want to know if you love my Lord![20]

These lyrics reveal the far-ranging impact of slave religion. From such a vantage point, one does not *believe* in Jesus; one *knows* and *experiences* him. Moreover, any person who does know Jesus is changed forever, much like the person who is well-loved and cared for by a parent in early childhood. The impact of such love extends far into the future, even after a parent's death, by leaving the affected person with an enduring sense of well-being and personal security.

Of course, the ability of African Americans to bond so strongly to Jesus was facilitated not only by the historical background of African spirituality, but also by a personal identification with the story of the life of Jesus. There were many parallels to the experience of slavery: A child of God, born of humble origins, forced with his parents to flee from oppressors, eventually captured, persecuted, tortured, and killed; there was much that was personally familiar. Most important, the Jesus story provided a reminder that although misunderstood and unappreciated by his captors, Jesus remained forever a child of God. To experience the love of Jesus, therefore, was to have a strong personal protection against external attempts to destroy completely one's sense of personal worth.

The scope of this chapter precludes a more thorough discussion of the multiple ways in which religious experiences and beliefs were manifested in the slave community and expressed outwardly in slave songs.[21] For the purpose of the present discussion, I want to emphasize the fact that the strong religious faith that existed among early African Americans established the basis for one of the defining elements of an evolving black American cultural ethos. While some later forms of black music have not been as manifestly religious as the spirituals, the unequivocally soulful character of virtually all black American music can reasonably be traced to the template laid down in the slave spirituals. In turn, the centuries-long African tradition of integration of spirituality into everyday life, combined with the specific religious developments shaped by slavery and a new Africanized Christianity, were powerful elements in the evolution of the spirituals.

The deep sense of spirituality that was present from the beginning of the slave experience and expressed so strongly in slave songs provided a firm basis for the use of music to buttress the self-esteem of Africans in bondage. This use of music was not, as commonly believed, primarily escapist in nature. The creators of the spirituals were much more interested in obtaining their freedom than they were in using their songs to create an imaginary vision of life after death.[22] The true power of the songs was contained in the alternative definitions of the self that they facilitated. Regarded by their

oppressors as chattel, Africans in bondage were able to retain their sense
of themselves as whole human beings, as children of God. One of the
greatest protest spirituals, for example, exclaims:

> I got shoes,
> You got shoes,
> All God's children got shoes.
> When I get to Heaven, gonna put on my shoes,
> And walk all over God's Heaven!

This song is not about wishing to die and going to Heaven. Rather, it
employs the imagery of Heaven, *in the imagination*, to construct a different
definition of life in the present. It is a statement of the singer's confident
knowledge that even though there are no earthly shoes (or other physical
comforts) provided to slaves, everyone is worthy of shoes, and everyone is
a child of God, despite external definitions to the contrary. In embracing
the song and its lyrics, the singer creates a new, here-and-now definition
of the self. As the contemporary African American activist Jesse Jackson
might say, the singer is proclaiming, in essence, that "I *am* somebody!"
The meaning of this self-proclamation is even clearer in the final lines of
each of the song's verses. There is a masked reference to the slavemaster:

> Everybody talkin' 'bout Heaven ain't goin' there,
> Heaven, Heaven;
> Gonna shout all over God's Heaven![23]

In other words, things are not as they might appear. The slavemaster, who
is always "talkin' 'bout Heaven," may believe that he has been divinely
appointed to assume a role of superiority in relationship to his "property."
However, in the singer's mind, the hierarchy is reversed, not just in the
future, but now. The slaveholder is regarded as a pitifully tragic creature.

This employment of subtle metaphor to effect a psychological reversal
of the publicly defined hierarchy of oppression is a device that has been
employed repeatedly by African Americans in a variety of cultural forms.
With its beginnings in the code of morality embodied in the spirituals, it
has become a signature feature of black American culture. For instance,
many of the blues songs of the early twentieth century painted graphic
images of white people in the victim role. In one song example provided
by historian Lawrence Levine, for example, the lyrics evoke a strong identification with the boll weevil, a tiny, weak-appearing creature who nonetheless has the ability to endure a great deal of punishment from its
"civilized" environment. In the process, the boll weevil gains the ability to
turn the tables by inflicting a great deal of damage. White people become
prime victims of the tiny boll weevil's newfound power:

Boll weevil said to the merchant,
"Better drink you cold lemonade;
When I git thru with you,
Gwine drag you out o' the shade—
'I have a home! I have a home!' "

Boll weevil said to the doctor,
"Better po' out all them pills;
When I get through with the farmer
He can't pay no doctor's bills—
'I have a home! I have a home'"[24]

When the boll weevil gets through, it has a *home*! The white man, on the other hand, is completely bewildered.

The ability to employ poetic imagery to reverse the hierarchy of oppression also provided the foundation for outward acts of resistance, both during slavery and at other times in African American history. During slavery, resistance took a variety of forms: arson, insurrection, murder, escape, calls for African emigration, and numerous other concrete actions by individuals, families, and bands of rebels.[25] In the slave community, such acts of resistance were accompanied by the singing of songs in which the brave acts of biblical freedom fighters received top billing. This employment of spirituals as a partner of protest and resistance was a preview of things to come at later points in history, including the use of improvised spirituals as freedom songs during the Civil Rights movement of the 1960s.[26]

Clearly, the spirits that inhabited the slave quarters were partners with African American captives in refashioning the intended order of things within the institution of slavery. The action of the spirits was particularly salient in the songs the slaves created. These songs facilitated both a strengthening of the inner will and a collective call to outward resistance. The foundation for the distinctly African American cultural attitude, which Ferdinand Jones has called "challenge" (see "Jazz and the Resilience of African Americans," Chapter 5 in the current volume), was contained in these early African American songs. The attitude of challenge redefines everything—self, community, and society—in distinctly soulful ways.

COMMUNITY

It is impossible to understand the cultural history of the spirituals without recognizing the strong community values of early African Americans. In many ways, this emphasis on family and community relationships is a direct extension of the strong religious orientation we have been discussing. Religious scholar John Mbiti has described the connection in African traditions between religious belief and interpersonal responsibilities: "Just as God made the first man, as God's man, so now man himself makes the individual who becomes the corporate or social man. *It is a deeply religious transaction.* Only in terms of other people does the individual become conscious of his own being, his own duties, his privileges and responsibilities towards himself and other people. . . . The individual can only say: 'I am, because we are; and since we are, therefore I am.' This is a cardinal point in the understanding of the African view of man."[27] (Emphasis added.) Furthermore, Mbiti explains, tribal communities in traditional African societies are basically kinship networks: "The kinship system is like a vast network stretching laterally (horizontally) in every direction, to embrace everybody in a given local group. This means that each individual is a brother or sister, father or mother, grandmother or grandfather, or cousin, or brother-in-law, uncle or aunt, or something else, to everybody else."[28]

In spite of the devastating emotional impact of tribal and family separations, there is considerable evidence that the tendency to understand and experience oneself in terms of an extended network of kinship relationships remained remarkably intact during slavery.[29] The lyrics of most of the spirituals reflect this worldview; nearly everything in the songs is filtered through the conduit of relationships with family and community members. Sometimes those relationships are implied, but frequently they are stated explicitly. One well-known spiritual, for example, describes the personal suffering of slavery through the image of a "motherless child." On one level, the image points to the frequent separation of families during slavery. On another level, the emotional brutality of slavery is portrayed through the metaphor of family separation. Since family relationships were so primary, and since the relationship between a mother and child is central to family functioning, there can be no more powerful image of suffering than an image of a child separated from its mother:

> Sometimes I feel like a motherless child,
> Sometimes I feel like a motherless child,
> Sometimes I feel like a motherless child,
> A long ways from home.[30]

Of course, an image of a motherless and homeless child would communicate the reality of suffering in any cultural context. However, the heightened emphasis on kinship in African cultural traditions makes the message even more powerful. There can be no question, therefore, that a situation of extreme personal anguish is being described.[31]

There are dozens of spirituals in which the image of family separation is less severe but nonetheless highly effective in what it communicates. Consider, for example, the lyrics of one verse of the spiritual "Peter, Go Ring Them Bells":

I wonder where my mother has gone,
I wonder where my mother has gone,
I wonder where my mother has gone,
I heard from Heaven today.[32]

The lyrics of this song, like most spirituals, can be interpreted on multiple levels. One likely meaning is the mixed feelings of jubilation and sadness one might experience in getting word about the successful arrival in Africa of a family member during the period of African repatriation. One would be happy to have "heard from Heaven" (Africa, in this case), but also saddened by the prospect of prolonged separation from loved ones.[33]

The employment of images of family separation in the spirituals not only highlights the painfully frequent occurrence of family disruption on the auction block, but also the continued emotional attachment to family members in spite of such disruptions. Moreover, in the early African American experience, the concept of kinship was extended beyond the boundaries of strict blood relationships to include functional relationships with community members to whom one was not biologically related. Terms like "brother" and "sister," therefore, convey the presence of feelings of intimacy attached to relationships with members of one's own community, regardless of blood ties. This is a cultural tradition that remains active today.

Some spirituals employ references to "brother" and "sister" for the purpose of calling attention to violations in the expected code of loyalty and respect among members of the slave community. In such songs of accountability[34] violators are often chastised with an implied challenge to correct their wayward ways and return to the fold. The call-and-response lyrics of the spiritual "Scandalize My Name" illustrate this kind of message:

I met my brother (sister, preacher, etc.) the other day,
Gave him my right hand;
But as soon as ever my back was turned,
He took and scandalize' my name!

You call that a brother?
No, no.
You call that a brother?
No, no.
You call that a brother?
No, no!
Scandalize' my name![35]

Implied in the message of the song is the notion that the violator can regain the privilege of being called "brother" if he abandons his scandalous behavior. But whether that choice is made or not, the community code (honor your brother, your sister, your mother, your preacher, and so forth) is clear.

The ethic of community connectedness is particularly evident in the large number of slave songs that employ the designations "Sister" and "Brother" to refer to biblical figures. In some of the verses of "Peter Go Ring Them Bells," for example, there are successive references to biblical figures: "I wonder where *Sister* Mary is gone; I wonder where *Brother* Moses is gone; I wonder where *Sister* Martha is gone; I wonder where *Brother* Daniel is gone."[36] This way of identifying characters from the Bible makes clear the strong psychological identifications with the stories of those biblical characters. With the simple change to "*Sister* Mary," the mother of Jesus Christ is transformed into a member of the slave community. Like any mother in that community, her pain and suffering in relation to the hardships faced by her child come alive in ways that are not possible when she is regarded simply as "Mary." There are similar patterns in the stories of *Sister* Martha, *Brother* Daniel, and *Brother* Moses; the stories all take on new life when they are told in such personally intimate ways.

Personalization of Bible stories illustrates another significant cultural value of the early African American community: the honoring of ancestors. In African traditions, ancestors are not simply dead relatives; they remain present in the community in the form of spirits who can be consulted for advice, guidance, and support.[37] Cut off from the specific memory of tribal ancestors, Africans in bondage in North America created, in effect, ancestral equivalents. Moses, for example, was not simply a figure from the Bible; he functioned as an ancestor. The story of the deliverance of his people out of bondage became an important source of inspiration for the freedom struggles of African peoples in slavery. Moreover, the spirit of Moses was ever present to provide support for those struggles. This was also true of other Old Testament heroes; they were regarded in some respects as ancestral freedom fighters whose stories were cherished by African American slaves who were struggling to find effective protest and resistance strategies.

In many ways, the relationship of the slave community to the stories of the Bible created a kind of timeless experience where past, present, and future were all part of one reality. Historian Lawrence Levine has argued that spirituals based on Old Testament stories were particularly important in this regard:

It is important that Daniel and David and Joshua and Jonah and Moses and Noah, all of whom fill the lines of the spirituals, were delivered in *this* world and delivered in ways which struck the imagination of the slaves. Over and over their songs dwelled upon the spectacle of the Red Sea opening to allow the Hebrew slaves [to] pass before inundating the mighty armies of the Pharaoh. They lingered delightedly upon the image of little David humbling the great Goliath with a stone.

These songs state as clearly as anything can the manner in which the sacred world of the slaves was able to fuse the precedents of the past, the conditions of the present, and the promise of the future into one connected reality.[38] (emphasis added)

The "connected reality" that Levine describes was also a source of support and inspiration for the people who emerged as leaders in the ongoing fight against slavery. From this perspective it is easy to understand why Harriet Tubman, one of the most effective "conductors" of the Underground Railroad (the informal network that assisted slaves in escaping into the Northern states and Canada), was often called "Moses."[39] A spiritual like "Go Down, Moses," in this context, acquires added meaning:

Go Down, Moses,
Way Down in Egypt land,
Tell ole Pharaoh,
To let my people go![40]

Similarly, the stories of Moses, Joshua, Daniel and other figures of the Old Testament were reembodied in the personhood of anti-slavery activists Nat Turner, Denmark Vesey, Gabriel Prosser, and numerous others. In this respect, the dozens of spirituals that reference Old Testament figures can be understood on a variety of levels.[41] At all levels, however, these songs served to reinforce community solidarity in the slave quarters in spite of external forces that were intended to break down any semblance of humanity.

Relationships among slaves were more intact than might be expected. Moreover, recent research by Civil War historians has confirmed the fact that the Emancipation Proclamation finally signed by Abraham Lincoln was a direct result of persistent work on the part of countless members of the slave community who repeatedly made it clear that they were determined to be free.[42] The unique sensibilities that helped African Americans to survive 250 years of bondage also made it possible for them to be major players in shaping the American dream of freedom and unlimited opportunity. In fact, as social critic Albert Murray has argued, early African Americans were at the very center of the process of extending the contours of that dream, despite their systematic exclusion from political power.[43]

MUSIC

In the slave community, music was far more than a diversionary experience; it was an integral, necessary part of community life.[44] The influence of music was so pervasive that it almost eludes description. Historian Lawrence Levine has perhaps come closest to capturing the essence of slave music. In describing the task of some historians (or other scholars) who are unfamiliar with this feature of black culture, he observes that "the study of slave songs forces the historian to move out of his own culture, in which music plays a peripheral role, and offers him the opportunity to understand the ways in which black slaves were able to perpetuate much of the centrality and functional importance that music had for their African ancestors. . . . Without a specific understanding of the content and meaning of slave song, there can be no full comprehension of the effects of slavery upon the slave or the meaning of the society from which slaves emerged at emancipation."[45]

Levine's statement provides an apt description of the role of music as it evolved among African peoples in North America. His comments apply not only to slave songs, but to later forms of African American music as well. It is instructive, for example, to note how ethnomusicologist Portia Maultsby describes contemporary black American music: "Music is integral to all aspects of black community life. It serves many functions and is performed by individuals and groups in both formal and informal settings. The fundamental concept that governs music performance in African and African-derived cultures is that music-making is a participatory group activity that serves to unite black people into a cohesive group for a common purpose. This use of music in African-American communities continues a tradition found in African societies."[46]

Maultsby's comments are strikingly similar to those made by Levine about the role and functions of slave songs. While the intensity of its impact has been tempered somewhat as time has passed, it is clear that black music has continued to have substantial functional significance in contemporary black American life.

As Maultsby indicates, the functions of African American music (including, especially, the creation of group solidarity) are similar to the functions served by music throughout the African diaspora.[47] However, it is also true that the protracted experience of oppression in North America has offered a uniquely American set of challenges. Life difficulties associated with the impact of racism and poverty, for example, have been salient parts of the black American experience. As we have already discussed, black American music confronts such troubles head-on, paradoxically yielding an entirely different set of self-references than might otherwise be expected from a community of would-be victims. Pain and joy, in other words, become two sides of a single process.

In the spirituals, this two-sided process of pain and joy is always present. "I'm troubled in mind," one traditional song exclaims; "if Jesus don't help me, I surely will die!" But Jesus, as we have seen, is surely close at hand, so the singer's plea is almost certainly heard: "Nobody know the trouble I see," (but) "Glory, Hallelu!" And as noted earlier, there is no greater suffering possible than the suffering which is described metaphorically by the spiritual "Sometimes I Feel Like a Motherless Child." Even here, however, there is another side to the story. Implied, even if not stated, is that "*sometimes* I do *not* feel like a motherless child; *sometimes* I feel like a child of God!" By confronting one's pain directly, one gains access to deeper, uncontaminated human reserves, gaining in the process renewed strength, renewed hope, and renewed humanity.

Later forms of black American music have continued this same paradoxical coupling of pain and triumph. For example, as theologian James Cone has noted, the blues tradition is a direct beneficiary of the spirit-based transformational energy contained in the spirituals.[48] In this context, the comments of writer Ralph Ellison are especially revealing: "The blues is an impulse to keep the painful details and episodes of a brutal experience alive in one's aching consciousness, to finger its jagged grain, and to transcend it, not by the consolation of philosophy but by squeezing from it a near-tragic 'lyricism'". Using the imagery of the blues to explain the emotional power of Richard Wright's autobiography, *Black Boy*, Ellison continues: "like a blues sung by such an artist as Bessie Smith, its lyrical prose evokes the paradoxical, almost surreal image of a black boy singing lustily as he probes his own grievous wound. . . . Their [the blues'] attraction lies in this, that they at once express both the agony of life and the possibility of conquering it through sheer toughness of spirit."[49]

Ellison's comments reflect his understanding that the blues tradition (or one might say the "black music tradition") is inextricably interwoven into the fabric of African American cultural life. The ability of black Americans to dance, laugh, and sing soulfully (regardless of life circumstances) is a transformational by-product of a deeply ingrained lyrical consciousness, which persistently encounters the spirits (named or unnamed) at the center of life.

ELEMENTS OF THE SPIRITUALS AS ART FORM

While the source of the psychological power of African American music is intangible ("it's just a *feeling*," some might say), it is important to delineate at least some of the specific elements that mark it as a unique art form. The spirituals are a good starting place, for much of what is now generally true of all black American music had its beginnings in the spirituals.

We have already discussed the religious nature of the spirituals, their community-galvanizing function, and the psychologically effective impact of many of the lyrics. In addition to these significant features of the spirituals, there are several specifically musical elements that contribute to their emotionally and spiritually communicative power. While a detailed technical analysis of the musical characteristics of the spirituals is beyond the scope of this chapter,[50] it is important to comment on some of these musical elements.

One of the most important elements is rhythm. In virtually all African societies, the drum was employed as the principal musical instrument. The rhythmic drive of the drum, considered a sacred instrument in most African societies, was thought to facilitate communication between the people and the spirits.[51] Although the use of drums by African captives in North American slavery was prohibited, it was impossible to eradicate the strong impulse to produce rhythmically centered music. In fact, as theomusicologist Jon Michael Spencer points out, "rhythm, not the drum, was the theological imperative in African religions."[52] It makes perfect sense, therefore, that enslaved Africans found many suitable substitutes for the forbidden drum. These included various improvised instruments, such as kitchen spoons, cans, pots and pans, and whatever else was at hand. Perhaps the most effective instrument of all—the body—was almost always used. Spencer observes that "their sacred music was embellished percussively by the bodily rhythms of hand-clapping, foot-stomping, body-slapping, and ring-shouting. Since response to rhythmic stimuli is instinctive and as certain as the physical reflexes, these bodily modes of percussive response to the rhythms in black music are intrinsic and immediate, for the bodily instrument is always at hand."[53]

To a significant extent, the specific context for such rhythmically oriented music making was the ring-shout, a dancing and singing ritual in which participants moved around a circle in a counterclockwise direction. This ritual was derived from similar ceremonies in western and central Africa.[54] The ring-shout was conducted in secret night meetings that often lasted well into the morning hours. The spirituals chosen for group singing in the ring-shout were frequently those with repetitively rhythmic verses. Historian Sterling Stuckey has described the effectiveness of the ring-shout in strengthening community bonds, particularly in circumstances where family separations were common: "The repetition of stanzas as the dancers circled around with ever greater acceleration reinforced and deepened the spirit of familial attachment, drawing within the ancestral orbit slaves who may not have known either a father or a mother, their involvement being an unbroken unity of the community. Familial feeling in the broad sense of clan and in the personal sense of one's own parents was a dominant, irresistible theme of slave consciousness."[55]

Stuckey's description of the ring-shout also helps draw attention to one other musical element that was prominent in the spirituals: the repetitive use of familiar verses. By employing words that were simple and familiar, and therefore easily conducive to communal singing, the spirituals helped ensure the creation of community rituals that were accessible to virtually everyone in a particular slave community. In so doing, they created a powerful medium of psychological transformation: group singing. In an oral culture, the practice of singing in group settings is employed to communicate, to teach values, and to facilitate contact between the community and the spirits.[56]

Historian, singer, and social activist Bernice Johnson Reagon has argued that singing in the African American tradition is also effective because of the emotional and physiological changes that accompany the production of sound in the body. In one of the many congregational singing workshops she has conducted, she had this to say about the reason that the singing in black congregational settings is so important:

Songs are a way to get to singing, though singing is what you're aiming for. And the singing is running sound through your body. You cannot sing a song and not change your condition. . . . I am talking about a culture that thinks it is important to exercise this part of your being. The part of your being that is tampered with when you run this sound through your body is a part of you that our culture thinks should be developed and cultivated, that you should be familiar with, that you should be able to get to as often as possible, and that if it is not developed, you are underdeveloped as a human being! If you go through your life and you don't meet this part of yourself, somehow the culture has failed you.[57]

Reagon's comments reflect her belief that independent of the other unique elements of the spirituals, singing in and of itself (especially in a group context, where singing is accompanied by body movement) is effective. She views the spirituals as important because they are part of a shared tradition that makes it possible for people to sing together without having to learn new songs or new words. From this perspective, it is ultimately the singing itself that is most important. There is much to be said for this point of view; this is a frame of reference that is reflected in the largely oral character of African American culture. It also helps explain why even in exclusively instrumental music making, as is often the case in jazz, imitation of the human voice is frequently a strong point of emphasis.

Many other cultures have discovered the spiritual and emotional power of singing and the even greater power that results from group singing. For example, Patricia Lawrence, a performing artist raised in the white American Baptist gospel song tradition, could easily be referring to black music when she writes that (white) gospel music is

participation music. It is going to stir up every cell in your body. Every ache in your heart. Every longing in your soul. It sends its laser beam deep into every corner of your being and unsticks the old junk hiding there. . . . So what is the release into energy and joy? The release is movement plus singing. Singing and swaying and clapping our hands, we draw what is stirred-up into our breath and sing it out on a wave of vibration and joyful expression. As energy fills our being we bring Spirit into our bodies and into the room. As the room fills with this energy, we open to each other.[58]

Lawrence may be unaware of the extent to which the evolution of music in white Southern churches was likely influenced by the tradition of music making among the slaves and servants with whom white Southerners have always had close contact.[59] Nevertheless, her passionate exhortation underscores the human functions served by participatory singing. As Lawrence points out, most indigenous cultures are familiar with the power of communal singing: "When we look to the remaining indigenous cultures on earth, or any of the writings and stories of old, we find singing to be the single most consistent element in any gathering, be it ceremony, ritual, or celebration. This is not insignificant. It is impossible to overstate the importance of singing in these contexts."[60] Thus, in their emphasis on collective singing, members of the slave community discovered one of the most effective psychological tools available to human beings anywhere.

One other musical element contributing to the power of the spirituals was the inclusion of songs that, because they were created out of any experience of deep suffering, assumed a kind of archetypal character that made (makes) them particularly powerful in their emotional and spiritual impact. Such power came not only from the symbolic or poetic poignancy of lyrics, but from inspired melodies as well.[61]

The power that is attributable to melody alone is not usually considered in sociological and psychological discussions of the spirituals, which typically focus almost exclusively on the poetry or lyrics. However, while there is much need for research into the contributing factors, experience teaches us that there are certain melodies that have the ability to reach us at a very deep emotional level. As such, they are timeless. In the European classical tradition, Beethoven's "Ode to Joy" would be one example of such a melody. It is strikingly simple yet intensely powerful in its emotional impact.

Of course, in the spirituals, we normally hear (or sing) both lyrics and melodies together, making it impossible to sort out the impact of melodies versus lyrics. This is as it should be; it is the combination of inspired poetry *and* inspired music (including both melody and rhythm) that makes most spirituals so effective. However, one experiential way to sort out the specific impact of a melody is first to try to speak the lyrics alone, and then sing the song with both lyrics and melody together. For example, one might experiment with a well-known spiritual like "Were You There?"

> Were you there when they crucified my Lord?
> Were you there when they crucified my Lord?
> Oh, sometimes it causes me to tremble, tremble, tremble!
> Were you there when they crucified my Lord?
>
> Were you there when they nailed him to the tree?
> Were you there when they pierced him in the side?
> Were you there when the sun refused to shine?
> Were you there when they laid him in the tomb?[62]

Most people will certainly be deeply affected by the poetic imagery of these lyrics. The words engage us at an intensely personal level; they place us right at the scene of the crucifixion of Jesus Christ. In addition, lines like "Were you there when the sun refused to shine?" communicate more information and emotion than an entire treatise on the social meaning of the crucifixion. In addition, it is clear from the lyrics that there is a close personal identification with the suffering of Jesus; it matches closely the suffering of many slaves. Despite such poignancy, however, most people will also find their understanding of this song deepened considerably when they sing it, or even when they hear it sung by someone else. The melody line, like the poetry, is simple and repetitious. Yet, it is strikingly effective in its impact on us personally. Not only does it communicate something of the slave's relationship to the crucifixion of Jesus, but also, like many other spirituals, it serves as a metaphor for suffering and as a vehicle for transcending the otherwise immutable impact of suffering. Both the lyrics and the music contribute to such an experience. One could say the same of later forms of black American music. The prolonged experience of oppression in America has contributed the same kind of power to the blues, gospel, and rap, for example. In all of these seemingly varied black art forms, music and lyrics combine to produce the intended emotional impact.[63]

There are many other musical elements that contribute to the effectiveness of the spirituals in their original form. These include the extensive use of improvisation, the emphasis on a call-and-response structure, the effective alternation of major and minor keys, the inclusion of "blue notes," and the emphasis on free expression of emotion through music.[64] As Portia Maultsby points out, most of these elements have become distinguishing features of all African American music.[65]

THE "ARRANGED" SPIRITUAL: THE IMPACT OF ASSIMILATION

One issue that arises in any discussion of African American music is the tension between the influence of traditional African versus European cultural influences. At what point in the evolution of European influences does the music cease being authentically black? This is a difficult, emotionally laden question with no easy answer. Thus Tilford Brooks, in his survey of "America's black musical heritage," makes it clear that he believes that a valid answer to such a question is nearly impossible.

There are those who are of the opinion that music written by Blacks in the European tradition is simply an imitation of the music of White composers, that Black music must be restricted to those musical forms that are Black in origin. There are others who contend that the Black musician who writes in the European tradition brings to that music a set of unique experiences that are manifested in this music; that regardless of the tradition in which the music is written, it is Black music providing it was written by a Black person who has lived the Black experience; and that even though it may not be written in one of the traditional Black music forms, this music is intuitively Black because of the cultural environment in which it was created.

There will be no attempt in this book to define Black music other than in its simplest meaning, . . . music that is indigenous to Blacks or composed by Blacks. Ideological questions as to what music is Black and what is not will not be considered here.[66]

Similarly, Eileen Southern, in her classic text on black American music history, takes essentially the same approach. By titling her book *The Music of Black Americans*, she avoids any attempt to outline any defining characteristics of African American music. She simply chronicles the history of music created *by* black Americans.

While it is tempting to follow the lead of scholars like Brooks and Southern, such a stance would avoid addressing some of the controversy surrounding the spirituals, where the question of cultural authenticity has been raised frequently. For example, ethnomusicologist John Storm Roberts voices a fairly typical view of the disjuncture between the original religious and musical experiences of slaves and the polished spirituals performed by the Fisk Jubilee Singers and other black artists trained in the European classical tradition. "The Fisk Jubilee Singers . . . appear not to have presented black religious music as it really was. Something of the style of the Fisk Jubilee Singers can be heard on recordings of later versions of the group. . . . The sound of these . . . make it obvious that the group's repertoire represented an art re-creation in a line that continued through the Eurocentric concert performances of Paul Robeson and Marian Anderson— music that had little to do with the worship of the black Christians who originated the spirituals."[67]

There is no question that Roberts is correct from a technical, musicological standpoint. The style of singing that was prevalent in the slave community was markedly different from most concert-based renderings of slave songs, including but not limited to singers trained in the European classical tradition. Of course, since there are no recordings of slaves singing spirituals, we will never know precisely how the spirituals actually sounded in their original forms. We do, however, have a record of the comments of observers. For example, Lucy McKim Garrison, one of the editors of the first notated collection of spirituals, which was published in 1867, had this to say about the singing of spirituals by slaves: "It is difficult to express the entire character of these Negro ballads by mere musical notes and signs. The odd turns made in the throat and the curious rhythmic effect produced by single voices chiming in at different irregular intervals seem almost as impossible to place on the score as the singing of birds or the tones of an aeolian harp."[68]

As Garrison indicates, attempts to notate what was up to that point a purely oral tradition were difficult at best. The use of western musical conventions in published collections of spirituals, therefore, resulted in an early and very significant alteration in the songs themselves.

One can gain some appreciation of original performance styles by listening to recordings of spirituals as they are sung by the residents of the sea islands off the coasts of South Carolina and Georgia, where African and early African American cultural retentions have remained potent.[69] In listening to such recordings, one gains increased appreciation for Lucy McKim Garrison's comments. The free improvisational style of group singing, which is evident on these recordings, is dramatically different from the polished melodies and harmonies of the spirituals as they are typically performed today by individual artists, ensembles, or church and community choirs. Undoubtedly, much has changed since the songs first appeared.

In addition to the effect of musical notation, the spirituals were changed substantially when they evolved from the spontaneous call-and-response music of field laborers to the concert repertoire of performers who sang *to* rather than *with* their audiences. Still, there was nothing inherently less black about any of these changes. Other forms of distinctly black music, including the blues, also evolved into performance rather than folk music. Moreover, *all* music evolves over time. Not only do social conditions change, but cultural preferences and styles change as well. What was noteworthy about the spirituals, however, was the fact that outside of black church settings, the most influential bearers of the spirituals tradition after the turn of the (twentieth) century were African American performers and composers who were trained in the European classical music tradition. In addition to classically trained black college choirs, the spirituals were performed in concert by such singers as Roland Hayes, Marian Anderson, and Paul Robeson. The style of such performances was dictated by the so-called arranged spirituals of such noted African American composers as H. T. Burleigh, Edward Boatner, Nathaniel Dett, William Levi Dawson, and Hall Johnson. These compositions were essentially the words and melodies of slave spirituals arranged musically in a form resembling the European art song.[70]

Historian Michael Harris has described another change that occurred in the years starting around 1915 and continued through the late 1920s and early 1930s. Many blacks who had migrated from the rural South to the urban cities of the industrial North established memberships in black churches in their new communities. The move by these rural blacks in an attempt to better their economic conditions was accompanied by a conscious push on the part of church leaders to encourage their congregations to leave their past, including black church songs, behind. In most of the large black Baptist churches in Chicago, for example, music directors were under clear instructions from their pastors to establish music programs that featured European classical works, the standard Bach, Beethoven, and

Brahms. In these settings, traditional styles of black worship, including shouting, witnessing, and improvisational singing, were discouraged. The singing of spirituals, at least in their traditional improvisational forms, was out of the question. However, some music directors attempted to address the hunger of churchgoers for traditional black music by making available their own arranged spirituals for performance by choirs as anthems.[71] One of the values reflected in this move was the idea that the spirituals would be more "developed" (that is, closer to a European aesthetic standard) if performed in the art song genre. John Wesley Work, one of the early directors of the Fisk Jubilee Singers, was a strong adherent of this point of view: "In truth, the general adaptability of this music to a high degree of development is its hope of gaining artistic recognition. It deserves to be put into a finished form; it lends itself admirably to such a purpose; and those who would keep it as it was first reduced to writing, in their mistaken zeal would doom it to stagnation and to the contempt of highly musical people."[72]

Harris argues that the emergence of gospel music was largely a result of attitudes like this. Gospel music was a blues-influenced genre that satisfied the needs of urban church goers to have more identifiably black music at the center of their worship services. Former blues musician Thomas Dorsey was one of the first to redirect black church music in this new, "gospel blues" direction. Edward Boatner, who was music director of Chicago's Pilgrim Baptist Church in the early 1930s and one of the most prominent composers of arranged spirituals, was vehemently opposed to the decision to include Dorsey and his music in Sunday morning worship services. In a 1977 interview, Boatner reaffirmed his disdain for Dorsey's work.

At that time I never knew what a gospel choir was. But I knew that when I heard him play the piano, I knew what was happening. He was sitting in the church one day and he was playing a gospel hymn or song for some lady who was sitting there. And it was nothing but jazz. You can look at any of them today, any of the gospel songs. They have that same jazz type of form. . . . I felt it was degrading. How can something that's jazzy give a religious feeling? If you're in a club downtown, a nightclub, that's all right. That's where it belongs. But how can you associate that with God's word? It's a desecration. The only people who think it isn't a desecration are the people who haven't had any training, any musical training—people who haven't heard fine anthems, cantatas, oratorios.[73]

The "training" Boatner refers to, of course, is training that is influenced by European conceptions of what "fine" music is. Given these beliefs, what is one to make of what Harris calls the "denatured" spirituals of Boatner, Work, or other composers of this persuasion? It is these "denatured" versions of spirituals that have been performed by black college choirs as well as concert singers from the day of Roland Hayes and Marian Anderson to

such current stars as Jessye Norman and Kathleen Battle. Should we conclude that spirituals performed in this concert tradition have evolved to the
point of being no longer recognizable as black music?

One's understanding of this issue is determined largely by the angle chosen to view it. From one point of view, the abhorrent comments of composers like Boatner and Work are enough reason to conclude that the music
they created is outside the boundaries of the black American music tradition. On the other hand, their comments aside, one must ask the question
why they went to such great lengths to compose dozens of arrangements
of slave songs. The argument that they were simply trying to appease
church members, or that they were attempting to rehabilitate what they
perceived as sick music, is unconvincing. If they truly believed that European music was the sole standard of excellence, they would have concen-
trated most of their time arranging and performing European music and
educating otherwise uninformed laypersons in the art of appreciating this
"fine" music. However, composers like Burleigh, Dett, Work, and Boatner
spent a substantial part of their professional careers creating arrangements
of slave songs.

It is also true that many of the singers of arranged spirituals performed
these songs out of a strong emotional identification with black music
traditions, including the music of slavery. Paul Robeson, who's father had
been a slave, used the arrangements of H. T. Burleigh when he performed
spirituals.[74] He also was known for his pride in black cultural traditions,
and the spirituals in particular. In his book *Here I Stand*, his feelings about
the spirituals are crystal clear: "Yes, I heard my people singing!—in the
glow of parlor coal stove and on summer porches sweet with lilac air, from
choir loft and Sunday morning pews—and my soul was filled with their
harmonies."[75]

Similarly, Roland Hayes, who started his career attempting to compete
with white singers of European classical music, was very definite in his later
years about the strong emotional connection he felt to traditional African
American culture and music: "I am embarrassed to recall that in my preoccupation with the European composers, and with learning French and
German, I had become neglectful of Afro-American music. . . . I was unconsciously putting myself into competition with white singers, whose spotlight I wanted to share. I had yet not received the revelation which was
presently to give my ambition its native direction. . . . It remained for me
to learn, humbly at first, and then with mounting confidence, that my way
to artistry was a Negro way."[76]

More recently, opera singer Florence Quivar, in the liner notes to her
recording of spirituals, *Ride on King Jesus*, offered her own testimony: "I've
grown up in a world of music all my life, and I've been truly blessed to
have been able to sing on so many great operatic and concert stages
throughout the world. But nothing has given me as much joy as working

on this recording of Negro spirituals. They are a part of my beginnings. Of my own roots. Of family. Of friends. Of an American Dream."[77]

In this same vein, for the past several years, scores of classically trained singers have assembled on Martin Luther King Jr.'s birthday in church venues in Harlem, New York. The purpose of their annual gathering is a vigil concert honoring Dr. King, consisting entirely of spirituals. The program, which is attended every year by a standing-room-only interracial audience, is hosted by Francois Clemmons, founder and director of the American Negro Spiritual Research Foundation and the Harlem Spiritual Ensemble. The concert typically begins in the early evening and extends into the early morning hours, with singer after singer performing spirituals, many of them using the arrangements of Burleigh, Boatner, Dett, and Work. Each year the church sanctuary is filled with palpable emotional energy as the singing binds the audience and performers together in the best possible honoring of the spirit of the late Dr. King. The vigil also provides a reminder of the transformed spirituals that became the freedom songs of the Civil Rights movement of the 1960s that Dr. King led.

All of these illustrations have bearing on the complicated issues of what music can be regarded as authentically black. From one perspective, which I believe is the most accurate, there is a robustness in the black music tradition that refuses to die, even in the face of considerable attempts at premeditated murder. Even when the spirituals have been concertized, smoothed out, refined, or "denatured," the soul remains. There is something about the power of the original melodies and lyrics that continues to exert its influence, even in the face of multiple transformations in form and style. As the annual vigil concerts in New York illustrate, even concertized spirituals can serve the group-galvanizing functions of the original call-and-response slave songs. Moreover, even in the face of a conscious disdain expressed by a composer like Boatner with respect to traditional black music traditions, Boatner and others of his persuasion managed to produce music whose "soul" has been honored by several generations of singers with strong emotional and spiritual ties to their African American roots. These facts would all suggest that the arranged spiritual is indeed a continuation of the black music tradition.

THE FUTURE

This chapter began with a reference to the ambivalence toward the spirituals that has been evident in the African American community since the end of slavery. Much of the ambivalence, I believe, has stemmed from the misdirected conception that the horrors of 250 years of slavery can best be dealt with by disconnecting ourselves emotionally from any identification with that period in our history. Beyond that, we also have allowed ourselves to believe, somehow, that we should be ashamed of the cultural heritage that is associated with our victimization. This blaming-the-victim (us) stance is obviously self-defeating. Moreover, as we have seen, the tradition of the spirituals, with the history it embodies, is a robust tradition that cannot die, even if we would wish it otherwise. It is also the foundation for what can now be regarded as the African American music tradition, broadly conceived. The use of the spirituals as a conduit for communion with the spirits, with one another, and with our best selves is the raw material out of which much of African American culture has been built.

The African American community will certainly be best off if we can embrace rather than avoid the memories of our painful past. This is the only way for us, and for the nation at large, to heal. There are some signs that this reality is beginning to be recognized in black communities nationwide. Ceremonies held in remembrance of the "Maafa" (Kiswahili for "unspeakable horror") are now becoming commonplace. There are also increasing numbers of people who are using the story of our people's successful triumph over slavery as an inspiration to face mounting contemporary problems like drug abuse and gang violence.[78] As this movement takes hold, it is just a matter of time before people make the conscious connection between the experience of slavery and the music created as an aid in the fight to end slavery.

It is encouraging to see some recent signs of resurgence of interest in the spirituals. For example, in the last few years, the Harlem Spiritual Ensemble has conducted many successful tours, performing all over the world. When Francois Clemmons and Louis Smart founded the Ensemble in 1986, there were many people who predicted that the group could not survive if it insisted on performing spirituals exclusively. This has not proved to be the case. After an initial period of struggling, the ensemble is now flourishing.[79] In addition to the Harlem Spiritual Ensemble, the female professional vocal group New Arts Six, based in Dallas, Texas, has also taken on the mission of performing and preserving the cultural heritage of the spirituals. Their work has also been well received.

Recently, there have been some unique recordings released that are particularly noteworthy. Cynthia Willson-Felder, another Dallas-based performer, has released a recording, *New Songs of Zion*, which presents spirituals performed in gospel style, thereby making the music more accessible to contemporary generations.[80] In a somewhat different vein, *Watch and Pray*, a recording that includes performances by several artists in honor of the work of heretofore little recognized African American women composers, has also been released recently. Included on the album are several arrangements of spirituals.[81] In addition, jazz artists Charlie Hayden and Hank Jones have released an innovative and stunningly beautiful album of spirituals, hymns, and folk songs illustrating the way in which black music forms overlap and interact. This jazz-based recording includes some of the most poignant interpretations of the spirituals available today.[82]

Paralleling these kinds of developments by performing artists, there are some contemporary African American churches that continue to recognize the importance of including old and new songs in a creative and ever-changing blend of community-empowering, spirit-enhancing music.[83] This tradition is honored by Bernice Johnson Reagon's compilation of songs from the congregational singing tradition,[84] complemented by collections of concert spirituals, community gospel and work by pioneering African American gospel composers, demonstrating the interconnection of all forms of African American sacred music.[85] These recordings are a follow-up to her successful twenty-six-hour series on black sacred music, which was aired for the first time in 1994 on National Public Radio.

All of these examples illustrate many of the changes now occurring that point to the real possibility of a significant revival of interest in the spirituals. My experience the last several years conducting lecture-concert programs on the spirituals, in cities throughout the United States, has provided me with a firsthand appreciation for the possibility of such a revival. I have been encouraged particularly by the consistently enthusiastic interest in the history, cultural legacy, and deeper meanings of the spirituals tradition. My experience has also reaffirmed my belief that African American culture thrives when of all of its historic music forms are honored, preserved, and reworked. This is because all African-derived cultures are at their best when the wisdom and stories of the ancestors are remembered and respected. The spirituals are an essential piece of that ancestral legacy.

NOTES

1. Eileen Southern, *The Music of Black Americans*, 2d ed. (New York: W. W. Norton, 1983), p. 67; Wyatt T. Walker, *Somebody's Calling My Name* (Valley Forge, Pa.: Judson Press, 1979), 38.

2. J. B. T. Marsh, *The Story of the Fisk Jubilee Singers* (Boston: Houghton, 1880).

3. For a comprehensive survey of the worldwide impact of the spirituals from the end of the Civil War through the first half of the twentieth century, see John Lovell, Jr., *Black Song, The Forge and the Flame: The Story of How the Afro-American Spiritual Was Hammered Out* (New York: Paragon House Publishers, 1986; originally published in 1972), 397–586.

4. W. E. B. DuBois, *The Souls of Black Folk* (New York: Bantam Books, 1989; originally published in 1903), 178.

5. See note 3 above.

6. Not only is there lack of knowledge of the cultural origins of the spirituals, but there is a waning familiarity with the songs themselves. Concert musicians who perform the spirituals frequently remark among themselves of their dismay at the fact that awareness of the lyrics and melodies of even the most famous spirituals is surprisingly low in contemporary African American communities. In formal surveys I conducted after some of my own lecture-concert performances in 1991 and

1992, I found a strikingly clear pattern. When I asked people to indicate which songs they heard in the concerts were "very familiar," "somewhat familiar," or "not familiar at all," people older than forty years of age tended to indicate "very familiar" or "somewhat familiar" for at least half the songs. People younger than forty tended to indicate "not familiar at all" for most of the songs, including such previously well-known spirituals as "Sometimes I Feel Like a Motherless Child" and "Joshua Fit the Battle of Jericho." While more comprehensive and systematic research is needed, there is no question that knowledge of the spirituals tradition has declined dramatically in recent years.

7. Lovell, *Black Song*, 384–385.

8. James H. Cone, *The Spirituals and the Blues* (Maryknoll, N.Y.: Orbis Books, 1991; originally published in 1972); Riggins R. Earl, *Dark Symbols, Obscure Signs: God, Self, and Community in the Slave Mind* (Maryknoll, N.Y.: Orbis Books, 1993); Arthur C. Jones, *Wade in the Water: The Wisdom of the Spirituals* (Maryknoll, N.Y.: Orbis Books, 1993); Cheryl A. Kirk-Duggan, "African-American Spirituals: Confronting and Exorcising Evil through Song," in Emilie M. Townes, ed., *A Troubling in My Soul: Womanist Perspectives on Evil and Suffering* (Maryknoll, N.Y.: Orbis Books, 1993); Lawrence Levine, *Black Culture and Black Consciousness* (New York: Oxford Press, 1977); Albert Raboteau, *Slave Religion* (New York: Oxford Press, 1977); Jon Michael Spencer, *Protest and Praise: Sacred Music of Black Religion* (Minneapolis: Fortress Press, 1990); Sterling Stuckey, *Slave Culture* (New York: Oxford Press, 1987); Walker, *Somebody's Calling My Name*; Delores S. Williams, *Sisters in the Wilderness: The Challenge of Womanist God-Talk* (Maryknoll, N.Y.: Orbis Books, 1993).

9. There once was a lively scholarly debate around the issue of whether the institution of slavery was successful in obliterating any remnants of African sensibility among enslaved Africans. In recent years that debate has been replaced by an acceptance of the fact that certain robust aspects of African-centered cultural consciousness have contributed significantly to the formation and evolution of African American culture. For extensive treatments of these issues, see Joseph E. Holloway, ed., *Africanisms in American Culture* (Bloomington: Indiana University Press, 1990); Jones, *Wade in the Water*; Lovell, *Black Song*; Peter Paris, *The Spirituality of African Peoples* (Minneapolis: Fortress Press, 1995); Raboteau, *Slave Religion*; Stuckey, *Slave Culture*. See John Mbiti, *African Religions and Philosophy*, 2d ed. (Oxford: Heinemann, 1989) for a broad survey of the traditional role of religion and spirituality throughout Africa.

10. For a detailed treatment of the evolution of religion in the slave community, see John W. Blassingame, *The Slave Community: Plantation Life in the Antebellum South*, revised edition (New York: Oxford Press, 1979); Raboteau, *Slave Religion*; and Stuckey, *Slave Culture*. For a detailed discussion of how this evolution was reflected specifically in the spirituals, see Jones, *Wade in the Water* (especially Chapter 4).

11. See Jones, *Wade in the Water*, Chapters 1 and 2.

12. Paris, *The Spirituality of African Peoples*, 22.

13. In addition to the discussion of African religion and spirituality throughout the diaspora provided by Paris, see Mbiti, *African Religions and Philosophy* for a similar discussion of the similarities and variations throughout the African continent.

14. As an instructive exercise, the reader is encouraged to compare any of Aretha's many rhythm and blues recordings with the communicative and expressive style she employs in her gospel album *Amazing Grace* (New York: Atlantic Recording Corporation, 1972; reissued as Compact Disk No. 2–906–2).

15. Malidoma Somé, *Of Water and the Spirit* (New York: Penguin Books, 1994), 23.

16. For a transcription of the verses and melody of this song as it has been passed down in the culture, see *Songs of Zion* (Nashville, Tenn.: Abingdon Press, 1982), Selection No. 105.

17. Dwight N. Hopkins and George C. L. Cummings, *Cut Loose Your Stammering Tongue: Black Theology in the Slave Narratives* (Maryknoll, N.Y.: Orbis Books, 1991), 5–7; Jones, *Wade in the Water*, 79–83; Lovell, *Black Song*, 230–233; Mbiti, *African Religions and Philosophy*, 29–34; Paris, *The Spirituality of African Peoples*, 27–49; Raboteau, *Slave Religion*, 8–12.

18. See a helpful treatment of this idea in Kelly Brown Douglas, *The Black Christ* (Maryknoll, N.Y.: Orbis Books, 1994). See Levine, *Black Culture and Black Consciousness*, p. 35, for a specific discussion of the intimate Christ as expressed in the spirituals.

19. See *Songs of Zion*, Selection No. 95.

20. For a modern adaptation of this song by composer Roland Carter, see *God Is a God: Six Negro Spirituals for Voice and Piano* (Hampton, Va.: Mar-vel, 1983).

21. The interested reader is encouraged to consult any number of excellent explorations of slave religion and the associated reflections in slave songs. The following sources are particularly noteworthy: Cone, *The Spirituals and the Blues*; Margaret Washington Creel, *"A Peculiar People": Slave Religion and the Community-Culture Among the Gullahs* (New York: New York University Press, 1988); Earl, *Dark Symbols, Obscure Signs*; Hopkins and Cummings, *Cut Loose Your Stammering Tongue*; Levine, *Black Culture and Black Consciousness*; Raboteau, *Slave Religion*; Stuckey, *Slave Culture*. For a sampling of direct testimony from ex-slaves, see Clifton H. Johnson, ed., *God Struck Me Dead: Voices of Ex-Slaves* (Cleveland: The Pilgrim Press, 1993).

22. Jones, *Wade in the Water*, especially pp. 39–63; Lovell, *Black Song*, 223–381.

23. See *Songs of Zion*, Selection No. 95.

24. See Levine, *Black Culture and Black Consciousness*, pp. 240–241, for his discussion of this traditional song.

25. See Vincent Harding, *There Is a River: The Black Struggle for Freedom in America* (New York: Vintage Books, 1983), for a chronicling of slave resistance movements.

26. See Jones, *Wade in the Water*, pp. 39–63 for a discussion of the role of the spirituals in supporting resistance attempts. See Levine, *Black Culture and Black Consciousness*, pp. 3–80 for a detailed treatment of the sacred undergirdings reflected in slave songs, particularly those based on Old Testament themes.

27. Mbiti, *African Religions and Philosophy*, 106.

28. Mbiti, *African Religions and Philosophy*, 102.

29. Andrew Billingsley, *Climbing Jacob's Ladder: The Enduring Legacy of African-American Families* (Simon & Schuster, 1992), 96–116.

30. See *Songs of Zion*, Selection No. 83.

31. See Jones, *Wade in the Water*, pp. 18–38, for discussion of images of emotional suffering and transformation in the spirituals.

32. See *Songs of Zion*, Selection No. 97.

33. See Jones, *Wade in the Water*, pp. 39–100, for a discussion of the multilayered meanings of many spirituals. "Peter Go Ring Them Bells" is discussed on p. 56.

34. See Jones, *Wade in the Water*, pp. 101–120, for a discussion of the theme of accountability as expressed in the spirituals.

35. See *Songs of Zion*, Selection No. 159.

36. See *Songs of Zion*, Selection No. 97.

37. Mbiti, *African Religions and Philosophy*, 74, 83–84; Paris, *The Spirituality of African Peoples*, 51–75.

38. Levine, *Black Culture and Black Consciousness*, 50–51.

39. Sarah Elizabeth Bradford, *Harriet Tubman: The Moses of Her People* (New York: Corinth Books, 1961; originally published 1886). See also an interview with Harriet Tubman recorded in John Blassingame, *Slave Testimony* (Baton Rouge: Louisiana State University Press, 1977), 458.

40. See *Songs of Zion*, Selection No. 112.

41. Jones, *Wade in the Water*, 39–55.

42. See Ira Berlin, Barbara J. Fields, Steven F. Miller, Joseph P. Reidy, and Leslie S. Rowland, eds., *Free at Last: A Documentary History of Slavery, Freedom and the Civil War* (New York: The New Press, 1992).

43. Albert Murray, *The Omni-Americans* (New York: Outerbridge & Dienstfrey; distributed by E. P. Dutton, 1970).

44. Jones, *Wade in the Water*, 1–17; LeRoi Jones, *The Blues People* (New York: Morrow, 1963), 28–29; Southern, *The Music of Black Americans*, 6–24.

45. Levine, *Black Culture and Black Consciousness*, 54–55.

46. Portia K. Maultsby, "Africanisms in African-American Music," in Holloway, *Africanisms in American Culture*, 187.

47. For a personal account of the role of music in traditional African societies, see Yaya Diallo and Mitchell Hall, *The Healing Drum: African Wisdom Teachings* (Rochester, Vt.: Destiny Books, 1989).

48. Cone, *The Spirituals and the Blues*.

49. Cited in Murray, *The Omni-Americans*, 162–163.

50. For a more comprehensive treatment of the distinctive musical features of the spirituals, see Henry Edward Krehbiel, *Afro-American Folksongs* (New York: Frederick Ungar Publishing Co., 1962; originally published in 1913). See also Tilford Brooks, *America's Black Music Heritage* (Englewood Cliffs, N.J.: Prentice-Hall, 1984), 32–42; Hildred Roach, *Black American Music: Past and Present* (Boston: Crescendo Publishing Co., 1973), 29–39; and Walker, *Somebody's Calling My Name*, 51–63.

51. See Diallo and Mitchell, *The Healing Drum*; Mbiti, *African Religions and Philosophy*, 80, 93, 180; Southern, *The Music of Black Americans*, 10–11; and Spencer, *Protest and Praise*, 136–138.

52. Spencer, *Protest and Praise*, 141.

53. Spencer, *Protest and Praise*, 141–142.

54. Stuckey, *Slave Culture*, 13–30.

55. Stuckey, *Slave Culture*, 29

56. See Jones, *Wade in the Water*, 13, 146 (note 32).

57. Bill Moyers with Bernice Johnson Reagon, *The Songs are Free* (Cooper Station, N.Y.: Mystic Fire Videos, #76204, 1991).

58. Patricia Lawrence, "Singing Together!: A Direct Line to the Spirit." *Open Air: A Publication Dedicated to Sound and Music in Health and Education*, Spring, 1995, 12.

59. Ironically, there once was a whole school of thought that maintained that the influence was forged exclusively in the opposite direction—white to black. See Lovell, *Black Song* for an extensive discussion of the independent evolution of early black American religious music and the subsequent widespread influence of this black music on a wide variety of other music and artistic forms. See especially pp. 75–126, 458–470, 541–549. See also John Storm Roberts, *Black Music of Two Worlds* (New York: Praeger Publishers, 1972), pp. 40–68, for a discussion of the two-way influences of music; white to black as well as black to white.

60. Lawrence, "Singing Together," 13.

61. See Jones, *Wade in the Water*, 13, 146 (note 32).

62. See *Songs of Zion*, Selection No. 126 for the words and melody of this song as commonly sung today.

63. In the case of rap, the "music" is enhanced by the prominence of complex and varied rhythmic layering. See Tricia Rose, *Black Noise: Rap Music and Culture in Contemporary America* (Hanover, N.H.: Wesleyan University Press, 1994) 62–96. See also Cheryl Keyes, Chapter 6 in the current volume.

64. See note 50 above.

65. Maultsby, "Africanisms in African-American Music."

66. Brooks, *America's Black Musical Heritage*, 1–2.

67. Roberts, *Black Music of Two Worlds*, 161.

68. Cited in John Rublowsky, *Black Music in America* (New York: Basic Books, 1971), 112–113.

69. See *Been in the Storm So Long: Spirituals, Folk Tales and Children's Games from John's Island, South Carolina* (Washington, D.C.: Smithsonian/Folkways Compact Disk No. 40031, 1990).

70. See Lovell, *Black Song*, 427–452; Brooks, *America's Black Musical Heritage*, 202–227; Southern, *The Music of Black Americans*, 266–278.

71. Michael W. Harris, *The Rise of Gospel Blues: The Music of Thomas Dorsey in the Urban Church* (New York: Oxford Press, 1992). 91–150.

72. Cited in Harris, *The Rise of Gospel Blues*, 112.

73. Harris, *The Rise of Gospel Blues*, 197–198.

74. See, for example, Paul Robeson, *The Power and the Glory* (New York: Columbia Records, Compact Disk No. 0–7464–47337–2, 1991).

75. Paul Robeson, *Here I Stand* (Boston: Beacon Press, 1958), 15.

76. Quoted in MacKinley Helm, *Angel Mo' and Her Son, Roland Hayes* (New York: Greenwood Press, 1942), 110–111.

77. Florence Quivar, *Ride On, King Jesus* (Hayes Middlesex, England: EMI Records, Compact Disk No. 7049885–2, 1990).

78. See Charisse Jones, "Slavery Becomes an Inspiration," *New York Times*, April 2, 1995.

79. The Harlem Spiritual Ensemble has also released two commercially available recordings: *The Harlem Spiritual Ensemble, in Concert* (New York: Arcadia Rec-

ords, Compact Disk No. 26072–1991–2; 1991) and *Free at Last* (New York: Arcadia Records, Compact Disk No. 26072–1995–2; 1992).

80. Cynthia Willson-Felder, *New Songs of Zion* (Burbank, Calif.: Warner Bros. Records, Warner Alliance Compact Disk No. WBD-4152, 1993).

81. Pamela Dillard, Ruth Hamilton, Robert Honeysucker and Vivian Taylor, *Watch and Pray: Spirituals and Art Songs by African-American Women Composers* (Westbury, N.Y.: Koch International Classics, Compact Disk No. 3–7247–2, 1994).

82. Charlie Hayden and Hank Jones, *Steal Away* (New York: Verve Records, Compact Disk No. 314–527–249–2; 1995).

83. See, for example, Walter F. Pitts, Jr., *Old Ship of Zion: The Afro-Baptist Ritual in the African Diaspora* (New York: Oxford University Press, 1993).

84. Bernice Johnson Reagon, compiler, *Wade in the Water, Vol. II: African American Congregational Singing* (Washington, D.C.: Smithsonian Institution, Smithsonian/Folkways Recordings, Compact Disk No. 8F 40053; 1994).

85. Bernice Johnson Reagon, compiler, *Wade in the Water, Vol. I: African American Spirituals: The Concert Tradition* (Washington, D.C.: Smithsonian Institution, Smithsonian/Folkways Recordings, Compact Disk No. 8F 40072; 1994); Bernice Johnson Reagon, compiler, *Wade in the Water, Vol. IV: African American Community Gospel* (Washington, D.C.: Smithsonian Institution, Smithsonian/Folkways Recordings, Compact Disk No. SF 40075; 1994).

BIBLIOGRAPHY

Abingdon Press, *Songs of Zion*. Nashville, Tenn.: Abingdon Press, 1982.

Berlin, Ira; Barbara J. Fields; Stephen F. Miller; Joseph P. Reidy; and Leslie F. Rowland, eds. *Free at Last: A Documentary History of Slavery, Freedom and the Civil War*. New York: The New Press, 1992.

Billingsley, Andrew. *Climbing Jacob's Ladder: The Enduring Legacy of African-American Families*. New York: Simon & Schuster, 1992.

Blassingame, John W. *The Slave Community: Plantation Life in the Antebellum South*, revised edition. New York: Oxford Press, 1979.

———. *Slave Testimony*. Baton Rouge: Louisiana State University Press, 1977.

Bradford, Sarah Elizabeth. *Harriet Tubman: The Moses of Her People*. New York: Corinth Books, 1961; originally published 1886.

Brooks, Tilford. *America's Black Music Heritage*. Englewood Cliffs, N.J.: Prentice-Hall, 1984.

Carter, Roland. "Is There Anybody Here?" In *God Is a God: Six Negro Spirituals for Piano and Voice*. Hampton, Va.: Mar-vel, 1983, 22–25.

Cone, James H. *The Spirituals and the Blues: An Interpretation*. Maryknoll, N.Y.: Orbis Books, 1991; originally published 1972.

Creel, Margaret Washington. *"A Peculiar People": Slave Religion and Community-Culture Among the Gullahs*. New York: New York University Press, 1988.

Diallo, Yaya and Mitchell Hall. *The Healing Drum: African Wisdom Teachings*. Rochester, Vt.: Destiny Books, 1989.

Dillard, Pamela; Ruth Hamilton; Robert Honeysucker; and Vivian Taylor. *Watch and Pray: Spirituals and Art Songs by African-American Women Composers*. Westbury, N.Y.: Koch International Classics, 1994. Compact Disk No. 3-7247-2.

Douglas, Kelly Brown. *The Black Christ*. Maryknoll, N.Y.: Orbis Books, 1994.

DuBois, W.E.B. *The Souls of Black Folk*. New York: Bantam Books, 1989; originally published 1903.

Earl, Riggins R. *Dark Symbols, Obscure Signs: God, Self, and Community in the Slave Mind*. Maryknoll, N.Y.: Orbis Books, 1993.

Franklin, Aretha. *Amazing Grace*. New York: Atlantic Recording Company, 1972. Rereleased as Compact Disk No. 2-906-2.

Haden, Charlie and Hank Jones. *Steal Away*. New York: Verve Records, 1995.

Harding, Vincent. *There Is a River: The Black Struggle for Freedom in America*. New York: Vintage Books, 1983.

Harlem Spiritual Ensemble. *Free at Last*. New York: Arcadia Records, 1992. Compact Disk No. 26072-1995-2.

————. *The Harlem Spiritual Ensemble, in Concert*. New York: Arcadia Records, 1991. Compact Disk No. 26072–1991–2.

Harris, Michael W. *The Rise of Gospel Blues: The Music of Thomas Andrew Dorsey in the Urban Church*. New York: Oxford Press, 1992.

Helm, MacKinley. *Angel Mo' and Her Son, Roland Hayes*. New York: Greenwood Press, 1942.

Holloway, Joseph E., ed. *Africanisms in American Culture*. Bloomington: Indiana University Press, 1990.

Hopkins, Dwight N. and George C. L. Cummings. *Cut Loose Your Stammering Tongue: Black Theology in the Slave Narratives*. Maryknoll, N.Y.: Orbis Books, 1991.

Johnson, Clifton H., ed., *God Struck Me Dead: Voices of Ex-Slaves*. Cleveland: The Pilgrim Press, 1993.

Jones, Arthur C. *Wade in the Water: The Wisdom of the Spirituals*. Maryknoll, N.Y.: Orbis Books, 1993.

Kirk-Duggan, Cheryl A. "African American Spirituals: Confronting and Exorcising Evil Through Song." In Emilie M. Townes, ed., *A Troubling in My Soul: Womanist Perspectives on Evil and Suffering*. Maryknoll, N.Y.: Orbis Books, 1993.

Krehbiel, Henry Edward. *Afro-American Folksongs*. New York: Frederick Ungar Publishing Co., 1962; originally published 1913.

Lawrence, Patricia. "Singing Together!: A Direct Line to Spirit." *Open Air: A Publication Dedicated to Sound and Music in Health and Education*. Spring, 1995, 11–15.

Levine, Lawrence. *Black Culture and Black Consciousness*. New York: Oxford Press, 1977.

Lovell, Jr., John. *Black Song, the Forge and the Flame: The Story of How the Afro-American Spiritual Was Hammered Out*. New York: Paragon House Publishers, 1986; originally published 1972.

Marsh, J.B.T. *The Story of the Fisk Jubilee Singers*. Boston: Houghton, 1880.

Maultsby, Portia K. "Africanisms in African-American Music." In Joseph E. Holloway, ed., *Africanisms in American Culture*. Bloomington: Indiana University Press, 1990, 185–210.

Mbiti, John S. *African Religions and Philosophy*, second edition. Oxford: Heinemann, 1989.

Murray, Albert. *The Omni-Americans*. New York: Outerbridge & Dienstfrey, 1970.

Paris, Peter J. *The Spirituality of African Peoples*. Minneapolis: Fortress Press, 1995.

Pitts, Jr., Walter F. *Old Ship of Zion: The Afro-Baptist Ritual in the African Diaspora*. New York: Oxford University Press, 1993.

Quivar, Florence. *Ride On, King Jesus*. Hayes Middlesex, England: EMI Records, 1990. Compact Disk No. 7-49885-2.

Raboteau, Albert J. *Slave Religion*. New York: Oxford University Press, 1978.

Reagon, Bernice Johnson, with Bill Moyers. *The Songs are Free*. Cooper Station, N.Y.: Mystic Fire Videos, #76204, 1991.

Reagon, Bernice Johnson, compiler. *Wade in the Water, Vol. I: African American Spirituals: The Concert Tradition*. Washington, D.C.: Smithsonian Institution/Folkways Recordings, 1994. Compact Disk No. SF 40072.

———. *Wade in the Water, Vol. II: African American Congregational Singing*. Washington, D.C.: Smithsonian Institution/Folkways Recordings, 1994. Compact Disk No. SF 40073.

———. *Wade in the Water, Vol. III: African American Gospel: The Pioneering Composers*. Washington, D.C.: Smithsonian Institution/Folkways Recordings, 1994. Compact Disk No. SF 40074.

———. *Wade in the Water, Vol. IV: African American Community Gospel*. Washington, D.C.: Smithsonian Institution/Folkways Recordings, 1994. Compact Disk No. SF 40075.

Roach, Hildred. *Black American Music: Past and Present*. Boston: Crescendo Publishing Co., 1973.

Roberts, John Storm. *Black Music of Two Worlds*. New York: Praeger Publishers, 1972.

Robeson, Paul. *Here I Stand*. Boston: Beacon Press, 1958.

———. *The Power and the Glory*. New York: Columbia Records, 1991. Compact Disk No. 0-7464-47337-2.

Rose, Tricia. *Black Noise: Rap Music and Black Culture In Contemporary America*. Hanover, N.H.: Wesleyan University Press, 1994.

Smithsonian Institution. *Been In the Storm So Long: Spirituals, Folk Tales and Children's Games from John's Island, South Carolina*. Washington, D.C.: Smithsonian/Folkways Recordings, 1990. Compact Disk No. 40031.

Somé, Malidoma. *Of Water and the Spirit*. New York: Penguin Books, 1994.

Southern, Eileen. *The Music of Black Americans*, second edition. New York: W. W. Norton, 1983.

Spencer, Jon Michael. *Protest and Praise: Sacred Music of Black Religion*. Minneapolis: Fortress Press, 1990.

Stuckey, Sterling. *Slave Culture*. New York: Oxford Press, 1987.

Walker, Wyatt Tee. *"Somebody's Calling My Name": Black Sacred Music and Social Change*. Valley Forge, Pa.: Judson Press, 1979.

Williams, Delores S. *Sisters in the Wilderness: The Challenge of Womanist God-Talk*. Maryknoll, N.Y.: Orbis Books, 1993.

Willson-Felder, Cynthia. *New Songs of Zion*. Burbank, Calif.: Warner Bros. Records, Warner Alliance, 1993. Compact Disk No. WBD-4152.

2

The Poetry of the Blues: Understanding the Blues in Its Cultural Context

Peter R. Aschoff

An important factor, which is only beginning to be appreciated by non-Africans, is that Western academic disciplines have separated out artistic phenomena that in Africa are conceived as a unit. Because an African mask can be enjoyed as a work of sculpture when torn from its context and isolated, immobile, in a museum case, Westerners tend to equate "African art" with sculpture. Africans, however, do not consider that mask a discrete entity; it is part of a costume, and it is of no importance until it is danced in, to appropriate music and lyrics. When an Ibo sculptor was asked to carve a mask that could be taken to America as an example of his work, he produced a carving of a human figure wearing the mask, explaining that the full beauty of the masquerade would not be seen in the mask alone.[1]

These are the canons of the cool: There is no crisis that cannot be weighed and solved; nothing can be achieved through hysteria and cowardice; you must wear and show off your ability to achieve social reconciliation. Step back from the nightmare. It is a call for parlance, for congress, and for self-confidence. . . . AfroAtlantic art forms are judicial and medical, as well as aesthetic. It is a very hard-nosed way to use art.[2]

This is no lie . . . I can be playin' the blues, and when I play the blues, I can feel somethin' goin' on and the next thing I know I'm feelin' good. . . . That's the Devil in me then. . . . It's like that song sing, "But got the Devil in my soul." . . . That's what it is. Then you go to playin' church songs and everything and then that feelin' come back, that Christian feelin' comin' back on you. . . . That's just the way that it is. The Devil got his work and God got his work.[3]

PREFACE

The anthropology of the blues is not the same thing as the history. If you want to talk about the blues as an element of culture, you have to recognize that the blues is, first and foremost, an oral art and a performance ritual; then proceed to talk about its role as an oral tradition; the beliefs, values, and world view it presents; the impact and effects of its rituals; and its importance as a cultural repository and an adaptive mechanism. To say that Bukka White, when he was released from Parchman Farm in 1940, took the train to Chicago where he recorded a series of 78s, many of which dealt with aspects of the legal system and prison life, in general, and his experiences with them, is a historical statement. The anthropological approach is to point out that in his "District Attorney Blues" White is singing about a district attorney who uses his reading of the weather to determine men's fates, revealing his conviction that the legal system is arbitrary and capricious.[4] White does so by symbolically and animisticly tying the decision making of the D.A. to weather changes so integral to White's agrarian culture, which White, and through him all the members of the blues culture, must cope with and endure but can neither predict nor influence without resort to animistic resources himself. As generations have done before him, he observes, documents, and instructs.

INTRODUCTION

"Ancient civilizations have crumbled, dynasties have fallen, rivers and lakes and oceans have been poisoned, men in funny rubber suits have provided diversion by walking on the surface of the moon. Yet the music of Charley Patton, a functionally illiterate rounder who sang for common laborers in an isolated geographical pocket that most of the rest of America had forgotten or never knew existed, still informs, entertains, and moves listeners all over the world."[5]

Its original cultural context and audience dwindling as a result of African American culture's continuing evolution, the blues appears to be changing from a culturally grounded, traditional art form into a financially fruitful, worldwide "pop" music. Although some people argue that "the postwar (WWII-ed.) transference of the blues tradition from an older black working-class generation to a younger white middle-class generation"[6] means that "there exists the possibility of some cross-cultural communication and even conflict resolution" by "breaking down cultural barriers and refashioning race and social relations along more egalitarian lines," such apologetic and ethnocentric revisionism may be unsupportable in light of Anglo-America's historical willingness to appropriate African American culture without attribution.

Jazz, modern gospel, and rock 'n' roll. All three began as unmistakably black music, the products of, and voices for, particular aspects of the African American experience. Over the years, however, the mass culture has redefined this music, removing any recognition of the importance of its cultural roots, so that the music can be claimed by the larger society. In jazz and soul music, even Kenny G and Michael Bolton are considered, by many, creative artists rather than interpreters. Rock 'n' roll has been so successfully appropriated (beginning that day in the mid-1950s when Pat Boone was hired to "cover" the hits of Little Richard) that the episodic appearance of a black rocker (for example, Hendrix, Prince, or Living Color) shocks by its singularity.

Since the 1960s, the blues too has become a citizen of the world and consequently lives simultaneously, in time if not in space, in two completely different environments—one of them dramatically removed from the context that gave it birth. The blues most known today is an internationally popular and commercially successful instrumental musical form, with trivial "throw-away" lyrics and lacking any cultural context save the rock 'n' roll world of *Rolling Stone* and MTV. These "new" blues are consumed in vast quantities, almost exclusively by people who are not part of the blues' original social milieu.

The second behavior called the blues, still extant and of interest here, is an element within the culture of a specific group of African Americans whose roots are Southern, rural, agrarian, and working and lower-class. Within this original cultural context, the blues is an *oral poetry set to music*, which stands as a seminal voice in the post-Civil War oral traditions of Southern black Americans, representing much of that society's world view and the proper values, behaviors, and rituals attendant to that reality. Ralph Ellison wrote of the blues: "they are an art form and thus a transcendence of those conditions created within the Negro community by the denial of social justice. As such, they are one of the techniques through which Negroes have survived and kept their courage during the long period when many whites assumed, as some still assume, that they were afraid."[7]

The importance of poetry to the blues in its original context can be seen in the fact that, while today's blues/rock guitar gods record thousands of hours of instrumental blues each year, instrumental blues are virtually nonexistent among blues recordings from the days when they were produced for an almost exclusively black market and listening audience. Even Robert Johnson, a man who (with Charley Patton and Son House) formed the Delta blues trinity of the 1930s and whose guitar innovations played a pivotal role in shaping the modern sound of the blues, rock 'n' roll, the electric guitar, and American popular music in general, recorded only one brief instrumental bridge among his forty-one extant recordings.[8]

From a cultural perspective, the blues is a music defined by its blackness, and the blues is an art that can be understood only in this original cultural context. Likewise, the rest of the culture cannot be understood in the round without coming to grips with a poetry, music, and social activity/ritual, which is one of that culture's most important expressions. The editorial policy of *Living Blues*, the world's leading blues journal (as stated by co-founder Paul Garon), has remained unchanged for more than 20 years: "The blues can only be understood and appreciated as an art with its own historical, cultural, economic, psychological, and political determinants. *Living Blues* does not accept an acoustic definition of the blues. We feel that the blues is a black American working-class music that developed in response to numerous determinants; that these determining factors were . . . specific to the black working-class is borne out by the fact that it was they, and they alone, who produced the blues. . . . Deprived of its historical base . . . the blues . . . is no longer the blues."[9]

Garon continues with an example that reveals the cultural hegemony of those who would deny blackness as a characteristic both necessary and sufficient in defining the blues: "A magazine dealing with Eskimo art would hardly be tempted to devote space to reproductions of Eskimo sculpture turned out by white suburbanites regardless of the quality of the suburbanite product."[10]

No matter how skillful the creations, the white suburban sculpture will never be Eskimo ivory carving because the suburbanites are not Eskimos. In "Welfare Store Blues," John Lee "Sonny Boy" Williamson (1940) sings: "Now, you need to go get you some real white man, . . . you know, to sign your little note. . . . they'll give you a pair of them keen-toed shoes and one of them ol' pinch-back soldier coats."[11]

T. C. Johnson was even more explicit in his recognition that the blues is inextricably tied to its cultural context when, with obvious cynicism, he sang in "Johnson's Blues" that he can't understand why white men don't have the blues since they have all those things that bring on the blues: money and brown-skin women![12]

When the blues is stripped of this cultural context, what remains is not the same as the original, no matter how much its admirers looking in from the outside might wish otherwise. For those who care to look, the blues provides a window through which a world and a culture, understandably suspicious of outsiders, can be glimpsed. With its defining blackness removed, however, the blues is little more than the twelve bars and three chord changes that gave us rock 'n' roll, and it's no accident that rock 'n' roll musicians took the music but not the words.

As is frequently the case in instances of artistic appropriation, the mass American culture has inflicted on the blues a sort of aesthetic revisionism, removing the blues from its cultural context, stripping away its original philosophical content, status, role, and function, and then reshaping what is left in a manner that renders the remaining exoskeleton more accessible to the mass culture. ("Remaining exoskeleton" in the sense of superficially appearing the same, but lacking the guts.) In this manner, the cultural process by which the music is created is held to be unimportant, and the aural surface structure that remains is held to be the art form in toto. This shallow and eviscerated product is then embraced and celebrated as the "real thing" by the mass culture until the original is all but forgotten; suddenly, Eric Clapton and Stevie Ray Vaughan are bluesmen. Over time, this new art comes to be accepted as the real thing, and John Hammond becomes an acceptable substitute for Jr. Kimbrough, just as Pat Boone became a permissible replacement for Little Richard and Michael Bolton, for Otis Redding.

Every now and then, however, a light shines in the wilderness. Alan Lomax's memoir, *The Land Where the Blues Began,*[13] whatever its methodological shortcomings, reminds us of Lomax's career-long insistence that the profoundly African nature of working-class, Southern black culture be acknowledged, and not just in the obvious areas of musical and religious continuities. Lomax has little time for those who see only faint and flickering glimpses of African culture at work in the Delta, for he, like Herskovits,[14] finds Africa everywhere he looks. In the dancers at a fife and drum picnic, he sees rituals of potency and unity with Mother Earth, while in the erotic poetry of the blues, he recognizes continuities with the sexual attitudes of West Africa. In the economically induced farming-out of children to more prosperous relatives, and those children's casual adoption into their new households, Lomax perceives the extended family structure of African societies. Again and again, where others see only "the culture of poverty,"[15] or where even black scholars as prominent as E. Franklin Frazier[16] found only a people who had no unique culture of their own, Lomax witnesses the dynamic strength of a society whose cultural base is Africa.

Similarly, the almost singular appearances of *Urban Blues,*[17] a reputed anthropological classic focusing on the unique cultural context in which the blues exists, and *Blues and Evil,*[18] one of the few recent works on the blues to argue forcefully that the blues' religious imagery and philosophy can be understood only from an African theological perspective, serve to underscore the larger culture's all too frequent inability to distinguish between the blues as an internationally successful pop music and the blues as an oral poetry and ritual set to music, inextricably tied to the culture that produced it. Existing within what art historian Robert Farris Thompson refers to as "the Afro-Atlantic cultural continuum,"[19] the blues is simultaneously a music, a traditional oral poetry, and a social and ritual experience, which lies near the heart of the Southern, rural, agrarian, and black experience in this country, providing one of that experience's essential voices. Like the African masquerade, the blues can be understood only in cultural context, as part of an interwoven and interconnected whole. Just as one could not understand a Catholic mass without knowing the Christian history and theology found in the Bible, the blues cannot be understood without an appreciation of the cultural context in which it exists.

In struggling to jettison the ethnocentric and self-serving concepts about the blues created by the larger society in order for the blues to be understood in its own context and on its own terms, two sets of general questions present themselves about blues poetry. First, what is the nature of the world created by, and represented in, the philosophy and theology found in the poetry of the blues? What are its fundamental organizing principles, and what is the nature of its cosmology, and what is the nature of the reality created by the poetry's structuring of perception? Second, what is the role, place, and proper behavior for human beings both male and female in that reality?

DEMOGRAPHICS OF THE BLUES

Born during the decades following the Civil War of secular music, both black and white; of work songs agrarian, industrial, and penal; of religious music and of African artistic aesthetics and retentions, at once musical, theological, and social—the blues quickly came to occupy a prominent role and status among Southern African Americans. Musically, only jazz equals the blues in its importance and originality as a musical expression of the African and African American experience and aesthetic in the United States. But the blues is distinct for three reasons. First, as a primarily vocal music, blues exists in the oral tradition of African American in a way jazz does not. Second, jazz is born, primarily, out of the rhythms of play; blues is born out of the rhythms of work. Finally, the blues is distanced from jazz demographically—both by class and geography.

Demographically, it is crucial to point out that the societal context in which the poetry of the blues is an oral tradition—and for whose members the blues in performance is a rite of social intensification and a ritual of emotional healing—is of a very specific and discrete group of black Americans. They are not simply black. One fundamental mistake Anglo-Americans have traditionally made regarding African Americans is the assumption of cultural homogeneity. The reality is that African American culture is, in many ways, as diverse as Anglo-American,[20] and what is true for one African American is not necessarily the case for the next. Nothing makes this cultural diversity more apparent than the blues.

Southern, rural, agrarian, working- and lower-class, and black. These are the demographics of the blues. Even in the cities of the North, the blues still compliments a lady by likening her to a "lowin' heifer," and at a West Coast festival, the Sam Brothers still sing "I'm a Hog for You." Standing on a cramped and dimly lit bandstand in the shadow of Chicago's "El," the bluesman tells her, "You're a no good weed . . . cows gonna mow you down." It is not a coincidence that cities with no history of a large population born in the deep South—cities like Boston, New York, or even Washington, D.C.—have very little in terms of an active blues community, either now or in the past. The cities with active blues communities, historically and today, are in the Mississippi River Valley, the Piedmont area of the southeast, and in a geographical swath, which, beginning in East Texas, stretched out during and after World War II to the West Coast.

But even to describe the people of the blues culture as Southern, rural, agrarian, working-class, and black does not adequately define the cultural milieu of the blues. More than being lower- and working-class, blues people are people whose roots are deep in traditional African American culture; the culture of the blues, existing today only in pockets (although sometimes very large pockets), is a culture that has resisted the enculturation into that more homogeneous American culture, which many of America's "ethnic" populations, including many African Americans, have to varying degrees adopted over the decades of the twentieth century.

The culture of the blues, today as in the past, is marginal even within Southern, black, rural culture; so are its people. They are a population that holds to and retains beliefs and values, deeply rooted in Robert Farris Thompson's Afro-Atlantic Cultural Continuum, which are passé even to many members of the African American lower- and working-class. The people of the blues are among America's least "Americanized" and, among Americans of African origins, they may be the last great North American repository of the original African American creole culture à la Mintz and Price[21] (although certainly not in a static form).

HISTORICAL BACKGROUND OF THE BLUES

The decades following "the time of freedom" were a period of tremendous upheaval for African Americans living in those states that had only recently been "in a condition of rebellion." The ravages of war had left the South's infrastructure virtually inoperable; emancipation had totally disrupted a social structure that—however unjustifiable—at least had rules known by all; and the endemic corruption and retribution of Reconstruction only exacerbated the situation. Finally, the period of Jim Crow and the Ku Klux Klan, which Reconstruction spawned, seemed to bring the whole episode full circle—returning to a legal servitude often differing from slavery only in the wording of its empowering legislation. No black person living in the old Confederacy wanted to turn back the clock, but sometimes the future didn't look so promising, either.

But things had changed and, in no small part, these changes can be seen in the freedom of movement, a new option that, in the blues, quickly came to be an overarching symbol for freedom itself. For the first time, a black person dissatisfied with his lot could move; a man who—to use bluesman Sam Chatmon's legendary phrase—"just got tired of smellin' mule farts," could abandon farming to try his hand in the lumber or turpentine camps, work as a gandy dancer on a railroad track maintenance crew, or skin mules on the levee projects.

Mobility also opened a myriad of artistic and creative possibilities for black Southerners, both urban and rural. Black minstrel, tent, and medicine shows; turpentine, levee, and lumber camps with their barrelhouse saloons, each with a piano in the corner; and the gambling dens, taverns, and sportin' houses along black working-class entertainment strips like Memphis's Beale Street, Detroit's Hastings Street, and Nelson Street in Greenville, Mississippi: All of these supported emerging legions of entrepreneurial, and often itinerant, African American musicians. Most professional were the black vaudeville and theatrical circuits, the most famous of which was the Theatrical Owners Booking Association—widely known as T.O.B.A. or "Tobey time" but whose initials were also said to stand for "tough on black asses."

Most important for an understanding of the cultural and social processes that gave rise to the blues is the observation that none of these artistic and economic opportunities for black Southerners could have appeared before emancipation. The thirty-five years between emancipation and the birth of the twentieth century was a period of unprecedented artistic exploration, hybridization, and creativity in African American culture, and nowhere more so than in music, as both the artist's world and his audience began to broaden. By the turn of the century, jazz, gospel as we know it today, ragtime, and indeed most contemporary African American music, including the blues, had seen their foundations laid in places as diverse as the tobacco towns of the Carolinas, the Mississippi Delta's cotton plantations and lumber camps, the brothels of New Orleans' Storyville, and the newly burgeoning Northern ghettos.

The broad distribution of early blues motifs, such as "Joe Turner" and "Boll Weevil," demonstrates that by the first years of the twentieth century, the blues—regardless of its place of origin and without denying the regional and local traditions that have always served to root it in its immediate environment—had already become a pan-Southern phenomenon. Memphis society bandleader W. C. Handy (one of the blues' earliest great black publishers and commercializers) was waiting to make a connection in a Tutwiler, Mississippi, train yard in the early years of this century, when he was first exposed to what he later remembered as "the weirdest music I had ever heard.[22] Played by a person Handy recalled as a loose-jointed, poorly clothed black man who delicately drew a knife's edge along the strings of a Spanish-style guitar as he sang "Goin' Where the Southern Cross the Dog," the blues was, by that time, already well-known throughout the South among working-class African Americans. (The Southern and the Yazoo Delta, and the "Yellow Dog," were trains whose tracks crossed at right angles in the Mississippi Delta.) When Mamie Smith went into the

Okeh Record Company's Chicago recording studios on Tuesday afternoon, August 20, 1920, to record Perry Bradford's "Crazy Blues,"[23] (the first commercial recording of a blues song sung by a black person), the blues was already well into its second generation of performers.

In later interviews, the earliest recorded bluesmen told of learning their craft from men who came out of the 1800s considering themselves to be bluesmen and adamantly distinguishing themselves from the minstrels, songsters, and "musicianeers" of an earlier yet continuing tradition. While minstrels and songsters played a wide range of musics, bluesmen primarily played the blues. In addition, to be a bluesman was far more than a simple indication that you performed the blues: The bluesman was also a well-defined social role, with its own unique set of rights, privileges, obligations, and responsibilities. This perception, common among bluesmen and their audience, that bluesmen stand apart from others in their society will, later, be seen to be crucial in understanding the role and status of the blues, and the bluesman, within their cultural context.

No slave ever sang the blues. Despite the tendency today for some people to dismiss blues as "that old slavery-time music," no slave ever sang the blues—although all slaves surely had the blues, and references to "the blue devils" as an emotional state can be documented as early as 1812.[24] The blues as a musical and poetic art, however, was created in the late 1800s by that first generation of black Southerners born outside of slavery, and one of the overarching themes of the blues is freedom, not bondage. Not the abstract and vague church-promised "someday" freedom of "Swing Low, Sweet Chariot"; not a picture of metaphysically pure and surely unobtainable freedom, but a freedom rooted in real life and based on re-alistic perceptions and expectations; freedom in a world where things aren't perfect, but where life can be dealt with in practical terms. No slave could have sung lines as resplendent in the freedom to travel as a significant life choice as are found in the blues. Consider this compendium of traveling blues sentiments:

"My home ain't here, I can leave this town."

"I'm a bad boy, just blowed in your town."

"Hard times here, but it's better down the road."

"Rocks is my pillow, cold ground been my bed."

"Leavin' in the mornin' . . . if I have to ride the blinds."

One of the finest statements of the blues as a celebration of freedom is a poetic figure that dates to the earliest years of the twentieth century and that found its most famous expression in the first line of Robert Johnson's "I Believe I'll Dust My Broom."[25] The entire song is, itself, a transcendent statement of freedom, although neither Johnson's world nor the freedom he finds in it is perfect. The song is nonetheless a statement of independence that could only be made by a free person.

(Note: To "dust" one's "broom" appears to combine two English colloquialisms that predate the blues. "To broom" is nineteenth-century slang meaning "to run away"; "to dust" appears to be derived from Matthew 10:14, which tells you, when leaving the home of "Whosoever shall not receive you, nor hear your words," . . . to be sure and "shake off the dust of your feet." In addition, a "doney" refers to a woman of low reputation, especially morally or personally. It is a pejorative term.)

> I'm gonna get up in the mornin', . . . I believe I'll dust my broom.
> I'm gonna get up in the mornin', . . . I believe I'll dust my broom.
> Girlfriend, . . . the black man you been lovin', . . . girlfriend, can get my room.
>
> I'm gonna write a letter, . . . telephone every town I know.
> I'm gonna write a letter, . . . telephone any town I know.
> If I can't find her in West Helena, . . . she must be in East Monroe, I know.
>
> I don't want no woman, . . . want every downtown man she meet.
> I don't want no woman, . . . want every downtown man she meet.
> She's a no good doney, . . . they shouldn't 'low her on the street.
>
> I believe, . . . I believe I'll go back home.
> I believe, . . . I believe I'll go back home.
> You can mistreat me here, babe, . . . but you can't when I go home.
>
> And I'm gettin' up in the mornin', . . . I believe I'll dust my broom.
> I'm gettin' up in the mornin', . . . I believe I'll dust my broom.
> Girlfriend, . . . the black man you been lovin', . . . girlfriend, can get my room.
>
> I'm gon' call up Chiney, . . . see is my good girl over there.
> I'm gon' call up China, . . . see is my good girl over there.
> If I can't find her on Phillipine's Island, . . . she must be in Ethiopia somewhere.

Only a free man could have challenged his mate's infidelity with the line "You can mistreat me here, Babe, . . . but you can't when I go home."

The blues is a music that celebrates freedom, even freedom in the imperfect, through the symbolism of travel and the ability to resolve problems by distancing one's self from them. The blues are resplendent with images of roads, rivers, and railroad tracks to be traveled; with cars, boats, and trains to serve as vehicles useful both in going to and coming from; and with oceans, mountains, and deserts to either be traversed in pursuit of a desire or placed in the path of pursuing troubles. The blues celebrates trains as "Smokestack lightnin'," that shine like gold. The train is freedom. Smoke is lightning, natural and elemental power. Gold is the ultimate symbol of freedom, at once its goal and its pursuit.

No slave ever sang the blues; as both a social role and as a philosophy, the bluesman has claimed freedom and personhood over everything else, no matter what the price. The price was often an economically and socially marginal existence even by the standards of his time and place. To be a bluesman, however, also provided high status within the tightly knit blues society. The rap artist of his time, the bluesman put the truth out there regardless of the mainstream's reaction to it and was granted harsh respect for his insistence on living life on his own terms. Living in a society structured by design to deny personhood to members of the blues culture, the bluesman's uncompromising claim to it is nothing less than revolutionary.

"BLUESMAN" AS A GENDER-SPECIFIC SOCIAL ROLE

I am well aware of the gender implications of the term "bluesman"; my use of it is conscious. Although late twentieth-century academia began to prefer gender-neutral language, to do so when describing the blues and its performers is to force on the blues a value system that it does not share. Although there admittedly were, and are, many great female blues performers, the social role of "bluesman" is quite gender-specific; to be a musician who performs the blues is a musical ability and occupation open to all, but to *be* a bluesman is a social role closed, by definition, to the distaff side. The blues itself makes clear that the role of bluesman falls under the heading of division of labor by sex. The poetry of the blues does not use the genderless terms "blues artist" or "blues singer." Also, the word "blueswoman" does not exist in the lexicon of the blues. The blues does not describe blues performers who are women the same way it characterizes "bluesmen"; rather, the term frequently used is "women blues singers." The term "blueswoman" is never used as a distaff counterpoint to "bluesman." This difference in vocabulary alone is a clear symbolic statement that the blues makes a sharp distinction based on gender among its performers.

For instance, there simply is no female equivalent to "I'm a Blues Man," by Z. Z. Hill who assertively defines himself as "a B.L.U.E.S. man" who was raised on whiskey, corn bread, collard greens, and black-eyed peas; who took his first bath in muddy water; who does whatever is on his mind; who's independent and totally free; who's proud and well-endowed and looking to get all the women he can![26]

Just as a woman cannot, by definition, be a Catholic priest, so a woman can never occupy the role of bluesman without gender ambiguity. In fact, it is in part the social and gender ambiguity of women blues singers that causes the mythology of the blues culture to recognize their sexual magic and, by inference, the sexual magic of all the women of the blues culture, as especially powerful and irresistibly siren-like.

NATURE AND SIGNIFICANCE OF BLUES RECORDINGS

It is worth noting that the enormous body of recorded blues, dating from the earliest years of the recording industry, is a unique, first-person legacy. The people of the blues culture were, and are, predominantly oral. They seldom wrote books or kept diaries; they did not record their culture and their experiences on paper, nor did they build archives (except those constructed of sounds and ideas). Without the recorded legacy of the blues, we would have almost no first-person "real time" documentation from the world of Southern, working-class African Americans during the first half of the twentieth century; we would be forced to continue relying heavily on the observations made of that world by outsiders (plantation records and diaries, local/country/state/and federal records, academics), memories and retrospective interviews, and the writings of statistically atypical, literate, and upwardly mobile "escapees" from the world under discussion. (There are, of course, exceptions. The work of Zora Neale Hurston[27] is singular and unique in the study of Southern black culture. Unfortunately, this early phase of Hurston's career is often overlooked in her (mostly literary) admirers' rush to proclaim her as one of America's finest novelists.)

Although entirely appropriate social science resources, these traditional sources do not contain the kind of information that is to be found in the oral creations of a people. As early as 1911, Odum[28] was calling attention to the fact that the songs of black Southerners were "most valuable to the student of sociology and anthropology, as well as to the student of literature and the ballad." The blues, especially the recorded legacy of the blues, is a time capsule, a time capsule containing the voices, experiences, and lives of the blues culture's people in the first person and in real time, not in recollections conjured up after the fact. When Charley Patton "(High Water Everywhere," Pts. 1 & 2)[29] and Mattie Delaney ("Tallahatchie River Blues")[30] recorded their experiences during the great Delta flood of 1927, or when Walter Roland's "Red Cross Blues"[31] preserved the thoughts of those black Deltans forced, in the flood's aftermath, into unwilling confinement as laborers in refugee camps, they provide us with singularly unique insight and perspective into those events. (Hills, by the way, was a popular chain of grocery stores in the South during the period.)

> Say, me and my good girl talked last night . . . you know, talked for an hour.

She wanted me to go to the Red Cross store and get a sack of that
   Red Cross Flour.
I told her "No," . . . Great Lord, said "Woman, I sure don't want to
   go.
You know you have to go to Hills, 'cause I got to go to that Red
   Cross store."

Say, you know them Red Cross folks there, they sure do treat you
   mean.
Don't want to give you nothin' but two, three cans of beans.
Now, I told 'em "No" . . . Great Lord, Girl, said "I don't want to
   go."
I said, you know I cannot go to Hills. I'm got to go yonder to that
   Red Cross Store.

But you know the governorment (sic) taken it charge, now, say they
   gonna treat everybody right.
They gonna guar'em two cans of beans, now, and one little can of
   tripe.
And I told 'em "No," Great Lord, Girl, says "I don't want to go."
I think I better wait till I get a job and go to Hills, 'cause I'm got to
   go to that Red Cross store.

Say, you go up there early in the morning, say, they ask you, "Boy,
   how you feel?"
. . . Gettin' ready to give you a nickel worth of rice and a bag of that
   foldin' meal.
And I told 'em "no." Great Lord, Girl, says "I don't want to go."
Said, you know I cannot go to Hills . . . I'm got to go yonder to that
   Red Cross store.

But you know, say, I got a girl, now, said she gonna get herself a
   job.
She gonna take care of me, now, while the times is hard.
And I told her "Yeah . . . Great Lord, then I won't have to go."
I said, "When you get paid off, we'll go to Hills . . . I won't have to
   go to that Red Cross Store."

But you know, say, a girl told me this mornin' that she loved me
   'cause I worked two days a week.
I told her I worked for the Red Cross, . . . didn't get nothin' but
   somethin' to eat.
She told me "No," . . . Great Lord, said "Man, I don't want to go."
She said, "Boy, there, you hav'ta carry me to Hills," . . . said "I got
   to take you to that Red Cross store."

The fact that black refugee camps were frequently viewed as readily available sources of cheap labor whose residents were often pressed into work gangs rebuilding the Delta's infrastructure, with meager pay often coming in the form of script good only at the camps' commissaries, is little documented from the perspective of those benefiting from such racist policies. It is worth noting, even if only in passing, that Roland spends just three of the song's six verses complaining about the conditions under which he is being forced to work. He is equally concerned with the impact the degrading practice of paying in commissary script has on Roland and his relationships with women; by inference, the disruption of his social world by injustice is as disturbing as the injustice itself.

On Patton, Delaney, and Roland's recordings, and on similar 78s by scores of artists, black people share with each other the great, shaping events in the modern history of their society; events often thought inconsequential by the larger culture around them. That these artists were documenting history in the first person and in real time—only slightly removed from the actual events and, as we shall see later, with little thought that outsider's ears would ever hear their very personal, and (for the times) racially incorrect, remarks—renders the recorded legacy of the blues stunning in its intimacy and immediacy. As a resource for the study of working-class black Southerners and their descendants throughout the United States, blues recordings made between the advent of home phonographs and the birth of an international audience for this music are absolutely unique.

The appearance, in the spring of 1994, of the cassette-only single "Ice Storm Blues," Parts 1 & 2, shows that, at its roots, the blues still exists as an agent of the traditional African American oral tradition. Written and performed by Clarksdale, Mississippi's, Big Jack Johnson "Ice Storm Blues" is about the legendary ice storm that hit North Mississippi that February and recounts the hardships that left scores of Delta towns like Clarksdale without electricity, water, gas, and telephones for a period of weeks as the area's entire utility infrastructure was rebuilt. Recorded locally and sold, essentially on a hand-to-hand and person-to-person basis, throughout the north Delta region, it stands as eloquent testimony to the tenaciousness with which the blues hangs on to its traditional cultural context and functions in spite of tremendous pressure for it to make concessions with the musical mainstream.

Because of the almost total lack of attention paid to the blues and its performers by anyone other than its primary consumers during its heyday, we are fortunate that from approximately 1920 to 1960, tens of thousands of blues recordings were released by major commercial recording companies that dominated the industry before World War II and the multitude of small "independent" labels that sprang up when the majors lost interest in "ethnic" music after the war. While some of these recordings—the more jazz or "pop" oriented—were made with an eye toward the white market, the vast majority were aimed exclusively at a black audience and were never expected to be heard, let alone bought, by white Americans. Usually released in separate series, often on subsidiary labels, and sold almost exclusively either in businesses in the black community or through the mail, these recordings, called "race records" by the industry, featured many musicians who enjoyed national recognition within the black community (although only one white person in 100,000 might have known of "Blind" Lemon Jefferson) as well as those whose reputations were only regional or local. Selling, collectively, in the millions, these recordings played an important role in the community and family lives of many African Americans.

The artists and the purchasers of these records (called "commercial" recordings by blues scholars and fans to distinguish them from "revival" recordings aimed at a predominantly white market) shared a common demography. Even in the urban North, the people making and listening to these records from the 1920s to the 1960s and even later tended to be migrants from the South looking for something familiar in a foreign land; it was a sound of home that helped to make more comfortable, and comforting, a new world in which much of what they had known previously was no longer true. "Goin back down South, where the weather suits my clothes," the bluesman would sing when the hawk (wind) came flying in off Lake Michigan and chilled him to his Southern bones.

BLUES RECORDINGS AS A SOCIAL SCIENCE RESOURCE

The blues falls on a continuum of all African American music with overlapping forms. The music is organized, usually although not always, into twelve bars and three chord changes, while the poetry of the blues follows an aab rhyme scheme and consists of many thousands of "blues couplets," which, with allowances for individual creativity, are used to compose the songs. This body of oral poetry is the commonly held cultural heritage of a specific group of black Americans. Other forms of oral tradition, of course, transmitted additional aspects of the culture.

The poetry of the blues exists at two levels: as personal statements of the individual artists and, in their totality, as cultural and social products—statements that transcend the idiomatic and personal to address the world of agrarian, black Southerners as agents of both enculturation and a historical repository. In fact, this ancient interaction between tradition and individual creativity results in a dynamic tension that lies at the heart of blues poetry and its power. Blues poetry runs the gamut from extremely autobiographical accounts of personal and local events and personages to questions of general concern, such as historical occurrences, religion, values, aesthetics, attitudes toward work, ethnic and social dynamics, and male-female relationships.

While the definitive discography, *Blues and Gospel Records, 1902–*

1942,[32] lists blues recordings made in the earliest years of the twentieth century, it was not until the 1920s that commercial recordings in general and blues records specifically appeared in large numbers. This was due to the increasing presence of phonographs in private homes, the later spread of juke boxes, and to improvements in recording technology. In the case of the blues, the development of practical, portable recording equipment meant that the record companies, which were invariably headquartered in the North, could send crews to the South to record artists.

The rationing of shellac during World War II—its impact compounded by the concurrent calling of a recording ban by the musicians' union to protest the threat to working musicians presented by the spread of the juke box—caused the cessation of recording from 1942 until the end of the war. After the war, the "majors" (those few record labels that dominated the recording industry prior to World War II) withdrew from virtually all activities related to "ethnic" recordings, including blues, to concentrate on recordings of a more homogeneous and mass appeal. As a result of the majors vacating the market, coupled with the appearance of relatively inexpensive acetate and tape recording equipment, scores of small labels sprang up to fill the vacuum the majors' departure had left. These "Indies," usually (but not always) white-owned, continued the prewar tradition of recording artists with no expectation that the records would be heard by anyone but black people.

Beginning with the folk boom of the early 1960s, blues artists and record companies became aware of a growing new audience for their music, an audience mostly middle-class and mostly white (and now international and transcending ethnicity). This new interest extended both to live performances and to recordings. As a result, an entirely new industry appeared producing recordings for this affluent market, including records by blues artists who had seen their commercial careers end years, even decades, earlier. Such recordings, of course, present an entirely new set of theoretical and methodological problems in terms of lyric content in oral tradition as the perceived audience changes.

Successful analysis of blues recordings requires recognition of several factors that came into play during the production of these records, beginning with the recording situation itself. Importantly, the recording situation was awkward and artificial, and certainly did not capture faithfully the blues as it was performed on a daily basis by the artists when they were working within African American society. This was not the goal; the goal was to make records that would sell. In addition, the record companies, and the people conducting the recording sessions, were invariably white, male, and often Northerners. (Black record executives like J. Mayo Williams were almost unheard of prior to World War II.) Thirdly, prewar technology limited recordings to only a little over three minutes (a tradition that, once ingrained, was continued even after the appearance of tape and LPs), even though blues in performance can easily run far longer. In combination, the technical limitations of the metal or acetate recording masters, the artificial nature of the recording session, and the racial etiquette that was frequently at work undeniably influenced what was performed and how.

Consequently, it is often argued that a more valid example of the blues in its natural context is to be found in what have come to be called "field recordings"—recordings made by folklorists and others who went into the homes, clubs, and front yards of African Americans to record the blues for the Library of Congress and other archival concerns. It is also unrealistic, however, to assume that field recordings present, by definition, a more accurate portrait of the blues as an oral tradition. In the first place, it must be accepted as a given that the mere act of observation changes that which is being observed. In both commercial and field settings, the recordings were conducted largely by white people who were not part of the society and cultural process at work. Consequently, the recordings obtained, in both cases, were colored by the presence of white outsiders.

Other advantages of field recordings (theoretically a more relaxed and less intimidating setting) are mitigated by the perception and knowledge on the part of the performer that recordings made by a folklorist in a "field" setting will be taken away, never to return to the community where they were made. The artist's primary interest, therefore, is to please the re-searcher in hopes of remuneration. When making a commercial recording, however, the artist has every hope that the recordings *will* return to his community to be played either in homes or on juke boxes. Consequently, the artist in a commercial recording studio has a vested interest in produc-ing a recording that will meet the expectations of a local audience, which is already familiar with him/her and his/her repertoire, as well as meeting local standards and expectations for the blues performance in general (in addition, of course, to pleasing the man in charge of the session). This perception reduces the influence of the commercial recording setting and encourages a performance that the artist feels will be acceptable to the blues' natural audience.

Obviously, neither the commercial nor the field setting will produce re-cordings that are completely faithful to the music when it is performed in cultural privacy, but it is not true, as has sometimes been argued, that commercial recordings are of limited use as historical and ethnographic sources. When properly utilized, they are, at the very least, as valuable as field recordings.

THE BLUES AS A CULTURAL ELEMENT

Long-term observation renders obvious the fact that two entirely differ-ent rituals are being performed as the blues eases back and forth between its traditional and revival audiences. When a blues musician plays a white club, what gets the audience out of their seats, clappin' their hands and stompin' their feet is the impassioned guitar (that's "git'tar") solo. White folks love to hear 'em play the guitar. When B. B. King plays in The Grove at Ole Miss, it isn't the words that get the kids crazy—it's the way the man can pick "Lucille." But when B. plays off a hay wagon during his annual Indianola, Mississippi, homecoming, his predominant black audience assumes he can play the guitar. For white audiences, B. B. King is a guitarist who also sings; for his black audience, B. is a singer who happens to also play the guitar. B. B. King's black audiences come to hear him tell stories about their lives, and it's the lyrics that reach B. B. King's black audiences. B. says

> I gave you a brand new Ford,
> and you said, "I want a Cadillac."
> I bought you a ten dollar dinner,
> and you said, "Thanks for the snack."
> I let you live in my penthouse . . .
> . . . you said it was just a shack . . .

and at that point the entire club just absolutely falls out, because everybody knows the next line.

> . . . I gave you seven children,
> and now you want to give 'em back.
> I've been downhearted, Baby,
> ever since the day we met . . .
> Love ain't nothin' but the blues . . .
> How blue can you get?[33]

Blues lyrics don't mean anything to the blues' new and non-Black audience. Blues poetry doesn't speak to their world, culture, history, or reality. B. knows it. When he plays for revival audiences, his show includes lots of instrumentals, lots of guitar breaks between verses, and way more up-tempo pieces than ballads. When he plays for a black audience, however, it's just the opposite; lots of ballads and slow blues, few instrumentals, and the vocals are up front in the mix.

"Not only do I not want *your* raggedy ass," she tells him in "How Blue Can You Get?", "I don't even want the fruit of your loins around as a reminder that you ever knew me that well!" Rock 'n' roll, built on adolescent concepts of gender and sexuality, almost never pays any attention to the adult and procreative implications of the act, while the blues man is always concerned about "a house full of children, don't none of 'em look like me."

It is small wonder, actually, that the lyrics are not important to persons of the Caucasian persuasion. The message of the blues is neither the prod-

uct nor the voice of Anglo-America. The poetry of the blues is an oral
tradition in twelve bars and three chord changes, composed of thousands
of poetic couplets that are the common heritage of African Americans.
Especially those African Americans whose heritage is Southern, rural,
agrarian and working- or lower-class. An oral tradition whose purpose is
to be the collective memory of the people, to be an agent of instruction for
the children, and a reminder to the adults; a reminder of where you've been
and what you're supposed to be about.

Denied full access to the written word until, at least, 1954 and *Brown
v. Board of Education* (with the *Ayers* decision indicating that "separate
but unequal" still exists, in the U.S. Supreme Court's eyes at a collegiate
level in Mississippi, if no where else) and coming from West African societies that built glorious empires on almost exclusively oral traditions, African America has remained an essentially oral society. It is within the
verbal culture of African America that many of its values, beliefs, and practices are maintained and passed from one generation to the next, from a
parent's lips to a child's ear. The truths of the blues are no less valid or
important for being unwritten, but they are not the truths of the world and
culture admiring the blues from the outside looking in.

The blues talks about a lot of things. It talks about travel and uses it as
a metaphor for freedom. It talks about work and the need to work for a
living. The blues talks about questions of justice and inequality. It sometimes talks about questions of caste as well as class. The blues is also the
repository for much of African America's earliest religious theology; "I got
my mojo workin', but it just don't work on you,"[34] or "I'm beggin', Miss
Mary Bell(e?), . . . to be careful in wha't you say or do. I'm jus 'tryin' to
. . . help you, darlin', . . . cause that unseen eye is watchin' you."[35]

In particular, the blues speaks of two fundamental concerns. First, blues
poetry creates an animistic worldview appropriate for one of the African-
based cultures of the diaspora; it is a world whose mythology, theology,
cosmology, and worldview is often remarkably different from that of the
greater European-based society around it. It is within the poetry of the
blues where much of African America's early and only partially Christian
religious theology and mythology are stored.

Secondly, the blues then discusses what it is to be a man, and what it is
to be a woman, and what should be the relationship between the two
within such a world; the blues teaches how to be a man, and how to be a
woman in a world where things aren't always fair, and how to do it with
some dignity and some style and some class.

This is not to say that every song in the blues addresses these issues or
that every blues couplet expresses the same opinion about them. (Indeed,
the blues' traditional practice of poetic construction through free and op-
positional association around a central theme, rather than through linear
narrative, allows for a wide variety of perspectives even within a single

song.) Taken as a whole, however, the poetry of the blues creates a constellation of poetic symbols that presents a specific worldview and cosmology and then presents the beliefs and behaviors appropriate for that reality.

THE BLUES AS RELIGIOUS MUSIC

Traditionally, the charge has been leveled against the blues that it is "the Devil's music," that it encourages people to engage in sin of all types. Implicit in this allegation is the assumption that the blues is a Christian music; the charge only has credibility if you accept that the teachings of the blues, whether sinful or not, exist within a Christian theological context. After all, something can only be a sin if the sinner participates (whether as saint or as sinner is immaterial) in the moral system defining the behavior as sin. I would suggest that the blues' conflict with the Christian church is not born of discord within the framework of Christian theology; rather, it is a conflict between two *different* theologies, with different attitudes toward certain human behaviors. (Spencer's is a brilliant discussion of this issue.)[36]

Christianity (especially the fundamentalist Protestant Christianity practiced by many working-class Southern African Americans) is a religion which views life as a continuing struggle between the sacred and the profane. The concept of original sin means that humans are inherently sinful, with a dual nature, and therefore the focus of life must be to constantly struggle against the profane side of our nature in pursuit of the sacred. The culture of the blues, however, being in important ways unacculturated and standing outside much of even working-class black Southern culture, can be seen as descending more directly from the original African American Creole culture born in the earliest decades of the African American experience. As a result, much blues theology does not trace its roots to Christianity but, rather, finds its origins in a much older tradition. In 1927, Texas bluesman "Blind" Lemon Jefferson recorded a blues song whose four-line stanzas betray its origins in the earliest days of the form.

> There's one kind favor I'd ask of you.
> There's one kind favor I'd ask of you.
> There's one kind favor I'd ask of you:
> See that my grave is kept clean.[37]

At first hearing, this is simply the plea of a man hoping that he not be forgotten after he has died. Please, he implores, don't disrespect me; I was . . . somebody! Don't disrespect me by allowing my grave to go untended and my name and my memory to slip from the mind and hearts of the living. But this couplet works at another, and much deeper, level, reflecting a religious philosophy that views the grave as the dwelling place of the soul and as the place where the relationship between the living and the dead is mediated. In fact, the keeping of bare-earth graves is only a part of a larger complex of African American burial practices, which have been repeatedly noted as being a direct retention of African burial practices followed by, among others, the Kongo people.[38] Since the grave is the dwelling place of the soul, the logic goes, the grave should be maintained as any other dwelling place; since the Kongo keep bare earth yards around their dwellings, that is also the way they keep graves.

Unlike Christianity, which teaches that, at the time of death, the human soul leaves for Heaven or Hell and ceases to be a part of this world, West African animists like the Kongo believe that the ancestral spirit remains a very real part of this world and thus must be dealt with as one would deal with any other member of one's family and society. In fact, Jefferson's lyrics reflect a religious system that is largely devoid of Christian theology; it is a world where ancestral spirits are real and where these spirits must be considered as actors in this world. It is a world where talented specialists are uniquely able to deal with spiritual matters and where charms, spells, and ties between behavior and well-being are very real. Eddie "Son" Thomas (1983) told a wonderful story that starts with the line "My Grandfather, he was a-scared of ghosts . . . He' as scared of dead folks."[39]

William Harris's "Bull Frog Blues"[40] is another indication of a worldview that falls outside the traditional Christian domain. Dismissed by the larger culture as superstition, the song clearly reveals a cosmology in which unnatural events are often omens that, to the attuned, can indicate auspicious events. In it the occurrence of unnatural events (dreaming of bull frogs, and the falling of rain while the sun is shining) serve as omens, intended to let the song's listener know that Harris has some important issues to discuss (the impermanence of interpersonal relationships in the symbolism of dreams and waking images) and that the listener should pay close attention.

The blues is not the music of the Christian devil; it is not Christian music at all. The blues recognizes no original sin, and it accepts no mark of Cain; the theology of the blues acknowledges that both the sacred and the profane are essential parts of the human experience and that the success or failure of our lives is determined by our ability to maintain the balance that should exist between the sacred and profane aspects of existence. Balance, however, is the key, and the bluesman who gains his abilities through a Faustian encounter with Legba has crossed over the line and has become a very dangerous, if powerful, person, indeed.

> Early this mornin', . . . when you knocked upon my door . . .
> Early this mornin', . . . ooh, when you knocked upon my door,
> and I said, "Hello, Satan, I believe it's time to go.

You may bury my body, . . . down by the highway side.
[SPOKEN:] Baby, I don't care where you bury my body when I'm
   dead and gone.
You may bury my body, ooh, down by the highway side, . . .
so my old evil spirit can catch a Greyhound bus and ride.[41]

The blues accepts, enjoys, and celebrates both the sacred and the profane sides of human nature. The blues people see no conflict. Did not God, after all, create them both? As Ida Goodson says in the film *Wild Women Don't Have The Blues*: "This is no lie . . . I can be playin' the blues, and when I play the blues, I can feel somethin' goin on and the next thing I know I'm feelin' good . . . That's the Devil in me then . . . It's like that song sings, 'But got the Devil in my soul' . . . That's what it is. Then you go to playin' church songs and everything and then that feelin' come back, that Christian feelin' comin' back on you . . . That's just the way that it is. The Devil got his work and God got his work."[42]

The theological opposition that exists between the blues and the church often creates for bluesmen themselves an internal ambivalence in their own lives. More than a few aging bluesmen, feeling death slipping down their lungs, have left their original calling and retired to the pulpit (preaching as only the most formerly unrepentant of sinners can). On a list that runs from Ishman Bracey to Queen Sylvia Embry, legendary bluesman Eddie "Son" House is the prototypic embodiment of the ambivalence felt by many bluesmen.

Son House was a giant. In his prime during the 1930s and early to mid-1940s, Son House may have been the greatest bluesman who ever lived, not because of his staggering skills on the guitar, but because of his voice and because of his deep understanding of the philosophical and religious implications of the blues poetry. He was born in Lyons, Mississippi, around the turn of the century, House, himself, wasn't sure exactly when. His manager during the 1960s, Dick Waterman, thinks Son may have been near one hundred years old when he died in 1989.[43] Standing between Charley Patton, from whom he learned, and both Robert Johnson and Muddy Waters, to whom he was mentor, Son House connected the earliest years of the blues with what would become "modern" blues. He was, without question, the finest Delta bluesman of his generation, and when Muddy Waters[44] talked about the concept of "Deep Blues," he surely had Son House in mind.

Although his handful of 1930s commercial recordings sold poorly, Son House was a major player in the Delta blues brotherhood of the day (even though he never did quite achieve the celebrity as an entertainer that was accorded Patton—House was too "deep" for that, and he dismissed much of Patton's performance antics as "monkey junk"). Muddy Waters later recalled, "When I was a boy comin' up, that man was King . . . King, you hear me? Folks came from miles around to hear that man play the blues."[45]

Son had been a preacher as a young man—his conversion to the blues came late—and he was a very intelligent man who fully understood the theological and philosophical implications of blues poetry. "Blues is not a plaything, like people think they are. Like youngsters today, right now, they take anything and make the blues out of it, just any little ol' jump somethin' or other and say, 'This is such 'n' such a blues.' No, it's not . . . that's no blues."[46]

He likened blues to deep love. Patting his chest over his heart, he said, "That kind of love, it goes here. That's where the blues start at."

House understood that blues is a music that accepts and celebrates the secular side of human nature, just as the Baptist church rails against it as strongly as it pursues the sacred. This ambivalence, this inability to resolve the conflict between the theological philosophies of a music and a religion that he loved equally, was at the heart of the emotional power of House's music.

Listening to House's music hints at the reason for this criticism; seeing him in action makes it perfectly clear. During the 1960s and early 1970s, in his later years and performing before throngs of young white fans who worshipped him as the very embodiment of deep Delta blues, the presence of an audience would prompt the preacher in him to the fore and House would sermonize at length.[47] He told his young parishioners that you can follow God or you can follow the Devil; there is no middle ground. Surely this message was not lost on House, who was himself trapped between the two. In "Preachin' the Blues"[48] he sings, "I had religion, Lord, this very day. But the womens and whiskey, well, they would not let me pray."

In the profound depth of his understanding of the ambivalent role of the bluesman, only Robert Johnson and perhaps Muddy Waters were Son House's equals.

As you read the following lyrics to "Preachin' The Blues," Pt. 1, notice how this ambivalence comes through in the poetic text. Being an example of blues composition at its finest, there is no linear narrative development; rather, it is a classic demonstration of composition by jazzlike improvisation. House picks a central theme—in this case the relationship between the profane and the sacred—and then associates freely around it. "Just because those words were the ones that got to be on the record don't mean that it was the only ones that could fit in there. We changed them songs around all the time. It don't matter what . . . (I sang on the record). I probably never done it again that way anyhow."[49]

The final product is a poem that speaks with equal enthusiasm from both sides of the issue without ever resolving the conflict.

Oh, I'm gonna get me religion. I'm gonna join the Baptist Church.
Oh, I'm gonna get me religion. I'm gonna join the Baptist Church.
I'm gonna be a Baptist preacher, and I sure won't have to work.

Oh, I'm gonna preach these blues, now, and I want everybody to
   shout.
Mmmmmmmmmmmmmmmmmm, . . . and I want everybody to shout.
I'm gonna do like a prisoner. I'm gonna roll my time on out.

Oh, in my room, I bowed down to pray.
Oh, I was in my room. I bowed down to pray.
Say the blues come along, and they drove my spirit away.

Oh, and I had religion, . . . Lord, this very day.
Oh, and I had religion, . . . Lord, this very day.
But the womens and whiskey, well, they would not let me pray.

Oh, I wish I had me a heaven of my own.
[SPOKEN:] Great God almighty.
Hey, heaven of my own.
Then I'd give all my women a long, long happy home.

Yeah, I love my baby just like I love myself.
Ooooooooooooooh . . . just like I love myself.
Well, if she don't have me, she won't have nobody else.

SEX ROLES AND SEX IN THE BLUES

The second thing the blues talks about—and these issues are not unre-
lated—is the one most commonly associated with the blues. Although often
dismissed as party music concerned only with drinkin', fightin' and cour-
tin', the blues is, its obvious entertainment value aside, a very sophisticated
discussion of what it is to be a man, what it is to be a woman, and how
to be a man and how to be a woman in a society where things are not
always fair, and how to be a man or a woman in that society with some
class and some dignity and some style.

Specifically, the blues presents a portrait of what it is to be a woman
that marks the blues as uniquely African American in its perspective. Central to the blues philosophy of what it is to be a man and a woman is the
blues' recognition of, and emphasis on, the magico-sexual power of
women. The blues teaches that a woman's sexuality empowers her. There
has never been a lyric, in the history of the form, that sang "The good
Lord gave him something, take him through this world," and yet "My Baby
ain't good lookin', and her teeth don't shine like pearls, but the Lord has
give her somethin' . . . that takes her through this world" is a very common

line in the blues when talking about women. "Jealous of him? Jealous of Him!?" the blues woman asks. "Why should I be jealous of him? With one of these I can get all of those I want."[50]

> I want you men to listen, to what I have to say;
> You'd better be in shape, when you come my way.
> Cause I'm a hard lovin Mama . . . healthy, firm and fine.
> If you mess around with me, I know I can make you mine . . .
>   anytime . . . anytime.[51]

"Anytime, anytime," the blues woman says. A woman of the blues culture knows that, as long as she can "keep her man's nose wide open," she can do just about anything she wants. (This image refers to the flaring of a stallion's nostrils during sex; the rural roots of the blues are constantly revealed in its poetic preference for metaphors based in rural, agrarian, and natural life.)

It is important to remember that many of the blues culture's women are descended from African traditions where the sexual magic of women is so powerful that, once a month, they may be secluded or become subject to various other taboos and required ritual behaviors. Perhaps it is because they are spiritually unclean or ritually polluted (and that is how the men might try to lay it off), but it is also because during this time, when a woman's magic is made manifest and its power is most evident, she is a challenge to the male-dominated public power structure. In the poetry of the blues, it is common for a woman's monthly cycles to be associated with the phases of the moon and for her sexuality to be capable of controlling a man. Indeed, through symbolic association with animistic powers and the attendant worldview, a woman's sexuality is presented as a force of nature, uncontrollable and irresistible. She might be the "somebody" who hoodoo'd the hoodoo man in Junior Wells's "Hoodoo Man Blues"![52]

While Tammy Wynette (one of the most successful female country and western singers) sings "Stand By Your Man"[53] in almost whining acceptance and supplication, Howlin' Wolf sings to his woman, "How many more years . . . have I got to let you dog me around?"[54] Not "How many more years . . . do you *want* me to let you dog me around?"; not "How many more years . . . do you *hope* to dog me around?"; not "How many more years . . . do you *think* you can get me to let you dog me around?"; but, "How many more years . . . do I have to let you dog me around?" in both recognition of and resignation to his inability to either impact on her actions or to resist her sway over him.

As an oral literary tradition, the poetry of the blues uses small constellations of symbols to speak volumes and to discuss issues of transcendent social importance. Creating symbolic constellations from commonly held poetic clusters, a blues will conjure up in the mind of artist and audience alike a shared societal discussion of a much larger issue. Of course, this poetic "shorthand" is more important within the artificial confines of recorded blues' traditional three-minute format, but, even in the open-ended structure of blues in live performance, it retains an essential and referential function.

Making use of what Robert Palmer has referred to as "symbolic compression," Howlin' Wolf, in the six lines of "How Many More Years," lays out the nature of the male/female tension, implicitly referencing a library of philosophical discussions that have spanned time and space. In three couplets, with the first line in each verse repeated to allow for the creation of tension through the delay of resolution and to provide time for construction of the concluding thought, the Wolf uses the experiences of everyday life to give flesh to a perception of a woman's sexuality and the male/female dynamic that has roots reaching into a distant and African past.

> How many more years . . . have I got to let you dog me around?
> How many more years . . . have I got to let you dog me around?
> I'd as soon rather be dead . . . sleepin' way down in the ground,

he asks in the first verse, referencing the blues culture's recognition that women are holding the boss card. A man can bluff, raise, and call, but the bluff won't work—she'll stay in the game; he can raise—but he's only setting himself up; and, if he calls, he's holding nothing but deuces. And yet, neither can he fold. The lure of the game is irresistible. The second verse reinforces his inability to influence the game:

> If I'd treat you right, you wouldn't believe what I'd say.
> If I'd treat you right, you wouldn't believe what I'd say.
> You'd think I'm half-way crazy . . . You'd beg on (back) and (I'd) let
>   you have your way.

Even if he does right by her, she'll continue to do him that-a-way. Indeed, his wishes and deeds are irrelevant both to her decision making and to her actions. (The words in parentheses were inserted by the author for purposes of lay intelligibility.)

In the final couplet, Wolf acknowledges that he has only one recourse that allows him to save face. Sometimes you have to cut your losses.

> I'm goin up stairs . . . I'm gonna bring back down my clothes.
> I'm goin up stairs . . . I'm gonna bring back down my clothes.
> If anybody asks about me, just tell 'em I walked outdoors.

Wolf can neither influence her actions nor will his ego allow him to continue subjecting himself to her controlling power. The song is an affirmation of the most important thing for any human being to know. What is it to be a man, what is it to be a woman, and what is the nature of the relationship between the two? Even when out of her presence, a man can sometimes not escape the power she holds over him. In "Somebody Put Bad Luck on Me,"[55] Baby Boy Warren believes it must be the enduring effect of a former lover that interferes with every relationship he tries to have with other women.

One should not assume, however, that the blues has a simplistic, one dimensional, or misogynistic view of women as manipulative and domineering. In addition to empowering her, a woman's sexuality is also seen as therapeutic, nurturing, and restorative. A woman, after all, can help a man "get right." Marvin Gaye's Motown hit "Sexual Healing" was not saying anything new; his was simply a modern pop restatement of an aesthetic as old as the blues itself, like Sonny Boy Williamson singing

> I remember one Friday mornin', we was lyin' down cross the bed . . .
> . . . Man in the next room was dyin' . . . Stopped dyin' an' raised up
>   his head, an' said . . .
> "Lord, ain't she pretty, and the whole state knows she's fine.
> Every time she start to lovin, she brings eyesight to the blind"[56]

In the culture of the blues, women deal from a position of power and strength and are not expected, or taught, to be pliant, submissive, and receptive, as is the case in much of Anglo-America's folk traditions. A woman will brag, "With what I got, I can make a rabbit hug a hound," or, as Blue Lu Barker said in so many words when recalling a song she sang in the thirties, "A woman's got everything she needs to control her man!"[57]

Because the blues theology holds that the goal of life is the successful balance of the sacred and profane spheres of existence, it logically follows that sex—being one of the most important parts of the human secular spirit—would be seen as not just an acceptable part of life, but as essential to a healthy, well-balanced adult life. As a result, it is assumed in the blues that all normal, healthy people, both male and female, are both sexual and sexually active. Indeed, contrary to European values, celibacy is perceived as actively unhealthy, because it causes imbalance of the spirit. As a result, and again differing strongly from traditional European values, the women of the blues culture are granted the same sexual interests, enthusiasm, and appetites as men. Women, like men, are entitled to get dressed up on Saturday night and go out lookin' for some stuff.

> Well, I've known some women have two men,
> Seen some women have three.
> Sometimes it look like like a woman can have any man she see![58]

Denise LaSalle looks out over her audience like a woman pickin' a melon: "Ooh, there are some pretty boys up in here tonight, ya'll!" she'll exclaim in absolute relish of the evening's work ahead. With her hands on her hips, a smile on her face, and a strut in her voice, she indulges herself in glorious Freudian imagery when she sings about a cheatin' man whose "key no longer fits her lock!"

Blues women, early on, sang songs rejoicing in the positive and empowering attributes of their sex and the blues woman's approach to life.

> I hear these women ravin' bout their monkey men, . . .
> about their triflin' husbands and their no good friends.
> These poor women sit around . . . all day and moan, . . .
> wonderin' why . . . their wanderin' Papas don't come home.
>
> But wild women don't worry.
> Wild women don't have no blues.
>
> Now, when you've got a man, don't (you-ed.) never be on the
>   square . . .
> 'cause if you do, he'll have a woman everywhere.
> I never was known to treat no one man right.
> I keep 'em working hard both day and night.
>
> 'cause wild women don't worry.
> Wild women don't have the blues.
>
> I've got a disposition and a way of my own.
> When my man starts kicking, I let him find another home.
> I get full of good liquor, walk the streets all night.
> Go home and put my man out if he don't act right.
>
> Wild women don't worry.
> Wild women don't have the blues.
>
> You never get nothing by being an angel child.
> You better change your ways and get real wild.
> I'm going to tell you something, I wouldn't tell you a lie.
> Wild women are the only kind that really get by.
>
> 'cause wild women don't worry.
> Wild women don't have the blues.[59]

Regarding "Wild Women Don't Have the Blues," it has been suggested that "monkey man" is a term that has its roots in the African folkloric tradition of the monkey as a trickster hero, and in the blues it is often applied to a woman's "back door man," especially if he is recognized as a talented lover or hustler whose faithfulness cannot be assumed. This motif is also found in formulaic toasts, such as "The Signifying Monkey" and in commonly held songs like "The Dirty Dozens." "Monkey and the baboon, . . . playin in the grass, . . . Monkey got mad and whipped his yas, yas, yas" and, more obscurely, in the doctor's warning that if Big Bill Broonzey doesn't quit drinking "I think I'm gonna have to give you monkey glands."[60]

A final aspect of blues poetry regarding men and women is worth attention. Occasionally, it will be suggested that the blues interest in the male/female dynamic is focused on the carnal to the exclusion of other facets of the relationship, implying (sometimes with a lack of subtlety that borders on racism) that the men and women of the blues culture do not desire relationships built on foundations of love, respect, trust, or any of the other "higher" emotions and that those relationships that do develop are, at best, transient and convenient means for attaining short-term goals.

It is true that the blues is able to distinguish sex from love, to recognize that the latter is not requisite for the former, and that sex for the sheer physical pleasure of it is no sin. (Bo Carter says it straight out when she sang about putting bananas in fruit baskets!)[61] To extrapolate from such boldness, however, that people of the blues culture do not desire and enjoy long-term relationships built on mutual love, trust, and respect is an unwarranted use of the data.

Occasionally, a blues song appears that beautifully blends genuine love with exquisite eroticism; such is the case with Bertha Lee's "Yellow Bee."[62] To fully appreciate the intimacy of this song, it is necessary to know that her husband at the time was Charley Patton; Patton was the greatest and best known Delta bluesman of his era and was the guitar accompanist on this song. As such, he was in the studio as it was being recorded.

Although Patton had a guitar and vocal style as "black" as any ever recorded, the one extant photograph of him shows a man who was, in fact, very "high yellow"; his skin was very light, his facial features were fine (with thin lips and nose and high cheekbones), and his hair was "good" (fine and wavy). He *is* the Yellow Bee of, and to, whom Bertha Lee sings in "Yellow Bee." In this setting, "Yellow Bee" is a loving and erotically charged song sung by a woman to her husband.

> Yellow Bee, Yellow Bee . . . please come back to me.
> Yellow Bee, Yellow Bee . . . please come back to me.
> He made the best ole honey, any yellow bee I ever seed.
>
> Well, he buzzed me this mornin', . . . been lookin' for him all day
>   long.
> Well, he buzzed me this mornin', . . . been lookin' for him all day
>   long.
> Had me to the place once, . . . hated to see Yellow Bee leave home.

Well, I just stand here . . . worried, worried, worried.
Come here, Yellow Bee . . . oooh, you know your stuff.
[Spoken, by Patton] You know you know it.
Ah, buzz me, Yellow Bee . . . 'til I gets enough.

Yellow bee makes honey, black bee make the comb.
Yellow bee makes honey, black bee make the comb.
If you wanta feel blue, stop into my honey comb.

Well, I just stand here . . . worried, worried, worried.
Come here, Yellow Bee . . . oooh, you know your stuff.
[Spoken, by Patton] Aw . . . I know you know it, Mama.
Ah, buzz me, Papa Charlie, . . . 'til I gets enough.

Aaaah, . . . stinger long as my right arm.
Aaaah, . . . stinger long as my right arm.
Had me to the place once, . . . hated to see my Yellow Bee leave
    home.

In the blues culture, men and women deal from positions, balanced although not alike—a necessary and mystical tension alloyed in a cauldron
fired by the interfacing sexual powers of both parties.

SUMMARY

People who take the position presented in this chapter are frequently
pilloried in the blues' journals as purists, at best, and, at worst, as fanatical
moldy figs with a museum mentality. They argue, essentially, that the only
appropriate definition of the blues that is both necessary and sufficient is
an aural one. Using a popular analogy, they feel that, like the duck, if it
sounds like the blues, then it is the blues. What they are saying, of course,
is that it is only the product that is important and that the cultural and
creative process by which art is produced is of no import to its identity,
understanding, and appreciation.

The "purists" take a different position, of course. They will readily admit
that Kim Wilson, a harmonica player with the Fabulous Thunderbirds, can
play in the style of Little Walter Jacobs with such unerring accuracy that
it is virtually impossible, aurally, to distinguish between them. It is the
position of the author and others of his ilk, however, that technical proficiency is not an adequate substitute for authenticity. To borrow a concept
from linguist Noam Chomsky, one should not be interested simply in the
shallow surface structure of art any more than that of language. Both are
the product of a unique cultural and creative process, and it is only through
an understanding and appreciation of this process that either can be fully
appreciated.

It is neither illegal nor immoral, of course, to enjoy the blues simply as an internationally popular and commercially successful instrumental musical form, with trivial, throw-a-way lyrics and lacking any cultural context as described earlier in this chapter, and that is exactly what the vast majority of listeners to, and fans of, this unique American music will continue to do. (More power to them. Stomp it on down to the bricks!) This makes it all the more important for those of us who take the blues seriously as a unique voice for, and product of, the African American experience to continue documenting the blues as a crucial part of the black oral and musical traditions, providing insight into the world of the blues, its culture, and its people in ways available nowhere else. Just because blues people are often poor, sometimes lack middle-class education, and frequently stand outside America's cultural mainstream does not mean they are stupid. They have much to tell us if we will only listen.

NOTES

1. Frank Willett, "Arts of African Peoples," in *The Encyclopedia Britannica*, William Benton, Ed., 1, 233. (Chicago: University of Chicago Press, 1983).

2. Robert Farris Thompson, *Flash of the Spirit: African and Afro-American Art and Philosophy* (New York: Random House, 1983).

3. Ida Goodson, *Wild Women Don't Have The Blues* (San Francisco, Calif.: California Newsreel, 1989), film.

4. Booker T. Washington, "Bukka" White, *District Attorney Blues*, 1940, Okeh Records matrix #WC-2987-A.

5. Robert Palmer, *Deep Blues* (New York: The Viking Press, 1981).

6. William Barlow, *Looking Up At Down: The Emergence of Blues Culture* (Philadelphia: Temple University Press, 1989).

7. Ralph Ellison, *Shadow and Act* (New York: Random House, 1953).

8. Robert Johnson, *Kindhearted Woman*, 1936, ARC master #SA-2580-1.

9. Paul Garon, Editorial, *Living Blues* 12 (April 1973).

10. Paul Garon, Editorial, *Living Blues* 13 (March 1973).

11. John Lee "Sonny Boy" Williamson, *Welfare Store Blues*, 1940, Bluebird matrix #053001.

12. T. C. Johnson, *J. C. [sic] Johnson's Blues*, 1928, Okeh matrix #400250-B.

13. Alan Lomax, *The Land Where The Blues Began* (New York: Pantheon Books, 1993).

14. Melville Herskovits, *The Myth of the Negro Past* (New York: Harper & Row, 1941).

15. Oscar Lewis, *La Vida: A Puerto Rican Family in the Culture of Poverty* (San Juan and New York: Random House, 1966).

16. E. Franklin Frazier, *The Negro Family in the United States*, rev. ed. (New York: Macmillan, 1957).

17. Charles Keil, *Urban Blues*, orig. ed. (Chicago: University of Chicago Press, 1966).

18. Jon Michael Spencer, *Blues and Evil* (Knoxville: University of Tennessee Press, 1933).

19. Robert Farris Thompson, "Canons of the Cool," *Rolling Stone* 435 (1984): 23–28, 81.

20. Vera M. Green, "The Confrontation of Diversity Within the Black Community," *Human Organization* 29, no. 4, (1970): 267–272.

21. Sidney W. Mintz and Richard Price, *An Anthropological Approach to the Afro-American Past* (Philadelphia: Institute for the Study of Human Issues, 1976).

22. W. C. Handy, *Father of the Blues: An Autobiography* (New York: Macmillan, 1942).

23. Mamie Smith, *Crazy Blues*, 1920, Okeh Records matrix #7529-C.

24. David Evans, Personal communication, 1990.

25. Robert Johnson, *I Believe I'll Dust My Broom*, 1936, ARC master #SA-2581-1.

26. Z. Z. Hill, *I'm a Bluesman*, 1983, Malaco LP #7415.

27. Zora Neale Hurston, *Mules and Men* (Philadelphia: Lippincott, 1935). See also "Voodoo in Haiti," in *Tell My Horse* (Berkeley: Turtle Island, 1983; reprint of 1938 edition) pp. 137–278.

28. Howard W. Odum, "Folk-Song and Folk-Poetry as Found in the Secular Songs of the Southern Negroes," *Journal of American Folklore* 24 (1911): 255–294, 351–396.

29. Charley Patton, *High Water Everywhere, Pts. 1 & 2*, 1929, Paramount masters #L-59-1 and #1-60-2.

30. Mattie Delaney, *Tallahatchie River Blues*, 1930, Vocalion master #MEM-785.

31. Walter Roland, *Red Cross Blues*, 1933, ARC master #13550.

32. John Godrich, and Robert M. W. Dixon, *Blues & Gospel Records, 1902–1942* (Essex: Storyville Publications, 1982).

33. B. B. King, *How Blue Can You Get?* 1964, ABC Records LP #509.

34. Muddy Waters, *Got My Mojo Workin'*, 1957, Chess master #8393.

35. Sonny Boy Williamson, *Unseen Eye*, 1957, Chess master #9840.

36. Jon Michael Spencer, *Blues and Evil* (Knoxville: University of Tennessee Press, 1993).

37. "Blind" Lemon Jefferson, *See That My Grave's Kept Clean*, 1927, Chicago: Paramount master #20074-2.

38. Robert Farris Thompson, *The Four Moments Of The Sun. Kongo Art In Two Worlds* (Washington, D.C.: National Gallery of Art, 1981).

39. James "Son" Thomas, *Monologue on Ghosts*, 1983, Personally recorded audio tape in possession of author.

40. William Harris, *Bull Frog Blues*, 1928, Gennet master #14318.

41. Robert Johnson, *Me and the Devil*, 1937, ARC master #DAL-398-1.

42. Ida Goodson, *Wild Women Don't Have The Blues* (San Francisco, Calif.: California Newsreel 1989), film.

43. Dick Waterman, "Son House Obituary," *Living Blues* 84 (1989): 48.

44. Muddy Waters, "Son House Obituary," *Living Blues* 84 (1989): 48.

45. Ibid.

46. Muddy Waters, Interview on Camera Three, 1968, WVBS-TV, New York.

47. Son House, and Bukka White, *Masters of the Country Blues* (Cambridge, Mass.: Yazoo Records, 1991), film.

48. Eddie "Son" House, *Preachin' The Blues, Parts 1 & 2*, 1930, Paramount masters #L-410-1 and #L-411-1.

49. Muddy Waters, "Son House Obituary," *Living Blues* 84 (1989): 48.

50. Anonymous, Personal communication with author, (ca 1980).

51. Chubby Newsome, *Hard-Lovin' Mama*, 1949, Regal master #1139-2+1.

52. Junior Wells, *Hoodoo Man Blues*, 1953, States master #1327.

53. Tammy Wynette, *Stand By Your Man*, 1968, Epic 45 rpm #10398.

54. Howlin' Wolf, *How Many More Years*, 1951, Sun master #U84.

55. Baby Boy Warren, *Somebody Put Bad Luck On Me*, 1953, 1954, Drummond master #310.

56. Sonny Boy Williamson, *Eyesight to the Blind*, 1951, Trumpet master #DRC-152.

57. Blue Lu Barker, *Wild Women Don't Have The Blues* (San Francisco, Calif.: California Newsreel, 1989), film.

58. Ferdinand Jones. Original composition, 1999.

59. Ida Cox, *Wild Women Don't Have The Blues*, 1924, Paramount master #1824–1.

60. Big Bill Broonzey, *Good Liquor Gonna Carry Me Down*, 1935, Bluebird master #96232–1.

61. Bo Carter, *Banana in Your Fruit Basket*, 1931, Columbia master #404923-B.

62. Bertha Lee, *Yellow Bee*, 1934, Vocalion master #14735–2.

3

The New Orleans Brass Band: A Cultural Tradition

Michael G. White

As the twentieth century closed, the perception of jazz as America's most significant artistic achievement gained momentum. The new level of respect is reflected in a steady increase of jazz activities and greater visibility for performers of all ages. Numerous jazz concerts, festivals, and educational programs are being sponsored and supported by an array of public and private organizations, major cultural institutions, and, most recently, the federal government. In addition, a growing interest in history and culture has focused attention toward Louisiana traditions, including traditional New Orleans jazz.

While all jazz styles, including swing, bebop, cool, and free jazz, have been associated with a wide range of sociophilosophical beliefs and behavior patterns, no form has had a more deeply rooted community-based existence than the Crescent City (New Orleans) jazz tradition. More than a passing fad or mere form of diversion, New Orleans jazz has existed for more than one hundred years as an indigenous multifunctional music that represents the ethos of America's most unique black subculture. Perhaps surprisingly, the typical six- or seven-piece ensemble that first brought New Orleans jazz to the American consciousness and to worldwide attention just before and during the 1920s has not been the most involving and significant musical form for locals. The New Orleans brass band, more than any formation in jazz or other musical styles, has been the longest running and most direct link to the true spirit and cultural heritage of the Crescent City.

As late as the mid-1970s, the most largely attended local functions involving traditional New Orleans jazz were community parades and funerals using brass bands. Thousands of local African Americans who rarely visited the French Quarter and would never attend a "traditional jazz" concert followed brass bands as if their lives depended on it. Until fairly recently, the New Orleans brass band tradition saw limited exposure outside of the Crescent City. In the history of jazz, brass bands were considered important mainly as having served as a training ground for early jazz pioneers.

To understand the cultural and musical implications of the New Orleans brass band tradition, it is first necessary to look at the unique social environment in which it was born and to contextualize the local tradition in the midst of America's long-term fascination with brass bands. Since its founding in 1718, New Orleans has had a nature and character very different from anywhere else in urban America. The city was first colonized by the French. As other colonies fought for independence against the British, Louisiana remained under French rule, except between 1763 and 1803 when it was governed by Spain. When the Americans came after the Louisiana Purchase of 1803, the original inhabitants steadfastly held on to their French language, customs, and traditions. The early settlers, formed partly from "less desirable" French outcasts, were characterized as hedonistic because of their constant preoccupation with food, music, dance, celebrations, and holidays.

Geographic location, economics, and a somewhat more lax Franco-Latin approach to slavery and race relations yielded the development of the most unusual and diverse black population in America. Because New Orleans was a growing port along the Mississippi River, many black slaves were imported for the slave trade, construction, maintaining docks and levees, and work on the boats. Unlike on rural Louisiana plantations, many urban slave owners had a very small number of slaves. Sometimes the slaves' services were rented out. Many were allowed privileges and "freedoms" unheard of outside of New Orleans. It was not unusual for local slaves to run businesses, earn salaries, and have time off during which they attended a variety of functions.

Miscegenation (racial mixing) came largely through the *plaçage* system— which was a common practice allowing French men, often married ones, to establish long-term relationships and families with women of color. These unions led to even more lax racial attitudes as well as the rise of a distinct social class known as "Creoles of color." This growing complex racial structure led to New Orleans having the largest free black population in America by the beginning of the Civil War. As Alfred Hunt points out, it was the actual physical conglomeration of African-blooded people from such varied backgrounds that spawned the development of "the most vibrant black subculture in the antebellum south."[1] Grossly oversimplified and misunderstood, the black population of New Orleans comprised many culturally different groups, which were affected by migrations, language, regionalism, miscegenation, social status, and religion. Just scratching the surface of African-blooded peoples in the New Orleans area reveals a high level of diversity: slaves from more than a dozen African nations, two nineteenth-century migrations of West Indians from Haiti, slave and American Indian mixtures, Anglo Africans (free and slave) from outside Louisiana, and local Creoles of color (free and slave). There was such an emphasis on racial classification and categories that more than a half-dozen terms were commonly used beyond the general "Creole of color" and "black (Negro)": quadroon, octoroon, griffe, mulatto, marabon, brique, and others. After the war, the black population increased in number and cultural diversity when ex-plantation slaves from Louisiana and neighboring states migrated to New Orleans. The percentage of blacks often equaled or exceeded that of whites during the nineteenth century, making New Orleans the first major American city with a large black urban enclave.

Given the city's complex social structure, cultural makeup, and penchant for excessive pleasure seeking, it is not surprising that music and music-related activities of all types would be an important part of New Orleans life. By the early nineteenth century, the city already had a healthy dose of regular musical events: opera, classical concerts, parades, and funerals. The most popular and least expensive pastime was social dancing. There were public and private dances and elaborate balls, including the famous "Quadroon Balls" (a common means of introduction between beautiful quadroon [one-fourth black] and octoroon [one-eighth black] women and potential French suitors). The most common and accessible activity was parades, complete with marching bands. Historian Henry Kmen observed that before the 1850s, New Orleans had become "undeniably the music capital of America."[2] By that time, the music trade was a major industry, having more than eighty businesses dealing with instrument sales, music publishing, sheet music, and instruction.

Blacks from all social levels were exposed to and participated in a wide range of musical activities since the earliest days of New Orleans. Many were involved in white European musical traditions. As early as 1799, there were descriptions of black balls similar in every way to white ones. Black fiddlers were especially popular at public dances and at formal balls for both blacks and whites. They played standard European dance music using European instruments. Interestingly, at many early nineteenth-century balls, concerts, and operas, segregated sections were reserved for free colored and sometimes for slaves who thus became familiar with overtures and operatic melodies. European classical music became an avenue that free blacks actively pursued. Many were taught by a number of professional musicians who were imported to work the opera and concert halls. In the 1830s, there were two black theaters and an active Negro Philharmonic Society. By the Civil War, black musicians like Eugene Macarty and Basile Bares were also teaching and composing classical pieces. Violinist-composer Ed-mond Dédé attained international prominence when he relocated to France where he became the conductor of a symphony orchestra in Bordeaux.

Though participation in European music traditions was strong among some blacks, it was a solid musical foundation formed from indigenous African practices passed along through slave work songs that gave the necessary spiritual, rhythmic, and melodic elements essential to the eventual creation of jazz. The post–Civil War migration of freedmen from plantations brought the Southern slave work song tradition to New Orleans. Many common characteristics of West African music, from which sprang the blues and spirituals, were thus present along the docks and levees. These slave work songs mixed with "Creole" folk songs, which had been developed by local slaves and sung in patois (Creole dialect consisting mainly of broken French). A unique custom of street cries has long been noted in New Orleans. Fruit venders, peddlers, shoe shine boys, and others developed singing styles that at times brought notoriety. One vendor, "Old Corn Meal," became so popular that in 1837 he appeared on stage at the St. Charles Theater and was said to have a major influence on the first (white) minstrels.[3]

Perhaps the most important aspect of early black music in New Orleans was a long tradition of African drumming and singing. Instead of resting on Sunday, many slaves celebrated their legal day of "freedom" by congregating in a designated area called Congo Square. There they traded, sold wares, drank, and participated in African ceremonies. Throughout various parts of the nineteenth century, slaves would beat out exciting polyrhythms, chant, sing in English or "Creole patois," and dance the bamboula, chica, calinda, congo, juba, and other African dances. A kind of "creolization" gradually took place as fifes and fiddles were sometimes added to the African stringed instruments, marimbas, and drums. The popular Congo Square gatherings were banned before the Civil War, but continued in underground voodoo ceremonies on levees and waterways along the outskirts of town.

As the enslaved Africans' "epic memory" encountered customs and traditions in America, the black man's characteristic process of "adaptation and reinterpretation"[4] gradually led to an "Africanization" of European practices. This synthesis can be seen in the popular New Orleans Mardi Gras tradition, which blacks transformed into a tradition of their own. Many took advantage of the temporary "freedom" and masking to either blend in with unsuspecting whites or to participate in an African-type ceremony centered around the exhaulted "King of the Wake" (a mythical figure whose charismatic presence and spiritual power drew large crowds of cheering followers). This social flexibility and restructuring, seen at Mardi Gras, extended to many "improvised" daily life encounters.

The New Orleans tradition of parades extends back to eighteenth-century French rule. The earliest parade marching bands were military and militia drum and bugle (or fife) units. These groups became accustomed to marching to commemorate holidays, feast days, military victories, elections, political rallies, weddings, and funerals. Parades became so common that they occurred any place and at any time. In New Orleans, as elsewhere, marching bands grew in popularity during the 1830s with the rise of improved and easily manufactured brass instruments. The imported European professional musicians both gave lessons on popular wind instruments and played in parades. The sight of marching brass bands and Sunday parades became so common that in 1838 the local *Picayune* noted "a real mania in this city for horn and trumpet playing." It went on to mention that on nearly every street corner people were "trying to blow horns," and that "our numerous martial bands are perhaps unrivaled on this side of the Atlantic."[5]

Brass bands got an additional boost by being used for both union and confederate forces during the Civil War. In the 1860s and 1870s, directors like Patrick Gilmore became nationally recognized for the large ensembles that they conducted. In 1880, the most popular marching band director/ composer in history, John Phillip Sousa, was helping to turn brass bands and parades into a national craze. By 1889, there were an estimated 10,000 active marching bands in the United States. These groups usually contained upward of eighteen players who became accustomed to a standard repertoire of heavily arranged written marches, patriotic songs, popular themes, ethnic folk melodies, hymns, dirges, and light classical pieces. In New Orleans, numerous civic and ethnic brass bands formed in this mold after the Civil War.

Blacks in New Orleans also shared in the local obsession with parades. Many black musicians got into parade music, as did their white counterparts, through militia company drum and bugle corps units. During the union occupation of New Orleans, large racially mixed marching bands paraded for funeral processions and special occasions. Parades with marching brass bands became a symbol of strength and triumph for blacks during Reconstruction. In the 1870s, groups like the St. Bernard, Kelly's, and the Oriental Brass Bands were commonly seen and well known. In this growing trend, popular black brass bands of the 1880s, like the Excelsior, Onward, and Pickwick, prided themselves on having only skilled readers, the latest in popular and difficult repertoire, and the finest of uniforms. These groups occasionally toured the states and fared well in national competitions. At home, black brass bands were heralded for participating in high-profile events, such as President Garfield's funeral commemoration and a parade for the 1885 New Orleans Cotton States Exhibition.

Despite the popularity and success of the black "Sousa-style" brass bands, by the 1890s it became apparent that a new trend was beginning to sweep the streets of New Orleans. This one, to the dismay of many trained reading musicians, depended more on spontaneous individual creation and less on written parts. In order to supply an increasing demand for brass bands in political rallies, dances, picnics, excursions, sporting events, and other functions, bands limited their sizes to between ten and twelve players. Because the need for bands had exceeded the amount of both reading professionals and written scores, nonreading musicians who played by "head" or "ear" began to appear on the streets. The combination of smaller bands, limited written scores, and nonreading musicians allowed for more personal and individual interpretation and improvisation.

Though the popularity of brass bands and New Orleans' traditional affinity for celebration are important to the development of jazz, it was an intense, evolving social and political climate (affecting the diverse black population) that became the spiritual basis for the musical "revolution." The post-Reconstruction period yielded many changes in the lives of local "people of color." Initially, the hope of finding true freedom and equality in America seemed within reach of the new freedmen and other blacks. During Reconstruction, many social and political gains were initiated and enforced by the federal government. As hopes remained high and the people of color began to unite under black Creole leadership, voting rights and black elected officials appeared. Soon a growing wave of revenge, greed, bitterness, and the desire by whites to regain Southern control reversed this trend. The result was an increase in racial violence, protests, Jim Crow laws, segregation, disenfranchisement, and the loss of many political, economic, and educational gains attained in previous years. The overall physical and emotional condition of blacks worsened as the result of poor health, disease, poverty, inferior sanitation and sewerage services, and unemployment. The disproportionate mortality rate among blacks was extremely high.

By the 1890s, life for many local blacks had become more difficult than before the Civil War. Adding to economic and social troubles was an increase of more than 30,000 rural black immigrants to New Orleans between 1880 and 1900. In addition to the loss of rights, events like the collapse of the Freedman's Savings and Trust Company in 1874 made it "practically impossible for Blacks to improve their economic position."[6] Though clubs, churches, homes, and businesses were lost, some blacks held on to trades, formed unions, and acquired property. In the face of social and economic uncertainty, many of them adopted a less frugal attitude, opting to "spend their money for immediate pleasure rather than to try to save for the future and be cheated out of it."[7] This posture became important because it fostered sponsorship of numerous jazz-related activities, thus providing many long hours and playing opportunities to a wide range of developing jazz players.

Several distinctive trends resulted from the social intensity of the post-Reconstruction period; each represented a response or reaction to a climate of increasing confusion, hostility, and anarchy. Various elements of the black community formed social organizations, secret societies, political groups, labor unions, civil rights demonstrations, and religious sects. A branch of spiritualism developed as an extension of the voodoo practices of Marie Laveau and others. On a folk level, black "Mardi Gras Indian" gangs and jazz emerged as "safer" ways of addressing life through artistic channels. It was particularly a synthesis between the two most historically distinct and isolated black groups that led to the vibrant new collectively improvised musical expression seen largely in brass band–related functions.

Much emphasis has been placed on physical appearance, especially complexion and hair texture, as the basis of a black obsession with social status. In reality, the main component in the long-standing divisive class structure among blacks in New Orleans has been the cultural differences between what W. E. B. DuBois called the "Latin (French) Negro" or Creole of color and the "Anglo-Saxon (American) Negro." Many blacks who migrated to New Orleans from plantations and neighboring states in the last half of the nineteenth century were ex-slaves, Protestant, poor, illiterate, unskilled, rural, and English speaking. The majority of black Creoles tended to come from backgrounds in which they were often free or privileged, Catholic, middle- or upper-class, educated, skilled tradesmen, urban, and French speaking. Creoles were generally used to a comfortable intermediary social position, between black and white. They tended to live downtown in "French" areas as opposed to living uptown in "American" areas. There were also radical differences in philosophy, thought, self-concepts, objectives, desires, and methods of responding to racism.

Despite historically conflictive cultural differences between blacks and Creoles, increased racial tension and prohibitive legislation, which classified anyone with one drop of Negro blood as "black," drew the two groups closer together. Clearly suffering from a common oppression, they began to unify: both sides realizing that there was strength in numbers. However, many Creoles resisted "Americanization" and withdrew into their own isolated world in which they tried to maintain their cultural values and identity. In this exclusive "nation," these Creoles used social institutions, language, religion, physical characteristics, cultural refinement, family background, and material possessions as important symbols in the constant need for self-validation.

The New Orleans black social structure, however, was full of complexities, uncertainties, and exceptions to the norm. As Joseph Logsdon and Caryn Cosse' Bell point out in *Black New Orleans*, there is "a danger in equating color, economic status and political conservatism in black New Orleans."[8] While "creolemania" was widespread, there are many examples of Creoles who were proud of their black African ancestry and looked down on the common practice of "passant blanc" (passing for white) by other Creoles. Numerous prominent, well-respected members of society described as "Creoles" were very dark complexioned. Legendary mahogany colored jazz drummer Warren "Baby" Dodds' childhood experiences and attitudes are typical of the common social interaction between blacks and Creoles and a definite sense of distinction between "them" and "us."

"In the downtown district where the Creoles lived, they played blues with a Spanish accent. We fellows that lived Uptown, we didn't ever play the Creole numbers like the Frenchmen downtown did . . . we played the blues different from them. They lived in the French part of town and we lived uptown, in the Garden district. Our ideas were different from theirs. They had the French and Spanish style, blended together. We had but one kind. That's negro. . . . Some of those people downtown didn't talk anything but Creole. Uptown, where I was, our people didn't talk like that. And, if someone moved in who did talk it, your mother kept you away from those people. . . . Now, my people, we were mixed with Indian, but we didn't want no parts of Creole talk. . . . If our mother would catch us trying to do that, she'd slap us in the mouth. . . . But in spite of that, I did have a little Creole friend they called Guito. . . . He was very dark. Darker than I was, and he couldn't talk nothing but Creole."[9]

Legalized segregation of blacks and whites and financial instability began to bring the two black groups closer together in schools, churches, neighborhoods, social life, and entertainment. It was the gradual cultural merger and acceptance between blacks and Creoles that formed the core of "Black New Orleans." Out of this "African-American Creole" merger, a blend of cultural elements from the entire spectrum of black-blooded people was now possible. In music, this meant a synthesis between African and Creole methods of learning, uses of music, instrumentation, repertoire, and rhythmic melodic and harmonic concepts. The Creoles had their own Afro-Creole folk songs, which were developed by early slaves and Haitian immigrants and sung in patois. More important, Creoles brought the European classical music tradition. Many of them taught instrumental lessons to other aspiring black musicians. The Creoles' musical standards remained high as they stressed reading music, "proper" playing techniques, good intonation, and correct fingering and blowing of instruments. They also brought a more professional approach to the business of music making. From the classical music repertoire, they brought themes and harmonic structures from the finest symphonies and operas as well as popular European folk songs.

The freedmen who migrated to New Orleans brought with them a music tradition heavily influenced by their "African cultural memory" and the Anglo music they encountered in America. Several elements that were crucial to the development of jazz evolved from slave work songs, including call-and-response patterns, emphasis on improvisation and individuality, polyrhythmic interplay, and a more emotional approach to melodic interpretation through growls, shouts, falsetto, buzzes, and bent "blue" tones. These common West African devices were characteristics not only of work songs but of the forms that developed from them—spirituals, black minstrel songs and the blues. Some of the fiery younger Creoles were drawn to the excitement of this African American folk music and soon attempted to learn it.

Thus during the 1890s, the blacks' and Creoles' need to express their musical traditions became a part of the social milieu. As hundreds became involved in music, varying degrees of teaching, exchange, and influence between untrained blues-playing improvisers and schooled readers took place. Unlike whites in New Orleans or blacks from anywhere else, local blacks were exposed to the widest possible range of musical styles. A pool of top-notch "legitimate" musicians, limited folk-level players, and everything in between were involved in thousands of performance opportunities; becoming part of an alternative spiritual outlet or "cultural paradise" created by an intense society in turmoil and in need of self-expression.

When legendary cornetist Charles "Buddy" Bolden and other uptown blacks first began to improvise and liven up standard themes and adopt blues vocal effects on wind instruments in the mid-1890s, they became unknowing participants in a musical and social revolution. At first, in the brass bands and later in smaller combined brass and string ensembles, they "synthesized several musical influences and expressed in music the spirit and emotion of the collective black New Orleans experience."[10] The new "ratty" style—not called "jazz" until years later—was a looser, freer, more swinging improvised approach to ragtime, marches, blues, hymns, waltzes, folk songs, and popular music. Despite some opposition from more genteel and "conservative" blacks and whites, the bouncy danceable tempos and sheer passion in the new, mainly instrumental style were too exciting to relegate to any one area, ethnic group, or social level. Soon the "hot" new music spread among local whites and to neighboring rural communities. In the early 1900s, jazz bands were traveling to northern states, and by the early 1920s, it had, in the face of harsh criticism, become a national craze and the conceptual basis for an entire generation in the "Jazz Age."

It was the typical six- or seven-piece dance ensemble—ironically first recorded in 1917 and popularized by imitative white New Orleans groups—that went on to millions of phonographs and international fame from northern city home bases like Chicago and New York. The raucous brass bands remained relatively obscure in the annals of jazz until several decades later. As the American obsession with more danceable ragtime and later jazz led to an early twentieth-century decline of Sousa-type brass bands, the New Orleans jazz-playing marching bands—now a separate institution—remained a highly visible and popular part of local culture. More than mere fun or entertainment among Crescent City blacks, brass bands were a multifunctional, necessary part of life. The music they played was a spiritual extension of a collective consciousness. It soon became apparent that freedom of expression within the confines of jazz could be an exercise in and a model for the type of democratic society that the black population sought. The brass band and related activities became a vehicle in which to express the aspirations, desires, spirit, and needs of black New Orleans.

The departure from rigid laws of European classical music was a move toward the collective expression of a defiant black ego. This first generation, born during the early Reconstruction period, found in their new music a way of expressing their hopes, fears, needs, joys, passions, and humor. In their hands, European instruments, harmonies, and melodic concepts were distinctly colored with new and altered themes, driving rhythms, growls, vibrato, and other elements from the African American vocal blues tradition. A solid, driving rhythmic underpinning served as a background for call-and-response patterns and collectively improvised musical "conversations."

The break of customary brass band style and format that started to gain attention in the 1890s did not mean a total abandonment of musical (and social) law and order. Freedom and creative improvisation were fitted into the confines of a musically logical collective or polyphonic approach. Feature solo playing was not characteristic of the New Orleans jazz brass band style. Generally the entire ensemble played throughout a song—expressing a combination of melody, counterpoint, rhythmic riff patterns, call and response, or playing "under" (lower volume) as someone played on "top" (lead-type improvisation). The individual was encouraged to create his own personal sound and expression based on the role of each instrument as it was derived from traditional European marching band format. Within the typical ten- to twelve-man New Orleans brass band, two or three trumpets played either the melody in part harmony or an improvised melodic lead. Two trombones punctuated rhythmic accents and sliding "tailgate" glissandi between phrases. The clarinet provided a soprano counterpoint to the brasses by exploiting the freedom to dance around the melody with obbligato fills and extended high notes. The tuba laid down the lower spectrum rhythmic foundation and ground beat by playing around arpeggiated chord tones accented on the first and third beats. Lower brass instruments (baritones and alto horns) played countermelodies and supportive rhythmic figures. Separate snare and brass drums established the tempo and strengthened the rhythmic pulse. The snare drum played off of military-style press rolls and cadences. The bass drum gave the New Orleans brass band its most characteristic sound—the exciting syncopated pattern derived from the type of African drumming heard at Congo Square. This "second line beat" is at the foundation of not only jazz but all locally interpreted musical styles.

The high level of syncronicity between African American, African Creole, and European musical systems as seen in New Orleans jazz-playing brass bands can be thought of as a musical representation of life. As such, there are no absolutes. The possibility for the expression of a wide range of moods, passions, and attitudes was in each performance. These "musical ceremonies" were open forums for active or passive self-expression. Call-and-response "dialogues" permeated each song. The "answers" to brief melodic statements could take on any of several forms: mere repetition, continuation or extension of melody, rhythmic support, complimentary counterpoint, to mention a few. The typical exchanges between instruments throughout the course of a song as they relate to the established European concept of melody are examples of "signifyin(g)." In *The Signifying Monkey: A Theory of African-American Literary Criticism*, Henry Louis Gates points out that the "repetition and revision or revision with a signal difference"[11] found in jazz are intrinsic to all black artistic forms. In traditional New Orleans jazz, as in other forms, the revision of melody can come from and project any number of moods and attitudes: sensuality, respect, mockery, playfulness, antagonism, competitiveness, and so on.

The most important vehicle in which the cultural and spiritual temperament of black New Orleans and its new musical expression openly interacted was in activities related to benevolent societies and social clubs. These groups, mainly under the categories of "Social Aid and Pleasure Clubs," "Mutual Aid Societies," or "Benevolent Societies," had origins among free Negroes before the Civil War and started off as parallels to similar white organizations. The popularity and strength of these groups were probably also influenced by West African social organizations and sacred societies. Many of the enslaved Africans who were brought to America had belonged to such organizations, which shared many of the same rituals, functions, and objectives as those that developed in New Orleans. The looser social structure and small amount of "freedoms" enslaved lives probably allowed for some type of covert social groupings that, like the practices held in Congo Square, wove other African traditions into the rich fabric of black New Orleans culture. In post–Civil War New Orleans, these self-help societies grew rapidly among all classes of blacks. A few, like the Eastern Stars and Odd Fellows, were local chapters of national organizations. While some of these groups grew out of and were related to churches, social class, and labor, many bypassed divisive categorization in the spirit of unity and good times. Social and benevolent organizations became so widespread that an estimated eighty percent of blacks in New Orleans belonged to at least one such group in the 1880s and 1890s.

Some organizations were formed strictly for educational, religious, or political reasons, but most were formed as a means of survival: to combat social and economic limitations caused by poverty, epidemics, and increasingly hostile racism. Among the many services that were provided to dues-paying members in good standing were pensions for the elderly, medical assistance, comfort for the sick, legal and political information, and burial insurance. In keeping with the festive spirit of New Orleans, the societies provided numerous sources of entertainment. Some clubs were mainly founded for pleasurable purposes. After all, social and financial hardships were no excuses for not having a good time. Picnics; excursions on wagons, boats, and trains; and dances were very common. Through their numerous social activities and celebrations of anniversaries and holidays, the benevolent and social clubs became the principle sponsors of brass bands. Several of the more than 250 organizations in New Orleans in the 1890s had their own brass band.

One of the most important and popular society functions was parades. Blacks had become accustomed to gigantic parades both as a show of strength and unity as well as for diversion. The cultural mixing between blacks and Creoles that resulted in the birth of jazz was also reflected in the parades and society activities. While initially critical of the Catholic tradition of holding parades and celebrations on Sundays, Protestants later found that the same emotionalism that caused them to shout, cry, and dance with the "spirit" could be expressed in parades. Soon, processions with brass bands became a common sight for Protestant church anniversaries and holidays. Logsdon and Bell point out that "by 1894, even the more disciplined black Methodist preachers . . . were 'sprinkling' banners, regalia, dolls and other paraphernalia and holding festivals on Saturday night that extended far into the Sabbath."[12] This blend of Protestant religious fervor and obsessive creole *joie de vivre* exemplifies the social homogeny that formed around the core of black New Orleans. This more practical and necessary linkage grew right in the middle of traditional Creole and black separatism.

It is in benevolent society processions that the social and spiritual values of the New Orleans jazz and brass band tradition can be viewed in a functional capacity beyond diversion or entertainment. In the face of worsening social, physical, and economic conditions, the African Americans of New Orleans needed to react. According to William Schafer, jazz in the brass bands was "born out of an intense emotionally charged desire of freedom and recognition," and it "reflects the great expectations of black people into the years following their official release from bondage."[13] The new music and activities around it offered a temporary alternative existence in which social pressures and anxieties could be forgotten, reinterpreted, or transformed. For thousands of musicians and community members, brass band functions were a practice of elusive democratic ideals that were foremost in the minds of local blacks. For many, the streets of New Orleans were transformed from being a connector between physical places to being a collective passageway to a spiritually free dimension.

Though the possibilities and implications of jazz could be far reaching and universal, its very nature embodied and put into practice freedom of expression, unity, creativity, and competition. Here, unlike in many aspects of daily life, the black ego could be challenged, expressed, and satisfied. The mutual triumph of both the collective and the individual were blatantly displayed in music and dance on the streets. Instead of being consumed by anarchy, self-pity, and lament for one's condition, why not turn the situation around and celebrate it? Rather than bemoaning what you hope will happen someday, make it happen now: "The sun's gonna shine in my back door TODAY! . . . and me and my boys are gonna wear our loud, fancy clothes and dance in it until it goes down."

The psychological effects of participating in the "jazz street culture" were sometimes far reaching. A sense of self-worth and value could be found in the massive parades in which thousands could follow and freely let go of inhibitions and temporarily transcend their earthly condition. In this "spiritual underground" one could be many possible things: free, proud, angry, majestic, militant, sensual, joyful, sad, equal, nonracial, judges, competitors, winners, escapists, truth seekers, signifiers, or even "royalty." The importance of these cultural exercises was reflected in the pride and elaboration that were given to manner of dress, attempts at strict processional order, and common band and society names that identified with positive affirmations in the "battle" for freedom: Onward, Olympia, Superior, Eureka, to name a few. The semblance of dignified order in the midst of the sometimes chaotic parades was even seen among the less-seriously named pleasure clubs like the Money Wasters and the Jolly Bunch.

The most common and widely attended brass band and jazz functions were club parades, church parades, and jazz funerals. The black New Orleans social aid and pleasure club and benevolent society parade (now commonly called "second line"), between 1900 and 1978, was truly a unique and exciting spectacle. It was formed by three dominant groups, the most important one being social club members, who sponsored the event and hired the bands. Club members, often from the poorer side of the working class, spent considerable money on elaborate colorful costumes, plumes, sashes, baskets, hats, shoes, umbrellas, fans, or anything that could be decorated. Clubs may have had up to several hundred members who formed into different "divisions," which were categorized by age, gender, seniority, or club status.

In between the divisions were up to three or four uniformed brass bands. In the early part of the century, standard band uniforms were used, but in later years, black pants, white shirts, black ties, and white policeman-type caps became the norm. The brass band was guided by a well-dressed grand marshall (in tuxedo and derby) whose function was to (try to) maintain processional order and serve as a beacon for the band to follow as he did a graceful strut to the music. Finally, there were the "second liners," the up to thousands of anonymous spectators who literally became a part of the parade. They seemingly appeared from nowhere at the first beat of the brass drum and followed the procession for hours in ninety degree plus weather without regard for time and space. As the parade proceeded along to military snare drum cadences, the procession was strangely reminiscent of soldiers returning from battle. Once the bass drum's characteristic three beats introduced a song, an almost magical transformation took place: The band began a hot, jazzy tune and the club members and second liners hypnotically followed along, dancing with their unusual gyrations. The second liners' dances, in time with the music, were all very different but somehow similar. There was no organized structure or uniformity to their movements, which were reminiscent of West African ceremonial dancing and the "spirit dances" of some black Protestant churches.

It was impossible for any observer to have seen and heard all or even most of the millions of subtle movements and sounds that occurred in a second line parade. At a glance, one may have seen dancers on top of cars, swinging from lamp posts, on the roofs of two- or three-story buildings, riding in tempo on the backs of others, or gliding belly down in the street, all the while keeping perfect time and pace with the procession. As the parade continued, the crowd grew larger, as many in various forms of dress (and undress) dropped what they were doing and joined in the celebration. Once the musical "call" was heard, the trance began, and those who were in tune to it had to follow and respond.

In the sea of various shades of black skin, there were young faces and old faces; soft faces and hard faces; faces on bikes, in cars, and in doorways, and windows. In the ongoing procession, weather, age, time, and physical ailments seemed to disappear in the midst of hot brass band music. Walking canes and crutches that almost never left the ground were suddenly hoisted high in mock imitation of the grand marshall's umbrella. Elderly faces, twisted, tired, and helpless from years in the struggle, now glowed as years were suppressed by joy. Bodies that had been bent by decades of hard times now straightened out, twisted, and gyrated with renewed vitality, saying that they would continue dancing "until the butcher cuts me down." Babies too young to walk wiggled in tempo with delight in their mothers' arms. Even animals within earshot were hopelessly drawn into the frenzy: "There's no music as exciting as New Orleans jazz brass band music. This scene shakes up all the neighborhood pets, dogs and cats. Dogs get excited, scamper and bark and create commotion at the action; you've never seen dogs act up as like at these funerals and parades. I have seen many jazz dogs get into the act just like their owners—really dance and jump about."[14]

To many non-New Orleanians, casual observers, and culturally isolated locals, the preceding scene may have seemed like madness—hundreds of blacks gone haywire at the same time. Yet in this temporary spiritual dimension, normal everyday worries and pressures were literally "stomped" or alleviated, as writer Albert Murray suggests.[15] Brass band music, and the improvised dances that were extensions of it, allude to a symbolic power from which one could overcome any obstacles that life, society, and nature have put in ones way. This new empowerment was commonly acted out as symbols of order, control, and restriction became not only non-threatening but also objects of incorporation. Countless examples exist of man-made structures that were used in second line dancing: fences, buildings, stop signs, fire hydrants, vehicles, telephone poles, and even the narrow rails of an interstate highway off-ramp. These symbols of earthly limitations became means of creatively defying, challenging, and playfully mocking authority (or even death). Elements of nature, like trees and bushes, could also be good second line "partners." A sudden rain would be cause for immediate dispersal of parades in any other place, but in the New Orleans second line "bad" weather brings on massive joyous screams of "Yeah!"—an opportunity to use umbrellas, wet clothes, puddles, and partially flooded streets to dance with (or in) as part of the ongoing celebration.

Just like at emotional religious services, not everyone present was "taken by the spirit." By their very authority-defying, excitement-raising nature, the parades sometimes involved isolated acts of violence. The extreme humid heat of ninety degree plus days, thousands of discombobulated people, and a length of up to eight hours of hysteria perhaps offered "too much" freedom for some. At times, entering rival neighborhoods, vengeance, racial assaults, and criminal mischief led to occasional fights and unlawful acts, which could go unnoticed or unpunished under the massive crowd cover and confusion. Parade-related violence reached a peak in 1978 when five people were murdered during the course of one Sunday afternoon parade. Since then, city intervention helped to curb crime, as routes were altered, parade lengths shortened, and mounted police patrols were increased. However the great majority of participants in club parades attended for the spiritual value, the expressive exciting music, or collective fun that these events offered.

For many, the club parade had a socially and psychologically uplifting value. Many of the downtrodden working-class club members looked forward to "their day" to shine and show off in their neighborhoods. It was a time to stand out and be respected and admired by the community. Indeed, many clubs, divisions, and individual members have become street legends because of their elaborate outfits and ways of second line dancing. There was usually much friendly competition among clubs to see which could outdo the other in terms of size, beauty of costume, and excitement generated by the bands. The competitive spirit did not exclude the bands, for many names like Black Benny, Alphonse Picou, and John Casimir remained on the lips of older parade goers. In a manner perhaps inspired by the nineteenth-century Africanized Mardi Gras figure, Buddy Bolden was chosen as jazz's first "King" by the "street subjects" he won over with his exciting new "hot" cornet style. His charismatic musical presence was like that of a minister or leader; his ability to "preach" a universal musical truth earned him much respect from the loyal following that he called his "children." Many spectators and club members picked out a player or band that they like and may have followed them all day and from week to week and parade to parade. Very spirited and spontaneous improvisation often resulted from the mutually inspiring exchanges between musicians and dancers.

The church parade was a smaller, less publicized, and a more toned-down version of club parades. These religious processions were usually held much earlier in the day and were shorter and more controlled. Instead of stopping at bars for rest and refreshments like the social club parades, these began and ended at churches. Interestingly, while church parades diminished among Catholics early on, they have remained common among Baptist churches into the present. Religious motivation, giving thanks to the Creator, anniversaries, and feast days were the main reasons behind church processions. Church parade divisions were more conservatively dressed in black and white. At the request of the reverends, bands played only up-tempo hymns and spirituals, not marches and blues numbers—but much of the improvisation and excitement in the music were the same. Church members "marched" or strutted with dignity and always maintained processional order. The isolated pride and majesty of church parades formed an interesting parallel to the benevolent society events, especially since this Sunday morning's church sister might have been next Sunday afternoon's club member.

The most well-known brass band function is the "jazz funeral." While funerals with music neither originated in New Orleans nor were an exclusively black tradition, they had become common in Louisiana since the eighteenth century. Inspired perhaps by "cultural memory" of parallel African traditions, blacks picked up the custom early on. After the Civil War, the practice of funerals with music was dominated by blacks. At some point during the 1890s, brass bands, using the principles and expressions of the "new" music, transformed this tradition into one of their own, expressing the West African concept of "rejoicing at death." In a culture which was learning to reinterpret its dualities, social condition, and very existence, it is not surprising that death would evoke sentiments of both sadness and joy in the music and celebration of its occurrence. The jazz funeral paid honor to the deceased by expressing sorrow at his or her earthly departure and by singing joy at his or her passing on to a "better life" in union with the creator.

As church or funeral home dismissal services were going on, the musical part of the procession began a couple of blocks away. A band dressed in black played an up-tempo hymn that decreased in volume as it approached the services. As the coffin was taken out to be placed in a hearse, a soft, sad dirge was played. A slow motorcade led by the band proceeded toward the cemetery as songs like "Nearer My God to Thee" and "West Lawn Dirge" were played ever so sweetly and mournfully. If the cemetery was too far away, the band divided into two lines and allowed the motorcade to pass through, thus "cutting the body loose." After a distance of a couple of blocks was established, the band began a lively up-tempo number like "Just a Little While to Stay Here" or "Oh, Didn't He Ramble," and the remaining mourners and onlookers danced the second line. The joyous revelry continued for a few blocks before dispersing. Seen as a sign of respect, these actions celebrated the ultimate "triumph" of death, "spiritual emancipation," and joyous resurrection to follow. To many black New Orleanians, a jazz funeral was an honor—the only way to be "sent off right." One social club member expressed a common attitude toward having such a funeral: "A woman's got to belong to at least seven secret societies if she 'specks to get buried with any style. . . . And the more lodges you belong to, the more music you gits when you goes to meet your Maker. . . . I'm sure lookin' forward to my wake. They is wakin' me for four nights and I is gonna have the biggest funeral the church ever had."[16]

As legendary jazz pianist Jelly Roll Morton put it, a New Orleans jazz funeral was "the end of a perfect death." These types of funerals were so common that even less desirables, like bums, hustlers, and gamblers, were often "sent off in style" by friends who would pay for the ceremony. Up until the 1980s, the most common jazz funerals were given for society club members and jazz musicians.

In line with its community-based origins, the New Orleans brass band tradition has evolved in accordance with changing social and economic conditions in the African American community. Because of its localized function and instrumentation, changes took place at a much slower rate than smaller dance band New Orleans jazz, which was more easily altered by outside influences. In the first decades of the twentieth century, brass bands gradually established the tradition of improvised jazz interpretation. The need for black organizations, and for spiritual release and fulfillment remained strong, to counteract violence, poverty, and other consequences of legalized segregation. A younger generation of musicians born between 1880 and 1910 would learn and further develop the brass band style and jazz. Dozens of regularly organized bands, pick-up groups, and individual musicians—either through direct family ties or "extended family" relationships—served as the inspiration and trainers of the next generation. Many of the legendary performers who moved outside of New Orleans and helped to infuse jazz into the American consciousness started out or learned in the brass bands: Joseph "King" Oliver, Louis Armstrong, Sidney Bechet, Johnny and Baby Dodds, Kid Ory, Red Allen, and others.

Many of the first- and second-generation New Orleans jazz brass band players had come from rural areas around the city after having been taught by teachers like Professor James Humphrey. Humphrey traveled weekly to small towns and plantations giving instrumental lessons, forming brass band, and writing musical arrangements. While generally not being a supporter of the "ragged" new music that his students were drawn to, Humphrey instilled high standards, which carried over into jazz.

As some of the conventional brass bands, like the Excelsior and Onward, struggled to maintain the "legitimate" approach by reading arranged scores, they were overshadowed by newer groups, like the Tuxedo Brass Band (formed in 1910), that played the newer popular style and repertoire. Brass bands continued to play for a variety of functions, but as the popularity of small band jazz increased during the twenties, musicians spent more time in these orchestral ensembles and less time in brass bands. Many players followed the exodus to northern cities during the latter part of the first and the early parts of the second decades, further depleting brass band ranks.

In 1920, a new group, the Eureka Brass Band, formed and throughout the decade was one of the few groups to maintain a high standard of band ethics by regularly rehearsing and playing an extensive repertoire of jazz and written pieces. By the 1930s, the Great Depression, a slightly more relaxed racial climate, and governmental assistance in some of the services that had been provided by benevolent societies caused a decline of the clubs and their activities. The 1940s brought major changes away from the insular nature of New Orleans. The widespread popularity of radio in many homes and the advent of World War II focused local attention in a more serious global direction. Younger black and white audiences developed more cosmopolitan musical tastes as they listened to, danced to, and performed music of the "swing era" big bands of Count Basie, Duke Ellington, Benny Goodman, and many others.

Despite decades of change and "modernization," brass bands continued to ignite the streets in community parades and funerals during the 1940s. The "New Orleans Jazz Revival," which began in 1942, was mainly one of outside interest and initially had little impact or visibility in the Crescent City's continuing traditions. The historical significance of the early revival is that it brought international recognition to several obscure older local players, and it also led to the first New Orleans brass band recordings. In 1945, producer Bill Russell recorded "Bunk's Brass Band" for his American Music label. The next year, writer/jazz fan Rudi Blesh recorded the "Original Zenith Brass Band." While these early efforts, especially with Bunk's Brass Band, are important links to how early groups may have sounded, both bands were smaller in number and had been put together solely for the recordings. The first true recording of a regularly organized working New Orleans brass band did not come until 1951 when two young white students from the North, Alden Asforth and David Wyckoff, recorded the Eureka Brass Band. Led by trumpeter Percy Humphrey, grandson of Professor Jim Humphrey, the Eureka had remained as the most traditional and representative group of the 1950s in terms of repertoire and style.

By the time brass bands came to the attention of out-of-town jazz fans, their sound signaled clear signs of change. In the late 1950s, John Casimir's Young Tuxedo Brass Band recorded on the Atlantic label. Though "Jazz Begins" remains one of the best all-time brass band recordings, influences of swing and bebop were evident. However, the solos, screaming high-note trumpet playing, swing-style saxophone riffs, rhythm and blues themes, and bebop lines did not completely alter the "traditional" or authentic feel because of the stable direction of Wilbert Tullman's swinging aggressive tuba and Emile Knox's driving bass drum rhythms. Time, economics, and age saw to it that a few younger men would enter the brass bands as they "came home" when work in other musical styles was slow. Much of the brass band activity of the 1950s occurred in the uptown Buddy Bolden neighborhood. There were only about six regularly organized brass bands and occasional "pick-up groups" then. In addition to the Eureka and Young Tuxedo, the Onward, George Williams, Silver Leaf, and Henry Allen Brass Bands were visible in community activities.

It seemed as if the 1960s would mark an end to the New Orleans brass band tradition, as several bands broke up, older members died, work was less frequent, and attitudes toward "traditions" changed. Some angry blacks of the Civil Rights movement viewed jazz and local customs like the "Zulu Club" Mardi Gras parade as "Uncle Tom" remnants of a shameful past and as passive acceptance of oppressive racial conditions. One black journalist complained, "This city has too many parades and not enough pickets." He considered it "nonsense" to have parades, joyous music, and dancing in "these times of national social unrest."[17] Rather than quietly dying out under the pressures of change, the New Orleans brass band underwent a resurgence during the 1960s and 1970s that would bring it to international attention and in the process establish patterns for its own continuity and transformation.

As the Civil Rights movement, the Vietnam War, political assassinations, riots, and "hippies" shook the American consciousness, New Orleans' image as a "fun" tourist escape grew tremendously. As tourists sought out a year-round Mardi Gras ambiance, the New Orleans business and political communities tried to satisfy their desires. For the brass band, this meant its entry into the commercial world. Many drastic alterations of sound, image, style, and attitude came with newer visibility, job opportunities, and nonlocal audiences. While a new market and increased economic potential were welcome changes, commercialism led to a decline of musical and cultural values that were essential to the tradition. Though brass bands still played in parades, funerals, and community events, they were just as likely to be seen on stages at tourist conventions, theatrical plays, nationally televised sporting events, festivals, and even in feature films. In the commercial arena, the brass band often became a scaled down "showpiece" that was flaunted like cheap, tacky souvenirs. Without the street environment and audiences who understood and participated in brass band functions, fundamental changes occurred that were of little concern in the midst of "pop culture" tourist mentality. As a result, band sizes became smaller and repertoires dwindled to a few recognizable standards. The formality of traditional band attire gave way to flashy colors, band T-shirts, and the draping of Mardi Gras beads, pins, and stickers on hats and instruments. Bands worked, cunning promoters made big money, tourists had fun—who really knew or cared about "authenticity" or "tradition" anyway?

Though the Eureka, Young Tuxedo, Onward, and lesser known nonunion groups like the E. Gibsong were still active, Dejan's Olympia Brass Band became the most visible, popular, and successful group of the 1960s and early 1970s. Founded in 1960 by saxophonist Harold Dejan, the Olympia—through good promotion, loyal supporters, and many high-profile engagements—achieved a level of recognition previously unseen by a New Orleans brass band. The group appeared on so many posters, films, television shows, and commercials, and played for so many openings, festivals, and high-profile engagements that the name "Olympia" was for some time synonymous with brass bands. It was not uncommon for brass band leaders and managers to receive callers seeking to hire "one of them Olympia bands."

A higher level of exposure and employment for brass bands came with the New Orleans Jazz and Heritage Festival, founded in 1970. Since then, marching bands were increasingly used as stage acts or for on-site parades in the international music festival market. Continued success in the community and commercial arena led to the development of more bands and younger players. In the early 1970s, two sources were responsible for the majority of younger brass band players who were to impact the tradition into the 1990s. One source was the Fairview Baptist Church Brass Band, a kids' group founded by veteran banjoist/historian Danny Barker in an effort to teach young people about their musical heritage. The other source of younger brass band musicians was trumpeter Ernest "Doc" Paulin, who repeatedly sought out younger players for his busy nonunion band. Paulin, a strict disciplinarian, stressed a high level of professionalism as he preached social and musical values of being a brass band and jazz musician. Through the Fairview and Doc Paulin bands, young players were exposed to traditional jazz repertoire, given the opportunity to develop through regular playing situations (often with experienced older players), and encouraged to explore the potentials of a music career or sideline. These two bands funneled several players through what was to be the last wave of authentic traditional New Orleans jazz in black community parades.

As the functional need of brass bands in the community continued, several simultaneous developments occurred during the middle and late seventies that altered the direction and future of the brass band tradition. In just a few short years, many bands and musicians who had been highly visible in community parades and funerals rapidly disappeared from the scene. Reasons for this occurrence vary: Several older players had either died, retired, or joined smaller bands in the less strenuous and more commercial arena; the rise of "Sunday Jazz Brunches" at hotels and restaurants drew many musicians away from afternoon parades; a growing opportunity to tour for festivals in groups, like one of the popular Preservation Hall bands, drew some jazz players away on weekends; the increasing cost of professional union bands was high for some clubs and families of deceased persons to afford; and a wave of parade-related violence turned some musicians away from the streets.

During the middle and late seventies, several new younger brass bands emerged to fill in the community void as traditional groups on the street became rarer and rarer. The ranks of younger bands were filled with musicians who rarely interacted with older players and had little, if any, contact with or "apprenticeship" in the authentic traditional New Orleans style. Since a once strong high school band tradition was beginning to decline, fewer younger players had training or development before becoming professional. Characteristic of many younger groups, which grew to dominate the streets by the early eighties, were unison section playing, "riff tunes," simplified harmonies, reduced number of keys, faster and more prominent rhythms, and smaller groups of about eight musicians. Instrumental shifts were also seen: The clarinet virtually disappeared, and the tuba and drums developed a more dominant role with rhythm and blues overtones. The overall sense of pride, professionalism, and seriousness gradually gave way to street clothes, baseball caps, and tennis shoes. Mixing all the musical elements around them—reggae, rhythm and blues, bebop, free jazz, high school band music, Mardi Gras Indian chants, current radio hits, and television themes—the younger bands brought a freshness and creative excitement to the streets that had been missing in the older traditional bands. Commercialism and the generation gap were the underlying causes of the older bands' dwindling repertoires, stagnation of styles, and a lack of new songs in the traditional groups.

Though outside influences and change had affected the brass band tradition since its earliest days, more direct and persistent attempts to alter the sound were apparent since the late sixties. Trumpeter and assistant leader of the influential Olympia Brass Band, Milton Batiste was responsible for incorporating and recording a vocal rhythm and blues style on brass band renditions of hits, like Professor Longhair's "Go to the Mardi Gras" and Smokey Johnson's "It Ain't My Fault." Reedman Himas "Flo" Ankle's Majestic Brass Band also continued the rhythm and blues approach. Along with the Olympia, Young Tuxedo, and Doc Paulin bands, the Majestic was among a half-dozen popular groups frequently seen in community parades during the transitory mid-1970s. The first revolutionary younger group was Leroy Jones's Hurricane Brass Band, which formed in the mid-seventies from the first generation of Fairview members. Soon the Hurricane, featuring Jones's blazing bebop trumpet solos over riffing saxophones and trombones, and the band's "blue-jeaned, T-shirted attitude" became a popular fixture in club parades. Jones soon set out on a solo career leaving the band out of work, after having generated interest in the new contemporary style that extended the Olympia's explorations. The short-lived Tornado Brass Band attempted to be a continuance of the Hurricane. In the meantime, second liners and musicians started listening to and "jamming" off a set of "modern" sounding tuba riffs that the Hurricane's (and later Olympia's) Anthony "Tuba Fats" Lacen played during parade rest stops.

In 1977, a few ex-Hurricane members joined with others to form the Dirty Dozen Brass Band, marking a major step in street band evolution. Driven by Kirk Joseph's dominant tuba lines and Roger Lewis's soulful bebop baritone saxophone solos, the Dozen was hailed as the "new thing" and soon became successful in the community and among festival promoters. Writers and community activists interpreted predominant bebop and rhythm and blues overtones and a casual approach to performance attire as defiant: "representing the real black spirit, unlike the traditional playing 'Toms' who were cast out of the community." Beginning with the Dirty Dozen, younger bands projected a sound and image that seemed to parody the authentic brass band tradition, as well as black stereotypes and themselves. It is ironic that some of the younger groups' more "educated" supporters identified so positively with band names and songs like the Dozen's popular "My Feet Can't Fail Me Now," that come from less admirable aspects of black history.

As the Dirty Dozen spent more and more time touring in the eighties, other young groups, like the Rebirth Brass Band, formed in 1982, became popular in community parades. The slower paced and funkier Rebirth exceeded the Dozen's success in New Orleans by being the only brass band to ever have a local "hit" record. "Do Whatcha Wanna" became a radio and Mardi Gras standard in 1990. Its bouncy tuba-driven rhythms and assertive shout vocal by trumpeter Kermit Ruffins seemed to sum up the philosophy and spirit of a new generation: "Do whatcha wanna, hang on the corner. . . ." Several other young groups formed in the late eighties and early nineties whose sounds, images, and styles continued to demonstrate and extend the more contemporary approach. Some of the newer groups still called brass bands including the Looney Tunes, Lil' Rascals, and Soul Rebels, incorporated elements of "hip-hop" and "gangsta rap" in street parades and club performances. The explosion of younger bands since the late eighties and their almost total dominance of the streets did not eradicate brass bands that played traditional New Orleans jazz. Though less visible in the community and press, bands like trumpeter Teddy Riley's Royal and Excelsior groups toured, worked steadily in hotels, and recorded. The Young Tuxedo Brass Band led by saxophonist Herman Sherman continued to bring in younger traditional-style players. Doc Paulin's band, the Chosen Few, the Majestic, and several pick-up groups still played for a few clubs, churches, and funerals.

In the early nineties, there was enough activity by both traditional and contemporary brass bands to reveal an interesting set of dualities, parallels, and mergers not uncommon to New Orleans culture. The yearly jazz festival has continued as a high-visibility employer for all styles of brass bands. By the mid-nineties, new "brass bands" seemed to spring up almost weekly. More than two dozen identifiable groups work in various forms of existence. Though many bands perform for a variety of situations, some play mainly for parades, others for conventions, and others for tours. Groups of between four and six very young children are often seen in the French Market and around Jackson Square playing a primitive "brass band music" for tips from tourists. In the nineties came the first "all girl" brass band, the Pinettes, and several white or white-led pick-up bands used mainly for tourist conventions. The most authentic traditional brass bands—the Young Tuxedo (the oldest continuing group), led by trumpeter Greg Stafford (since 1985) and clarinetist Michael White's Liberty Brass Band (formed in 1987)—have remained active and visible in festivals and more upscale venues. Traditional groups like the Onward rarely perform except for the local jazzfest. Other bands like the Treme, Pinstripe, Paulin Brothers (formed by six sons of Doc Paulin), and Algiers have found a comfortable niche in a stylistic "merger" between traditional and more modern styles. A new outlet for brass bands, the small neighborhood bar, has been a boost for younger and intermediary style groups. Housed in very small spaces and using a minimum of finances, more than a half dozen of these bars have regularly featured brass bands in recent years.

While evolution and change are in some ways necessary and inevitable, the open-ended, free-spirited nature of the New Orleans tradition has allowed for so much change that in terms of function, spirit, music, and image, little of the brass bands original meaning and distinguishing stylistic characteristics remain. As always, the brass band tradition's development has been shaped by social and economic forces surrounding it. Though still a visible and widely discussed topic among locals, Creole culture has diminished, becoming heavily fragmented, and is no longer a separate major force in New Orleans. Over two dozen benevolent societies and social aid and pleasure clubs still exist and continue to sponsor year-round parades and funerals; however, the role and activities of these organizations show increasing signs of decline resulting from change, economics, the "modernization" of New Orleans, and alternative lifestyles of younger generations. Many of the cultural trends and problems that characterize contemporary urban life in America have affected brass bands. The fast-paced transitory nature of today's world, and an endless number of instantly gratifying options in this "age of the self," are hardly conducive to the team mindset, self-discipline, and artistic sensibilities necessary for collectively improvised creation essential to playing traditional New Orleans jazz.

Another important change has been the virtual disappearance of the middle-class from street culture. Whereas much of brass band history shows a blend of middle- and lower-class people, values, and aspirations, better educational opportunities, computers, cable television, and more cosmopolitan attitudes have drawn most of the educated and stable youth away from having "traditional" inclinations. Having a greater range of choices and options in travel, employment, lifestyles, and diversions, most descendants of jazz families and early generation pioneers like the Humphrey's, Kid Ory, Sidney Bechet, and others have not taken interest in the tradition of their ancestors. Though jazz was passed on for several generations, today's younger descendants are likely to be office workers, program directors, lawyers, doctors, college professors, or politicians. Educated middle-class black youth who follow music careers generally prefer contemporary or classical forms. The few who do enter the jazz field know very little about the history or stylistic basis of "the New Orleans thing," which at times they may "fake" when financial opportunity arises.

Many harsh realities of contemporary inner city life—drugs, crime, violence, poverty, illiteracy, unemployment, and the decay of social institutions and values—are abundant in New Orleans. Some current street band "favorites" are indicative of the level to which the society has fallen: "Leave That (Crack) Pipe Alone Lil' Brother," "Food Stamps," "Drop Dem Drawers," and "Pop That Coochie." Though greatly diminished, parade-related crime still occurs. In August 1995, several people were wounded or killed by automatic weapons–toting thugs who randomly shot into a second line crowd. The once reverent and respectful jazz funeral has become a pale shadow of its original character. Since the late 1960s, jazz funerals, still mainly given for older musicians and club members, increasingly took on a carnival-like atmosphere. News cameras, disrespectful second liners, and tourists (often literally) came between the ranks of processions disrupting the funeral's focus in order to get closer to the "fun" and free show. By the eighties and nineties, publicity surrounding jazz funerals caused an increase in the legions of people seeking a continuation of Mardi Gras or jazzfest; and in scores of cunning filmmakers, photographers, and writers who sought to earn money and reputations. Since the late 1980s, a new trend in jazz funerals has become popular as a result of the "drug wars." Rebirth leader/tuba player Phillip Frazier shed some light on the realities of contemporary brass bands and jazz funerals in a 1989 interview: "You think about what's going on in your neighborhood—people growing up, struggling, those that make it and those that don't. . . . Since 1987 there've been families calling us for jazz funerals when someone dies. We've played more than 100 crack funerals."[18]

Such funerals are not limited to the Rebirth band's experiences. A 1995 funeral of a sixteen-year-old musician was typical of the genre. The teenage band members wore cut off jeans, tennis shoes or sandals, and T-shirts— as did the deceased in the coffin. During the slow procession of the motorcade, fast riff songs predominated by rap-style vocals like "I'm A Sixth Ward Nigga" went on for several blocks. During the ceremony, an incredible array of surrounding events took place: the coffin was removed, brought into the boy's house, and possibly opened; beer and marijuana smells competed with oxygen for space; a repeated loud banging noise turned out to be from the new "custom" of stop-sign punching; as the coffin was being placed back in the hearse, beer was poured over it by several second liners; and as the procession made a stop in a nearby housing project, the boy's mother did a second line dance on top of the casket.

Although the spectacle of "crack funerals" and other highly publicized ones are common, the rare, orderly traditional jazz funeral does still occur. Some have been noted for the spiritual beauty, reverence, and poignant hymns and dirges. Danny Barker, whose efforts helped to keep brass bands alive, had requested that he not have a jazz funeral, citing the "mockery" that they had become. At the urging, promises, and watchful eye of Young Tuxedo's Greg Stafford, Barker was given a very reverent and dignified send-off.

The 1995 death of trumpeter Percy Humphrey seemed an appropriate time to reflect on the brass band tradition during the "centennial of jazz." As the consummate symbol of traditional brass band leadership and musical values since the Eureka band's early years, Humphrey was critical of newer trends in the local music scene. It seems appropriate that the last jazz funeral with written scores (held in 1977) was among his Eureka band's last formal engagements. Humphrey was the last direct link in a tradition partially evolved from values and musical standards taught and maintained by his grandfather. He was part of the old jazz family lineage— his father was a jazz musician, so were his brothers Willie and Earl, and so were several other relatives. Percy Humphrey left his mark on the New Orleans community through the masterful trumpet phrases and sweet melodies that passed from Africa and Europe to Congo Square, to the Creole seventh ward, uptown to Buddy Bolden, and on to Percy and others like him. Weakened, though not expired, that initial spiritual flame that told the story of black New Orleans continues to "sing on" from the hearts and souls of those "faithful" heirs whom his generation inspired. In many parts of Europe and Japan, New Orleans–style brass bands patterned after early recordings sound refreshingly close to their models. As the memory of Percy Humphrey and all those who marched the streets alongside him lingers on, questions about the future of the New Orleans brass band resurface again and again as they have for decades.

The Crescent City brass band tradition predated jazz. A fusion of musical and social elements led to its function as a vehicle for expression of the collective creative black New Orleans spirit and as an open cultural exercise in democracy. Its gradual evolution occurred partly as a response to economic and social conditions in the community. Future developments in brass band nature, style, sound, and social significance will follow the same course. As traditional, contemporary, and intermediary styles exist among brass bands, the end results of this transitory state remain unclear. Already, the "new," younger brass band movement is more than twenty years old. Some of its more visible and influential participants have moved on in other directions: The Dirty Dozen is no longer considering itself a brass band as it moves more toward electronic instruments and a "funk" style; the Rebirth's Kermit Ruffins has embarked on a successful solo career in the post-1920s-Armstrong-popular-entertainer mode. Several other younger musicians coming either from the street bands or associated with schools like the New Orleans Center for the Creative Arts, the public school system's Jazz Outreach Program, the University of New Orleans, and Xavier and Dillard Universities are beginning to wear more "traditional" brass band attire and to address early traditional jazz songs and styles.

The influence of the New Orleans brass band tradition is reflected in various places. Smaller traditional jazz groups continue to play marches and hymns and imitate street band styles. Modern jazz drummers who were born in New Orleans, like Vernel Fournier and Ed Blackwell, have become legends for the "parade beat" variations they have used since the 1950s. Many hit records of early rhythm and blues artists, like Fats Domino and Little Richard, were backed by horn arrangements, themes, and rhythm sections that clearly showed brass band influence. Popular New Orleans funk bands, like the Meters and the Neville Brothers, have also used street band rhythms and themes. In the commercial world and the local parties, dances and weddings, mock "second lines" with twirling umbrellas, waving handkerchiefs, and sometimes comic attempts at second line dancing are common. Most NFL football fans who see the New Orleans Saints team on national television have no idea where the frantic dancing, umbrellas, and handkerchiefs of the spirited local crowd come from. Hardly any event with music in New Orleans today can be considered complete without playing "Bourbon St. Parade," "Second Line," "When the Saints Go Marching In," or some other themes that were popularized by brass bands.

The future of the New Orleans brass band may be influenced by a number of external forces in addition to pervasive social conditions. Recognition of the artistic and cultural merit of early jazz and brass band music has led to several high-level attempts at education, preservation, and perpetuation. Since the late-1980s, influential jazz trumpet virtuoso Wynton Marsalis has included adaptations of his native New Orleans brass band style in several performances and on acclaimed national radio and television productions. A series of jazz videos, documentaries, and record reissues have placed traditional styles along side more contemporary ones. There are public brass band radio programs and staged "battles" that feature more modern groups. Occasionally, authentic traditional brass bands are hired by the city to parade in the popular French Market.

One thing seems certain, the New Orleans tradition of marching street bands will have a future. What that future will be is perhaps only known by the Creator, ancestral spirits, and the Crescent City herself. New Orleans is still a mystical, magical place. Her streets hold the secrets of 10,000 years. Here, cemeteries are the resting places where the practitioners of opera, work songs, symphonies, and the blues danced the bamboula and quadrilles, waltzes, and the calinda. In their Africanized Francophone-American-Indian-Anglo-European-Caribbean wisdom, these spirits know that the "voice" of Buddy Bolden, the voice that arose from the deepest and most glorious side of human nature and that told all of our stories for so long, is an immortal flame to be passed on forever. Perhaps the spirit of the New Orleans brass band tradition is to continue on in a mystical dimension, like those who created it—for as Young Tuxedo Brass Band clarinetist and leader John Casimir once said "Nobody here [in New Orleans] ever really dies. . . . They're all still here like you and me. . . . We just don't see them anymore."[19]

NOTES

1. A. Hunt, *Haiti's Influence on Antebellum America* (Baton Rouge: Louisiana State University Press, 1988), 75.

2. H. Kmen, "The Music of New Orleans," in Hodding Carter, ed., *The Past as Prelude: New Orleans, 1718–1968* (New Orleans: Tulane University Press, 1968), 21.

3. H. Kmen, *Music in New Orleans: The Formative Years 1791–1841* (Baton Rouge: Louisiana State University Press, 1966), 237–245.

4. L. Jones, *Blues People* (New York: Morrow Quill Paperbacks, 1963), 27.

5. H. Kmen, *Music in New Orleans: The Formative Years 1791–1841* (Baton Rouge: Louisiana State University Press, 1966), 204, 212.

6. J. S. Blassingame, *Black New Orleans: 1860–80* (Chicago: University of Chicago Press, 1973), 215.

7. Blassingame, *Black New Orleans: 1860–80*, 67.

8. J. Logsdon and C. Bell, "The Americanization of Black New Orleans," in J. Logsdon and A. Hirsch, eds., *Creole New Orleans* (Baton Rouge: Louisiana State University Press, 1992), 197.

9. B. Russell, *New Orleans Style* (St. Charles, La.: G.H.B. Publishers, 1994), 23.

10. M. White, "Evolution of a Cultural Tradition," *Cultural Vistas* 2, no. 4 (Winter 1991): 18–38.

11. H. L. Gates, *The Signifying Monkey: A Theory of African-American Literary Criticism* (New York: Oxford University Press, 1988), xxiv.

12. J. Logsdon and C. Bell, "The Americanization of Black New Orleans," in J.

Logsdon and A. Hirsch, eds., *Creole New Orleans* (Baton Rouge: Louisiana State University Press, 1992), 224.

13. W. Schafer, *Brass Bands and New Orleans Jazz* (Baton Rouge: Louisiana State University Press, 1977).

14. D. Barker, *A Life In Jazz* (London: McMillan Press, 1986), 50.

15. A. Murray, *Stompin' the Blues* (New York: McGraw Hill, 1976), 45–54.

16. L. Saxon, E. Dreyer and R. Tallant, eds., *Gumbo Ya Ya* (Gretna: Pelican Publishing Co., 1987), 302.

17. R. Mitchell, *All on a Mardi Gras Day* (Cambridge: Harvard University Press, 1995), 47.

18. J. Berry, *New Orleans Brass Band Revival*. Reckon Premier Issue, 1995, 32.

19. A. Rose, *I Remember Jazz* (Baton Rouge: Louisiana State University Press, 1987), 6.

BIBLIOGRAPHY

Asante, M., and K. Asante. *African Culture: The Rhythms of Unity*. Trenton, N.J.: African World Press, Inc., 1990.

Charters, S. *Jazz: New Orleans 1885–1963*. New York: Da Capo Press, 1983.

Hall, G. *Africans in Colonial Louisiana*. Baton Rouge: Louisiana State University Press, 1992.

Hazen, M., and R. Hazen. *The Music Men*. Washington, D.C.: Smithsonian Institution Press, 1987.

Hirsch, A., and J. Logsdon, eds. *Creole New Orleans*. Baton Rouge: Louisiana State University Press, 1992.

Jacobs, C. "Benevolent Societies of New Orleans During the Late Nineteenth and Early Twentieth Centuries." *Louisiana History*, 1988.

Jacobs, C., and A. Kaslow. *The Spiritual Churches of New Orleans*. Knoxsville: University of Tennessee Press, 1991.

Lomax, A. *Mr. Jelly Roll*. Berkley: University of California Press, 1950.

Marquis, D. *In Search of Buddy Bolden*. Baton Rouge: Louisiana State University Press, 1978.

Richards, D. "The Implications of African-American Spirituality." In M. Asante and K. Asante, eds., *African Culture*. Trenton: Africa World Press, Inc., 1990.

Walker, H. *Negro Benevolent Societies in New Orleans*. Unpublished Ph.D. Dissertation. Nashville: Fisk University, 1936.

White, M. "The New Orleans Brass Band: Nature, Style, and Social Significance." *Xavier Review* 4, nos. 1 & 2 (1984): 23–35.

4

Why We Sing: The Role and Meaning of Gospel in African American Popular Culture

Angela M. S. Nelson

Throughout American history, there is ample evidence of attempts by European Americans to deny the personhood of people of African descent. This denial by whites of black humanity has resulted in slave mentalities, inferiority complexes, and low self-esteem among many African Americans. While blacks have a peculiar history related to their introduction to Christianity, it is *because of* and *within* Christianity that many African Americans have found a Father and a Friend "closer than a brother." In short, an African American form of Christianity has allowed many African Americans to gain a positive sense of their personhood and to develop positive self-esteem in overcoming inferiority complexes.

Gospel music is the contemporary musical expression of the African American Christian's belief in God. The most recent gospel development—Urban/Contemporary—has been propelled by three factors: (1) African-derived aesthetics for music making, including rhythm, percussiveness, and call-and-response; (2) social, cultural, and historical contexts of black gospel music traditions and life in America, including white racism and black Christianity; and (3) black economic empowerment leading to increased utilization and diversification of instrumentation and technology. The purpose of this chapter is to investigate the theologies within the texts (or lyrics) of black Urban/Contemporary Gospel composers, including a close examination of the life and music of composer John P. Kee of Charlotte, North Carolina.

THEOLOGY

Theology is the rational and subjective discourse reflecting on the human encounter with God and the interpretation of that experience in faith and practice. This includes the study of religious beliefs of individuals and groups in both historical and contemporary life. The theologies of black Urban/Contemporary Gospel composers will be analyzed in order to examine how a significant number of (if not most) African Americans psychologically negotiate their existence in contemporary American society.

In order to situate my discussion of Urban/Contemporary Gospel (circa 1981), I will now turn my attention to a brief overview of the history of black gospel music styles, its pioneers, and its theologies. In addition, by focusing on the contexts and textures (or aesthetics) of black gospel, I will also illuminate the fact that so-called black American "sacred" and "secular" musics in fact do not actually exist. In other words, as I discuss the contexts and textures of gospel (commonly referred to as black sacred music), I will also make lateral references to rap music (commonly referred to as black secular music) in order to highlight and illustrate the similarities between these seemingly disparate forms of music.

Black gospel developed around the turn of the century. It has its origins in the spirituals (the first group of black religious songs), camp meeting songs of the early nineteenth century "Second Awakening" revivals, white gospel hymnody of the Protestant City-Revival Movement of the 1850s, and the hymns of white composers David Sankey and Homer A. Rodeheaver.[1] The term *gospel* is assigned to these songs because many of the texts are derived from the first four books of the New Testament, which proclaim the "good news" of the life and ministry of Jesus Christ. Furthermore, gospel became a part of the regular services of the black church and addressed itself, more often than not, to common life experiences of blacks in urban settings.[2]

There are three major periods or styles of African American gospel music: (1) the transitional period, or PreGospel, from 1900 to 1930; (2) the Traditional Period, or Classic Gospel, from 1930 to 1969; and (3) the Modern Period, or Contemporary Gospel, from 1969 to the present.

PRE-GOSPEL

The first period of black gospel began with the gospel hymns of Charles Price Jones, the founding bishop of the Church of Christ (Holiness) U.S.A., and Charles Albert Tindley, a Methodist minister from Pennsylvania. Jones was a prolific composer of more than 1,000 songs, publishing his first collection in 1899 entitled *Jesus Only No. 1*, followed by his *Jesus Only Nos. 1 and 2* in 1901.[3] Tindley, the first prominent gospel hymn composer, began copyrighting his songs in 1900 and published a collection of his hymns and songs in 1916 under the title *New Songs of Paradise*.[4]

This period of black gospel was represented by gospel hymns. As such, its primary instrumentation was the piano and congregational singing. In terms of melody and harmony, Pre-Gospel combined popular tunes of the day with spirituals, blues, and jazz harmonies. Gospel hymns of the Transitional Period were congregational songs that, textually, incorporated black folk imagery. They attempted to interpret the oppression African Americans faced as they settled in the cities of the North.[5] Another realm of this early form of black gospel included various male quartets of the 1920s (following in the tradition of the jubilee choirs formed at many black colleges in the mid- to late-nineteenth century), singing preachers and their congregations including Reverend J. M. Gates, Reverend A. W. Nix, Elder Bryant, Elder Lonnie McIntorsh, and soloists Arizona Dranes, Laura Henton, and Blind Willie Johnson, among others. These soloists and ensembles were extensions of the black folk tradition and illustrate the first major move within gospel music away from congregational singing. (More about this point later.)

CLASSIC GOSPEL

The next major period of black gospel (from 1930 to 1969), which crystallized it into a distinctive music form, was the Traditional Period of gospel dominated by the Baptists. This period of gospel, sometimes called "Classic Gospel," gained momentum under Thomas A. Dorsey, a Baptist songwriter influenced by the gospel hymns of Tindley and also by Dorsey's early days as a barrelhouse joint blues piano player.[6]

Dorsey, founder of the Chicago school of gospel and often called the "Father of Gospel Music," was the prolific composer of nearly 1,000 gospel songs of which more than half were published during his lifetime.[7] Dorsey is significant to black gospel music because he was the first person to call the black church songs he was composing "gospel songs."[8] Other pioneer gospel composers of this period included Lucie Eddie Campbell-Williams, who composed exclusively for the National Baptist Convention, U.S.A. from 1930 to 1962 and was influential in setting the standards for performance of religious music in the African American Baptist church; William Herbert Brewster, Sr., the composer who gave black gospel music its first million-dollar sellers; Roberta Martin, who developed the piano style of gospel accompaniment and the choral sound of the 1930s and 1940s; and Kenneth Morris, gospel music's most influential publisher, choral arranger, composer, and innovator, who introduced the electric Hammond organ into the African American church.[9]

Just as female classic blues singers of the 1920s were the first significant "stars" of city blues music, similarly the stars of Classic Gospel were women. Innovative singers included Mahalia Jackson, "Sister" Rosetta Tharpe, and Mother Willie Mae Ford Smith. A close relationship between the composers and performers of Classic Gospel essentially made them co-equals in the propagation and spreading of black gospel music. Together these musicians transformed the congregational gospel hymn of the Transitional Period into the solo, ensemble, and choral gospel songs of the Traditional Period.[10]

In particular, this change in grouping is important to Urban/Contemporary Gospel because the primary vocal units for it are soloists, ensembles, and, to a lesser degree, choirs. In general, the transition from congregational hymns to songs for specialized soloists, ensembles, and choirs also had important sociological consequences. While the former song form united worshipers through collective activity of singing and declaring theological and doctrinal commonalities, the new style required the congregation to assume the role of audience. Therefore, unlike what occurred in the performance of spirituals where there was no audience, Classic Gospel music created such a category. Now, the most the congregation could do to share in these musical events was to give affirmative "amens," nod, hum, clap, stand and sway their bodies, or occasionally sing along on choruses and vamps.[11]

Aside from this transformation of early gospel songs, the musical characteristics of this period included reinterpretations of performance styles and instrumentation. In Jones's and Tindley's gospel, piano and (congregational) voices were the principal instruments, whereas the Traditional Period is marked by the addition of drums, electric organs, amplified guitars, percussion instruments, and more subcategories of vocal arrangements. In addition, the gospel keyboardist, who remains *the* central figure in creating and performing gospel music, moved from playing strictly blues harmonies with little modulation and improvisation to a chordal piano style with complex chord usage and creative embellishments.[12] Textually, Classic Gospel songs, especially those by Dorsey, reflect the "heavenward polarity" of Charles Tindley that depicted heaven as *the* ultimate triumph over earthly oppression.[13]

BLACK GOSPEL AS POPULAR MUSIC

Economically, the transformation from communal participation to performer-and-audience participation illustrates the effects of the American popular music industry on black gospel music and also establishes a foundation for an urban/contemporary style of black gospel. Black popular music authority Portia K. Maultsby states that black gospel music became an "economic commodity in secular contexts" around the 1920s when its performers were broadcast over network and independent radio stations; recorded by independent record companies; and showcased in large concert halls, coliseums, theaters, jazz festivals and nightclubs. In other words, when black gospel went outside of the sanctuaries of the church, it expanded the American music consumer market and was appropriated by purveyors of secular music forms.[14] While Maultsby's observations are indeed accurate, the phenomenon of black gospel sheet music has been overlooked. Considering its development, I believe it is safe to conclude that black gospel became an economic commodity *before* the 1920s.

The first popular songs were published in America with words and no music on broadsides and songsters in the early 1700s. When songs were published individually rather than in sets, this marked the beginning of sheet music. During the nineteenth century, sheet music became the basis for the entire popular music industry later called Tin Pan Alley.[15] It has been well documented that the first black gospel songs were in fact gospel hymns published in the form of sheet music as early as 1893.[16] Therefore, the black gospel song actually became an economic commodity and officially entered the arena of popular music when the publication and sales of gospel sheet music began. Not only were black gospel composers then concerned with the spiritual or inspirational aspects of composing, they also became concerned with making certain that their music was copyrighted, published, promoted, and distributed.[17]

Such African American composers as W. C. Handy and Harry Pace in the 1920s had already demonstrated that African Americans could be viable competitors in the market for the sale of sheet music and recordings based on black popular music forms.[18] The significance of the gospel song dissemination lies in the fact that through sales and distribution, its composers witnessed a phenomenal growth within African American religious circles for the most part without the promotion of the white dominant American popular music industry. However, as with other forms of black music, such as blues and ragtime, when white record store owners, agents, and publishers began to recognize that there was a high demand for black gospel, they could no longer ignore it.[19] In addition to black gospel composers looking to make a living from their compositions and arrangements, at this point black gospel became more involved with the white mainstream music industry. Nevertheless, the manner in which black gospel composers carefully controlled and monitored the development and growth of an indigenous music form that met the psychological, emotional, and spiritual needs of its consumers is definitely a significant step forward for African Americans in the creation and commercialization of their own music. Also, as the economic well-being of all blacks in general and black gospel composers in particular improved, their access to instruments and technology became less restricted. While these expressive means were not indigenous to African American culture, African American musicians nevertheless expanded their use of an African-derived aesthetic of music making on to

European-derived instruments. Every period or style of black gospel (as well as black secular music forms) has seen this, as the discussion of the next style of black gospel will demonstrate.

CONTEMPORARY GOSPEL

Following Classic Gospel is the Modern Period of black gospel, which commenced in 1969 with the Edwin Hawkins Singers' recorded arrangement of the nineteenth-century Baptist hymn "Oh Happy Day."[20] Just as enslaved African Americans created spirituals by borrowing from psalms and hymns, Edwin Hawkins created a new gospel song by borrowing from a traditional Baptist hymn.[21] What made "Oh Happy Day" different from Classic Gospel was its crossover appeal. In fact, "Oh Happy Day" was programmed as gospel and soul on black-oriented radio stations and as pop on Top 40 stations. Moreover, Hawkins's song (and other Contemporary Gospel songs after it) consciously integrated elements from contemporary black popular music styles.[22] The leading representatives of this period were Holiness-Pentecostal musicians of the Churches of God in Christ, Inc., particularly siblings Edwin and Walter Hawkins along with Walter's ex-wife, Tramaine Hawkins, and Andrae and Sandra Crouch, all from Los Angeles, California, and the Clark Sisters of Detroit, Michigan.[23]

Black gospel witnessed further growth during the Modern Period as composers and performers of this style introduced electronic instruments into gospel music performances and recordings and created a supplementary unit of strings, woodwinds, and brasswinds.[24] Textually, however, the theological worldview of this period can be classified as traditional in that the themes are essentially consonant with those of Tindley and Dorsey.[25]

The advances made in Contemporary Gospel opened the door for Urban/Contemporary Gospel. However, by and large, the composers and performers of Urban/Contemporary Gospel represent another generation of African Americans coming out of the urban context and their experiences with contemporary popular music greatly influenced their own music.

THE SOCIAL, CULTURAL, AND HISTORICAL CONTEXTS OF URBAN/CONTEMPORARY GOSPEL

The Urban/Contemporary Gospel style originated from Contemporary Gospel. Its pioneering figures are members of the male sextet called Commissioned and a quartet of brothers simply called "The Winans," whose album in 1981 began a new and exciting progression in gospel performance and recording. As seen in American popular music in general and other such popular African American music forms as blues and soul, the predominant composers and arrangers of Urban/Contemporary Gospel are African American men. They include brothers Marvin, Carvin, and Benjamin (or

"BeBe") Winans; Michael Brooks; Fred Hammond, Mitchell Jones and
Parkes Stewart; Mark Kibble; Claude V. McKnight III; Mervyn Warren;
and John P. Kee. Performers include most members of the Winans family,
who, incidentally, are sometimes called the "First Family of Gospel." They
are the Winans, composed of brothers Ronald, twins Marvin and Carvin,
and Michael; BeBe and CeCe Winans, the seventh and eighth children of
David and Delores Winans; Angie and Debbie Winans, the ninth and tenth
siblings of the family; and Vickie Winans, wife of Marvin Winans. Other
performers of this style are soloists Vanessa Bell Armstrong; Earth, Wind
and Fire's Philip Bailey; Helen Baylor; Fred Hammond; Lexi (or Alexis
Nucklos); Donna McElroy; Vernessa Mitchell; John P. Kee, and Keith
Staten. Also, small ensembles Billy and Sarah Gaines; Commissioned,
founded in 1982 and now consisting of Maxx Frank, Fred Hammond,
Mitchell Jones, Karl Reid, Marvin Sapp, and Michael Williams; Take 6,
consisting of Alvin Chea, Cedric Dent, Joel Kibble, Mark Kibble, Claude
V. McKnight III, and David Thomas; Witness, composed of four women:
Tina Brooks, Diane Campbell, Yolanda Harris, and Lisa Page; and choirs
Kingdom and Sounds of Blackness. In addition, there are Christian rap
performers Michael Peace, recognized as the pioneer of Christian hip-hop,[26]
Mike-E., Stephen Wiley, JC and the Boyz, D-Boy Rodriguez, D. C. Talk,
Fresh Fish, Rite Choice, Transformation Crusade, SFC (Soldiers for Christ),
ETW (End Time Warriors), and PID (Preachers in Disguise).

Urban/Contemporary Gospel encompasses performers outside of the basic rhythm and blues/soul sound (which is the melodic and harmonic foundation of most Contemporary Gospel). It includes those performers who
are natives to cities outside of the Detroit area. It is my contention that (1)
Urban/Contemporary Gospel began in Detroit and that (2) the Winans and
Commissioned are its chief pioneers, innovators, and propagators. At this
point, I will limit my analysis to gospel composers from Detroit, Michigan,
and I will show how Commissioned and the Winans family are indeed its
exemplary representatives. First, I will turn my attention to what makes
this style—the Urban/Contemporary Gospel style—unique and separate
from Classic and Contemporary Gospel and African American secular music forms.

There were several factors ushering Urban/Contemporary Gospel into the
early 1980s. For one thing, its chief composers were influenced by the secular music of their day, such music forms as rhythm and blues, soul, funk,
and rap and, to a lesser degree, jazz.[27] Indeed, the "electronic echo memory" of these African American composers is quite prevalent. For example,
in Take 6's release of *Join the Band*, echos of Earth, Wind, and Fire and
Al Jarreau can be heard. Also, the echos of funk band Cameo can be heard
in John P. Kee's *Colorblind*. Urban/Contemporary Gospel pioneer Michael
Brooks said that he listened to all kinds of music while growing up in
Detroit including classical music and to such white popular performers as

James Taylor, ABBA, Chicago, the Doobie Brothers, and the Partridge Family. Overall, Brooks added that he particularly liked all black popular music and he saw these as significant influences on his own writing style.[28]

In addition to being influenced by the gamut of black musical styles present at that time, musicians of this style recognized the potential for having careers in music that would allow them to remain true to their Holiness-Pentecostal upbringings while not crossing over into "secular" music. This development is due in part to the formation of Christian independent record labels, major record companies establishing Christian labels within them, and the vigorous drive of these companies to recruit contemporary black gospel artists.

Finally, child and spousal abuse, murders and crimes related to the outbreaks of crack-cocaine addiction, the AIDS epidemic, racial unrest, the sharp rise in the homeless population for both individuals and whole families, and unemployment were on the rise or more prevalent in America in general, and in African American communities in particular, by the early 1980s. Observing these developments in Detroit through the lenses of their own religious training prompted Urban/Contemporary Gospel composers and performers to suggest that people suffering from these problems need Jesus in their lives. Essentially, these musicians see their music as one way to "tell the good news" about him. Commissioned's cofounder Fred Hammond expresses this sentiment when he comments on the focus of his solo recording debut entitled *I Am Persuaded*. Hammond says he geared this album toward teenagers and young adults.

The world is saying it's cool to smoke and drink. I want to tell kids it's cool to be saved. . . . it's cool to be with the Lord. So many secular acts promote drugs and sex. I want to be one of the guys who sets the standard as a role model for kids, like the Winans were for me. I want to tell them that now is the time to get as close to the Lord as they can.[29]

Also, Carvin Winans reiterates this point concerning adults and young people when discussing his and his brothers' recording *All Out*. (It is safe to assume that his inclusion of country music is an obvious attempt to attract white Americans to their album.

We want this album to reach all phases of music. The country, the pop, R&B, the gospel, rap. We want to take out all the stops and let people know in all walks of life, the message of The Winans, which is Christ is soon to come. We were fortunate to be brought up in a Christian home with parents that cared about and loved us. Everybody hasn't had that. But we want to let people know that no matter how you were brought up, no matter a person's situation, that [He] knows and there's not a situation that [He] can't handle. That's [our] goal for this album; for it to go all [out] in the highways and byways, wherever that might be, reaching and touching everybody.[30]

This practice of "preaching" or spreading the Word of God through song began historically with Mother Willie Mae Ford Smith when she established the tradition of introducing songs at her services with a brief sermonette including explications of the text in her performances.[31] Likewise, Brooks said that the thrust of his composing is to write songs that involve taking biblical principles and phrasing them in such a way that people in the 1990s will understand them and to be able to apply them to their lives.[32] In short, Brooks sees his music as a ministry.

Noted black sociologist C. Eric Lincoln and sociologist Lawrence Mamiya trace this development of "music as a ministry" up to the Modern Period, and they state that musicians of this period use the "gospel medium as a new homiletical instrument."[33] If Brooks can be viewed as a norm for other black Urban/Contemporary Gospel musicians (which I believe he does represent), then they *are* "ministers" (literally in most cases) who "preach" their compositions to an affirmative "congregation/audience." Brooks's, Carvin Winans's, and Fred Hammond's claims, therefore, support Lincoln and Mamiya's contention that Contemporary Gospel performers use their music as a "homiletical instrument." Further, it shows that Urban/Contemporary Gospel composers see music inspired of God as a powerful tool that can effect a positive change in a person's spiritual and mental state. CeCe Winans, responding to questions regarding criticisms that she and other performers in the Contemporary Gospel style are expanding their music just for money, said this: "The gold records and Grammys aren't the important thing; it's when someone comes up to you and says that your record changed their life."[34]

THE URBANIZATION OF BLACK GOSPEL MUSIC

While I have shared several reasons for why black Urban/Contemporary Gospel developed when it did, the question of "Why Detroit?" still remains. In fact, it is this aspect of Urban/Contemporary Gospel that most effectively connects it with rap, for both were created in the city. Sociologists and urban city planners may well agree that Detroit, Michigan, is perhaps one excellent example of an American city that had been at a zenith at one point in its history but has become handicapped because of drugs, crime, a lowered tax base resulting from among other things "white-flight," and unemployment resulting from businesses moving out of the city. Even as grim as this statement may be about Detroit, it is my contention that it was *because* of all of these and other factors that Urban/Contemporary Gospel originated and developed in Detroit, a city with a history in many ways like the South Bronx where hip hop culture was conceived and grew. Three important factors unique to Detroit support my thesis: (1) Detroit inhabits a large population of African Americans; (2) the Churches of God in Christ, Inc., (or COGIC) and other Holiness-Pentecostal denominations

are a formidable presence in the city; and (3) Detroit is the founding home
of Motown.

The fact that Detroit has (and has had) a large concentration of African
Americans is significant because that means that the city has established
within it a strong cultural base from which Urban/Contemporary Gospel
could develop. Like Motown founder Berry Gordy, many Detroiters were
blacks who migrated from southern states in search of jobs with the Ford
automobile plants just prior to, during, and after World War I.[35] These
new city dwellers brought with them traditions from their southern roots.
Part and parcel of these traditions were religious and secular music. In
short, Detroit was burgeoning with various forms and styles of black music.
This storehouse of music (actually a storehouse of the black music aesthetic
that includes rhythm, percussiveness, and call-and-response) is a necessary
prerequisite for the creation of new black music forms, whether they be
sacred or secular. Urban/Contemporary Gospel is one such form that especially illuminates the fact that all African American sacred and secular
music are essentially the same if their categorization is restricted to an examination of contexts and textures.

The Church of God in Christ (COGIC), Inc., denomination is also significant to my discussion of Urban/Contemporary Gospel. Lincoln and Mamiya note in their study that Pentecostalism (of which COGIC is the largest
segment) has performed an indispensable service in the development and
acceptance of Contemporary Gospel music. As I have mentioned earlier,
performers reared in the COGIC church have pioneered in the creation of
Contemporary Gospel.[36] Therefore, it is not strange to discover that black
Detroit musicians would have an important hand in the creation of this
microstyle within Contemporary Gospel since their religious affiliation has
been such a significant force behind the development and progress of *all*
black gospel music.

Another important point that is connected to COGIC and is related to
almost all black musicians, deals with how they learn their craft. Most
black gospel musicians are self-taught, but they learn about instrumental
technique and harmonization from observing and working with other musicians in the church context. Composer Michael Brooks noted that "coffee
houses" (places where Detroit's black churchgoers would congregate after
night worship services in order to eat and listen to gospel music) were also
significant to his training in composition, playing, and directing of gospel
music. Ortiz Walton notes that it is this collective participation in African
American musical performance that has functioned as a "teaching tool" in
place of the European-style conservatory.[37] Urban/Contemporary Gospel
composers are no exception. For instance, both Mike-E. and Fred Hammond did "apprenticeships" of sorts with the Winans, and they both clearly
state that they were influenced by them. Along these lines, as is expected

to occur in most apprenticeships, Hammond and Mike-E. left the Winans and went on to work together in the all-male ensemble named Commissioned.[38]

The training of rappers and deejays is like that of black Urban/Contemporary Gospel composers in terms of their learning the necessary skills of the art in a communal, collective, and participatory manner. However, it is at this point that many of the similarities end. A few black Urban/Contemporary Gospel composers may be especially critical of rap because of more than its nihilistic and violent lyrics. It could be because rappers and deejays do not recognize the traditional Western European rules of harmony, melody, and rhythm, and they do not recognize what has become the established boundaries of sound engineering.[39] This does not appear to be a major bone of contention with Urban/Contemporary Gospel composers for two major reasons: Even though Urban/Contemporary Gospel composers play traditional European instruments (that is, piano, drums, organ, guitars, saxophones) it is clear that they do not play these instruments in traditional European ways and they most certainly do not produce traditional European sounds out of them. In addition, as far as sound engineering is concerned, Urban/Contemporary Gospel composers also extend the boundaries of the usage of low-sound frequencies, just as rap producers do. This shows their participation in the continuity of the black music aesthetic, which highly values density, timbral differentiation, and percussion and percussiveness.

In a city with a large black population and a plentiful source of churches, Urban/Contemporary Gospel composers were also intimately exposed to the music of Motown because its headquarters was located in Detroit.[40] The Winans were only permitted to listen to gospel music inside their home when they were children,[41] but Helen Baylor, Fred Hammond, and rapper Mike-E. have stated that they listened to and were influenced by the music of Motown.[42] Motown is significant because one of the strengths of this black independently owned label was its synthesis of rhythm and blues, pop music, gospel, and big band music. Another feature that singles out Motown was Berry Gordy's desire for "polished" recordings that would attract the white teenage mainstream market. "Polished" recordings, made possible with multitracking, is a unique characteristic of black Urban/Contemporary Gospel. Perhaps this desire for artfully constructed Urban/Contemporary Gospel recordings on state-of-the-art equipment was a seed planted and nurtured by their knowledge of Gordy's insistence on the same thing in all of the early Motown recordings. However, it is these polished recordings that form one significant criticism of black Urban/Contemporary Gospel by gospel traditionalists. Electronic sound technology illustrates one important link between Urban/Contemporary Gospel and rap.

URBAN/CONTEMPORARY GOSPEL: THE ULTIMATE
SECULARIZATION OF BLACK GOSPEL

One of the primary criticisms of all black gospel music has been and still is its "secular" manifestations. Many African Americans, especially those from old mainline religious denominations, view the music and its secular influences as blasphemous toward God and essentially "unspiritual."[43] However, it is these so-called secular influences that demonstrate the sameness of all African American musics. These complaints began even before Classic Gospel performers moved to venues outside of the church to sing their music. Criticisms have only continued to increase since the first time "Sister" Rosetta Tharpe appeared as a part of Cab Calloway's show at the Cotton Club in New York in December 1938.[44]

Lincoln and Mamiya observed that many critics of Contemporary Gospel music generally dislike its tendency to include secular metaphors and musical embellishments that may not be suitable for the worship setting.[45] Not only are secular metaphors, musical embellishments, and performance styles not suitable for worship, according to John Styll, editor of the Nashville-based *Contemporary Christian Music Magazine* (CCM), such contemporary Christian music forms as gospel (Christian) rap are *entirely* unsuitable for the worship setting: "It's not church music. And I think that's an area where people have some of their biggest problems. They can't imagine these rappers doing their thing on Sunday morning. Well, frankly, neither can I. It's not intended for Sunday mornings."[46] Al Hobbs of the Gospel Music Workshop of America, Urban/Contemporary Gospel's leading organizational proponent, concurs: "It's not primarily to be used in worship, nothing you play Sunday morning. It's for the concert halls, electronic media and radio."[47]

Again, this seems to be the bone of contention between Urban/Contemporary and Classic and Contemporary Gospel listeners; if the music is not suitable for the black worship setting then traditionalists do not view it as fit to be called "religious" at all. Some traditionalists go as far as to "demonize" certain secular forms of black music. For example, Classic Gospel singer and choral director Reverend Milton Brunson of New Jersey identifies rap and rhythm and blues as "devil music." All in all, Brunson does not view the inclusion of rap into recordings of groups like the Winans, BeBe and CeCe Winans, and Commissioned as positive characteristics.[48]

Nevertheless, the process of secularization continues on more than fifty years after "Sister" Tharpe's (re)introduction of black sacred music into American secular culture with the Urban/Contemporary Gospel group Commissioned, in their recording *Matters of the Heart*. This recording demonstrates the continued legacy of secular influences. Commissioned performs a song entitled "Another Day in Paradise," written by Phil Collins, on this CD, and they perform with converted rappers Run-D.M.C. on

"You Can Always Go Home."[49] Also, the Winans, who are no strangers to criticism of their music, have recorded songs with such mainstream "secular" artists as Kenny G, Gerald LeVert, Stevie Wonder, Anita Baker, Michael McDonald (formerly of the Doobie Brothers), Lalah Hathaway, country music star Ricky Van Shelton, Teddy Riley (creator of the "New Jack Swing" style in American popular music), Kenny Loggins, and rapper R. Kelly. They have been featured guests on such television programs as *Soul Train* and *The Arsenio Hall Show*, and they sang backup on Michael Jackson's socially conscious song "Man in the Mirror."[50] In 1985, the Winans signed with Quincy Jones's Qwest label, a secular label affiliated with the record company giant Warner Brothers, becoming the second black gospel group to make such a deal.[51] Almost fifty years earlier, "Sister" Tharpe in 1938 signed a recording contract with Decca Records, thus becoming the first gospel singer to record for a major commercial company.[52]

In addition, BeBe and CeCe Winans recorded "Bridge Over Troubled Water" written by Paul Simon,[53] and they have performed with pop star Whitney Houston,[54] rapper [MC] Hammer, and R&B/Soul balladeer Luther Vandross.[55] The brother-sister duo also have appeared on *Soul Train* with Mavis Staples singing a cover of the song "I'll Take You There" that the Staples Singers made popular in the early 1970s,[56] and in 1991 they were featured in advertisements for McDonald's restaurant.[57] Furthermore, in perhaps what is the epitome of secularization, the entire Winans family organized a Christmas special for television that has aired for several years in syndication.

I have briefly outlined some of the activities of Urban/Contemporary Gospel performers that are in conflict with black gospel traditionalists. Now it is necessary to delineate exactly what these "secular" influences are on the Urban/Contemporary Gospel style. The major manifestation of the secularization in Urban/Contemporary Gospel surfaces in the way that its recordings increasingly utilize techniques of the American popular music industry. These techniques can be grouped into four categories: (1) studio recording, (2) publicity and promotion, (3) vocal instrumentation, and (4) song composition.

In the area of studio recording, Urban/Contemporary Gospel composers include synthesizers producing synthesized string and woodwind sounds, and complex echo and reverberation effects. Also, multitrack recording or overdubbing[58] allows them to produce multiple layers of sound. Publicity and promotion of a new product is crucial to the dominant (secular) American popular industry. Recording companies have found that, in order to sell their Christian recordings, they must have their performers *look* as much as possible like the general American public and the performers must be seen visually through advertisements so that potential buyers can gain face-recognition with the music being released in record stores and on radio stations. Therefore, the current clothing and hair styles are as significant to

Christian performers as they are to secular performers. Gospel performers who wear flashy and up-to-date clothing illustrate for some traditionalists a move away from the Church and, ultimately, a move away from God.

Another definite sign of the secular pop industry's influence on black Urban/Contemporary Gospel, and indeed on all Contemporary Christian music, is the use of music videos. In fact, the cable channel MTV was established exclusively on the concept of showing promotional videos provided free by the record companies (based on the model of free records provided to radio stations) in order to sell the rock stars' records.[59] Christian record labels are essentially no exception. While the message in most Christian recordings is related to Jesus and his relationship to human beings, record company executive directors are also interested in selling the performers' records. Therefore, they too film videos to accompany title cuts of recordings. Such music videos can be seen on Family Channel's (FAM) *CCM* program on Saturday evenings and on both the *Bobby Jones Gospel Hour* and *Video Gospel* programs shown on the Black Entertainment Network (BET) on Sunday evenings.

Vocal instrumentation in black Urban/Contemporary Gospel borrows from the rhythm and blues traditions of the 1940s and 1950s, which includes a backup vocal group that emphasizes fragments of the lyrics through repetition or use of counterpoint.[60] While lyrics emphasize some aspect of Christianity, Urban/Contemporary Gospel composers borrow from popular music traditions by arranging repetitious sections, or refrains, within their compositions that will ensure that the refrains will be easily remembered. (Actually, black music has always included refrains and repetitious sections because the songs were usually learned orally.)

In addition, another aspect of these lyrics that points to its secularity is the obscurity of the subject matter. Some compositions by Urban/Contemporary Gospel composers do not directly address or name God or Jesus. The Reverend Milton Biggham, executive director of Savoy Records, the oldest Classic Gospel label in the United States, sums up this practice when he says "God is excluded from the picture" when "[p]roducers and company heads [. . . convince] artists to mention Jesus less in the song and to use personal pronouns such as He, I, Him and You."[61] This constitutes one problem that even Contemporary Gospel listeners have with the Urban/Contemporary form of gospel. In short, the criticism is that Urban/Contemporary Gospel performers are focusing more on production and less on the "mission of gospel," which is to spread the "good news" about Jesus.[62]

A final illustration of secular influences in Urban/Contemporary Gospel is shown in song compositions where entire songs are "covered," and where melodies and harmonies—effected by the urgency of "electronic echo memories"—are borrowed from white pop songs and other African American popular music forms such as soul, rhythm and blues, funk, and rap. For instance, in their *Matters of the Heart* recording, Commissioned included

a song written by Phil Collins entitled "Another Day in Paradise."[63] While
the song does speak about homelessness, which seems to be a reasonable
subject of concern for the Church, the composer of the song, Phil Collins,
is neither recognized in the black Holiness-Pentecostal Church as "saved"
nor even remotely considered to be religious. Nevertheless, Fred Hammond's inclusion of this song shows that black Urban/Contemporary Gospel composers and performers are not afraid to utilize music that will drive
home a point, no matter *where* the music originated.

THE TEXTURES OF URBAN/CONTEMPORARY GOSPEL

Urban/Contemporary Gospel uses many techniques found in black secular and sacred musics. In fact, these seemingly disparate aspects of black
and sacred musics are joined by the fact that all forms of African American
music share a common black aesthetic for music making and these include
(1) rhythm and rhyme, (2) percussion and percussiveness, and (3) collective
participation and call-and-response patterns. It is primarily these textures
(or rituals) that can be found in all African American expressive arts that
connect them. There is really no such thing as "sacred" and "secular"
because the music *sounds* the same!

The ritual of rhythm is evident in Urban/Contemporary Gospel through
the heavy use of syncopation and steady bass riffs, principally in the key-
boards, bass guitar, drums, and various synthesizers. *USA Today* black
music critic James T. Jones IV's description of Urban/Contemporary Gospel
as gospel with "inspirational or religious lyrics over *hard-driving beats*"[64]
more than adequately supplies meaning to my analysis of gospel music.
Rhythm is seen as a necessary part of black music whether it be gospel or
rap. Even though rhythm is significant to the composition of Urban/Con-
temporary Gospel and rap, in Urban/Contemporary Gospel the performers'
reference to "rappin' good rhythms and rhymes" is nonexistent. The reason
is obvious. If gospel performers or composers accentuated the fact about
how good *their* "rhymes and rhythms" were, the focus would be on that
particular person and not on God. Therefore, since the black aesthetic dic-
tates the presence of rhythm, it is most assuredly heard in Urban/Contem-
porary Gospel. However, attention to the performer(s) of it would not be
appropriate. Please note that the acknowledgment of this fact does not take
away from my contention that all black sacred (gospel) and secular (rap)
musics are actually one music. It only delineates the nuances of contemporary African American values and beliefs: Those African Americans in
the church (gospel singers) will direct attention to their leader—God—and
those at the party (rappers) will direct attention to their leader—themselves.

While rhythm is indeed a significant element in the composition and
performance of Urban/Contemporary Gospel music, the use of percussion
instruments and a percussive approach to music making are also important.

Percussion instruments are instruments that are struck, scraped, scratched, shaken, or rubbed. From the earliest days of Classic Gospel to the present, drums have been a core instrument of the rhythm unit alongside the piano (or organ in many black Holiness-Pentecostal churches). However, in black Urban/Contemporary Gospel, the "drum or bass concept," which is the organizing time and pulse structure underneath all black folk and popular music forms, has been extended into the use of drum and bass synthesizers. Obviously, this electronic expansion permits composers to create more percussive basal sounds than one drummer or bass guitarist could do alone, and it provides additional percussion instrumentation for such sounds as claves and triangles, without employing the assistance of several percussionists. As one may recall or expect, the drum machine and synthesizer also figure prominently in rap music, and their uses in both forms of music illustrate the perpetuation of the same black (music) aesthetic.

A percussive approach to music making also extends the idea and practice of how percussion instruments are used. This is evident in the "pounding" or "hammering" technique of Urban/Contemporary Gospel keyboardists and bass guitarists and in the inclusion of handclaps on recordings. Black gospel music scholar/director Mellonee Burnim attributes this desirable percussive sound to a "very flexible wrist."[65] The important idea here is that even when Urban/Contemporary Gospel composers and performers are not physically hitting a drum or some other "officially designated" percussion instrument, they do, however, treat other instruments or objects in such a way that it takes on the appearance of striking, scraping, scratching, shaking, or rubbing.

Rhythm and percussiveness go hand-in-hand in producing the Urban/Contemporary Gospel sound (as well as in all African American expressive cultural products). Another characteristic element is the call-and-response pattern and collective participation. Call-and-response is manifested in several ways on Urban/Contemporary Gospel recordings. These include antiphonal interactions (1) between the soloist and the backup vocal group, (2) between the soloist and the instruments of the rhythm and supplementary units, (3) between the backup vocal group and the rhythm and supplementary units, and (4) between the rhythm unit and the supplementary unit. While we may know the names of individual singers within Urban/Contemporary Gospel groups, all of the persons involved are collectively participating in making the music event occur and making it occur correctly.

Overall, rhythm, percussiveness, and call-and-response patterns encourage and maintain a sense of group solidarity, and they validate African American aesthetic and cultural values.[66] The same values are upheld equally in African American secular music (rap) and in African American sacred music (gospel). However, as I will discuss next, the primary way in which African American Urban/Contemporary Gospel composers explain and discuss their beliefs and attitudes is through their words, and their words form the basis for the so-called distinction between "sacred" and "secular" in African American music forms. By examining what they have to say, I will show that Urban/Contemporary Gospel lyrics reflect a theological worldview that paradoxically is similar and dissimilar to Classic and Contemporary Gospel. Also, it is these theologies that will give us an idea of how gospel is used psychologically by urban/contemporary African Americans.

THE TEXTS OF URBAN/CONTEMPORARY GOSPEL

Although black gospel has always been unique for its documentation of experiences common to blacks in urban areas, what makes Urban/Contemporary Gospel different from the other styles that went before it is that composers of this style pay particular attention to such urgent social issues as racism and homelessness, and they make a call encouraging Christians to become actively involved in resolving these and other societal problems. Racism has been thematized in the Winans's *Decisions* album[67] and in the songs of the gospel rap group PID (Preachers in Disguise). To date, PID is one of the few black sacred groups that has tackled the issues of homosexuality, sexually transmitted diseases, and homelessness in American society.[68] This aspect of Urban/Contemporary Gospel—its concern about social issues related to divisiveness—challenges theomusicologist Jon Michael Spencer's assertion that "the Lord essentially is not portrayed as [a] Reconciler" in black gospel. Spencer, in his study of anticulturalism in gospel, contends that "Customarily gospel does not command individuals to love those who despitefully use them but rather to turn away from them. This turning away from the world heavenward to the Ultimate Alternative [Jesus] is an end in itself rather than serving as a means of turning back toward friend, kindred, and neighbor in reconciliation."[69]

Through writing (or composing) about racism, which divides racial and ethnic groups and which depicts examples of being "despitefully used," and through writing about homelessness, which divides families and communities, Urban/Contemporary Gospel composers are indeed preaching a Word based on reconciliation. Black "secular" rap also does this. However, most rappers encourage African Americans to reconcile within and among themselves. For example, when Sister Souljah says "Always encourage a brother or sister to do what is right, Turn all of your talents and skills in a Black business,"[70] based on the general knowledge of Sister Souljah and her relationship with rap group Public Enemy, we know that she is not encouraging African Americans to reconcile with whites. Rather, she is telling African Americans to support themselves and their communities economically. In short, she is saying "Empower yourselves!"

Black Urban/Contemporary Gospel composers, on the other hand, have a more broad-based universal approach to reconciliation. Most times, they are specifically speaking about reconciliation between blacks and whites, effectively putting the "past behind." Marvin Winans (cowriting with Percy Bady and his brother Ronald) says that "love has no color" and that it shows "no evil to no people."[71] The point is driven further by the inclusion of white pop performer Michael McDonald on this particular recording.

While these contemporary issues addressed in Urban/Contemporary Gospel, more often than not, distinguish it from most Classic and Contemporary Gospel, in order to fully examine the theological worldview of Urban/Contemporary Gospel composers, it is also necessary to review those texts that are comparable to the theological worldviews of Classic and Contemporary Gospel, thereby demonstrating Urban/Contemporary Gospel's connection with prior gospel styles. In order to do this, I found it helpful to divide these lyrics into two subcategories consisting of (1) theologies and (2) theodicies. (*Theodicy* is the term for the propositional answers to the "question" or "problem" of evil. Human beings posit different theodicies in an attempt to explain how a good God permits evil and suffering in the world.[72])

After examining the lyrics of composers Michael Brooks, Fred Hammond, the writing team Mitchell Jones and Parkes Stewart, and Winans brothers Benjamin and Marvin, I found four central themes including one theodicy. They are (1) testifying about God's desire to heal and protect all people (His goodness), (2) spreading the "good news" about the life and ministry of Jesus, (3) expressing faith and hope in God, and (4) demonstrating how liberation, redemption, and self-affirmation can occur in God. Furthermore, the single theodicy is the "work of the devil" theodicy, including the personification of Satan.

The Urban/Contemporary Gospel composer's practice of personifying God and Jesus is especially unique to black gospel. These lyrics give God a "personality" and a "human voice," and they help to extend the "myth" of God and Jesus in African American culture. This point is especially significant because of the circumstances under which African Americans came to know about the God and Jesus of Christianity. Owing to the differences in social and cultural contexts, the Jesus that African Americans call on is going to be quite different from the one which European Americans call on. Cultural critic Amiri Baraka (LeRoi Jones), commenting in 1966, said almost matter-of-factly that "[T]he God spoken about in the Black songs is not the same one in the white songs. Though the words might look the same. (They are not even pronounced alike.). . . . [I]t is a different quality of energy they summon."[73] Likewise, theologian James Cone artfully illustrates this point in context when he says: "It is absurd on sociological, psychological and theological grounds to contend that the Ku Klux Klansman and the black person who escaped him are shouting for the same or similar reasons in their respective church services. Because whites and blacks have different historical and theological contexts out of which their worship services arise, they do not shout for the same reasons."[74]

Translating Cone's observation into the language of black inner-city males coping with white police brutality of the 1980s and 1990s, rapper KRS-One, the central figure and lyricist of Boogie Down Productions, notes that there are policemen who are "killing blacks, and calling it the law." What is bothersome to KRS-One is that these same policemen are "worshipping Jesus, too."[75] KRS-One's statement explicitly suggests that the same white policemen who harrass black men are also the same policemen who religiously attend church services. However, KRS-One is also implicitly suggesting that when these police officers are "worshipping Jesus" they are not doing it for the same reasons as the black men who endured their harrassment. Of course, Urban/Contemporary Gospel composers will not be as direct as KRS-One and other secular rappers. However, the social situation (or context) of gospel is the same as rap, and gospel composers (males especially) no doubt know about that which KRS-One speaks.

Simply put, African Americans in general and Urban/Contemporary Gospel composers in particular humanize God and Jesus by creating a voice in speech and music that can be understood in contemporary terms and that can fulfill certain psychological needs. Therefore, in Urban/Contemporary Gospel, we will find a God who is personified as an understanding "person" and One who is omniscient. In "Heart of Mine," written by Fred Hammond, God explains to this brokenhearted person that He knows that they are hurting and that he knows that the tears they cry are not tears of joy.[76] God reassures this believer that if she stands her ground, her "suffering and pain" will be rewarded with "great gain" in Heaven.

Testifying about the goodness of God is expressed in "Goodness, Mercy and Grace" written by Marvin Winans.[77] This believer says that if it had not been for the "goodness, mercy and grace" of God, he would not be able to go "to the corner store," "ride in a city street car," "take a trip out of town," or even "stay at home" without worrying about something happening to him. Testifying about God's desire to heal and protect all people in "Hold Me," Mitchell Jones and Parkes Stewart portray a believer asking the Lord for protection.[78] Gospel has always been based on telling the good news about the life and ministry of Jesus. In "Go Tell Somebody," written by Michael Brooks, believers are urged to "tell some lost soul about Christ" and to "tell them Jesus loves them" and that "He died for their sins."[79] The obvious result is redemption, liberation, and reconciliation.

The theology of faith and hope is addressed in "Meantime" by Benjamin Winans.[80] In this expression of faith and hope in God's promises, this believer states that even while he does not know how, he does know, however, that he will definitely survive his trials. Furthermore, even though he does not know when, he does know that Jesus will surely assist him through his difficult times. Liberation and self-affirmation are expressed in "Breaking of Day," written by Marvin Winans.[81] In this song, the believer is so joyful that Jesus passed his way and rescued him from a death-like condition, that likens it to the dawning of a new day and its accompanying promise.

In addition to the four theological themes found in these lyrics, theodicy is another recurrent theme. Just as in black spirituals of the nineteenth century, black Urban/Contemporary Gospel lyricists of the late twentieth century see Satan, or the devil, as representing the "concrete presence of evil in human society."[82] Theomusicologist Jon Michael Spencer calls this belief the "work of the devil" theodicy. In explicit agreement with Spencer's findings for blues music,[83] religious urban/contemporary blacks also blame the devil for the moral and natural evil in the world.[84] In "Hide the Word," by Michael Brooks, the devil is described as a "temptor" who sends temptations in the path of believers.[85] As a result, this sometimes prevents believers from "hiding the Word" of God in their hearts. When Marvin Winans asks God "Are We Really Doing Your Will?" he reminds God that in everything he does for him, the devil intrudes.[86] In this song's lyrics, the devil is seen as a persistent challenge to the workers of Christ.

Compositions by both Winans brothers, Hammond, Brooks, and Jones and Stewart basically represent fundamental ways African Americans relate to God. Having this outlet in music provides African Americans with a mechanism for dealing with life in America. One composer who has been tremendously influential in many black gospel church choirs is John P. Kee. In fact, several of his choral compositions are used as standard songs in many black churches. Therefore, it is worthwhile to review Kee's life, music, and theologies to better understand his appeal to many black church choirs and how he addresses the psychological needs of many African Americans through his music.

JOHN P. KEE: A BRIEF BIOGRAPHICAL SKETCH

John P. Kee, born in Durham, North Carolina, was introduced to the Pre- and Classic Gospel styles while growing up in Baptist and Holiness churches in North Carolina. He was a child prodigy in voice and classical piano and enrolled in the North Carolina School of the Arts when he was eleven years old. He graduated from high school at age fourteen and was soon introduced to drugs at age fifteen while playing in secular bands.[87] After a short stay in Yuba City in northern California, by age nineteen, Kee was back in North Carolina. Kee's return to North Carolina would mark the beginning of a significant change in his life because up until this time, he was a user and dealer of cocaine. Kee's change came when he decided to make Jesus the Lord and Savior of his life after witnessing the murder of a friend who was also involved in drug dealing. Kee believes that it was the grace of God that allowed him to survive this drive-by shooting. In response to his friend's death, Kee decided to commit his life to Jesus and to compose and perform gospel music. Also, when Kee asked the Lord to "deliver" him from the "hold" of cocaine, he says a miracle was performed in his life, and he is no longer addicted to cocaine.

Composing and performing gospel was not difficult to do, for Kee had already been playing for Jim and Tammy Baker's PTL (Praise the Lord) Club even while he was a drug addict and dealer. After his conversion, Kee continued to work there for several years after the murder incident, rehearsing with various groups at the PTL Club and with small choirs in the community. He did not talk about how God delivered him from cocaine or how God spared his life until he received more opportunities to display his anointed musical talents.

Kee's first entrance into gospel music recording came in 1985 when James Cleveland, the "King of Gospel," gave him an opportunity to teach two songs at the Gospel Music Workshop of America. Also, in 1986 at the urging of gospel singer Daryl Coley, Kee submitted a song to Edwin Hawkins and unexpectedly recorded it at the Hawkins Music and Arts Seminar in Houston, because the intended lead singer backed out. In the meantime, Kee's own group, originally formed in 1981, grew from a combo to the New Life Community Choir, based in Charlotte. By 1987, Kee had begun discussions with Dr. Leonard Scott of Gospel Excellence Ministries and Tyscot Records to negotiate his first album with them, and not long after in that same year, he released his debut album entitled *Yes Lord*.

Around 1990, Kee was "called" to preach. Far from being a traditional minister, Kee can be appropriately described as a street corner preacher with a "congregation" of about 75 young people who were "on fire" for the Lord.[88] He has a special concern for young people because of his own experiences with cocaine. In addition, he recognizes that by going out to the young people on the streets and by creating music that is "in between," there is a chance of leading young people to God.[89]

KEE'S MUSIC

Indeed, it is Kee's "in between" music and traditional music that have attracted many black church choirs to his compositions. John P. Kee is unique in that his compositions successfully combine elements from black Pre-, Classic, Contemporary, and Urban/Contemporary Gospel. A sampling of Kee's music will alert any listener to the multiple influences on his music, both sacred and secular. Some of Kee's musical experiences included performing with jazz trumpeteer Donald Byrd, white pop singer James Taylor, the rhythm and blues/funk band Cameo, and in numerous studio recording sessions with various artists in southern California before returning to

North Carolina in 1981. In addition to his own secular performance experiences, Kee was influenced by his brother Al who was a guitarist with the jazz band Weather Report and music director of the Staple Singers.

Kee's principal contribution to black gospel and American music is as a composer, arranger, and choral director. In addition, Kee is a proficient singer, bass guitarist, and keyboardist, playing piano, organ, and synthesizer equally well. Kee is a producer for Zomba Records and is an astute businessman and community activist, having established a "Feed-the-Hungry" program for Charlotte's homeless persons, an "Adopt-A-Kid" program, and Basketball Camp for Kids. Another unique aspect of Kee's ministry is his relationship to the members of the New Life Community Choir. Through his New Life Ministries, the members of the choir are salaried employees. This arrangement allowed them as a group to take Kee's ministry outside of Charlotte when they took truckloads of food and supplies to families devastated by the Miami hurricane in 1993. These activities show that John P. Kee is not only a gospel performer but also a contemporary "race man" who not only wants to uplift African Americans spiritually but also physically by providing jobs, guidance, and food when needed. However, it is in Kee's music that his "calling" can be clearly seen and heard.

Kee's recording *Colorblind* illustrates his abundant Urban/Contemporary Gospel sound. In fact, Kee intentionally recorded a solo work that would include rap, jazz, funk, rhythm and blues, and soul in order to attract young people: The hope is that, first, they would be attracted to the music, then secondly to the message. After the message is heard and received, perhaps young people would decide to develop a personal relationship with God.

Even while it is evident that Kee's diverse use of musical styles is unlimited and quite contemporary, he also clearly exhibits control over the composing and performance of the earliest form of gospel, Pre-Gospel. Of the thirty-six songs examined, six are folk-based or contemporary arrangements of spirituals and gospel hymns, while two are gospel hymn versions of the same song in Contemporary Gospel style.[90] Five are sung with instrumental accompaniment and one is sung a cappella (or without accompaniment). These songs exhibit Kee's virtuosic skill for African American music making in general; a skill that was acquired from Kee's close relationship to the Black Church. In other words, Kee still interacts with the "folk" of the Black Church who created gospel music out of a need to cope with city life and out of a need to cope with being black in America. Because of his own experience with city life and drugs, and because of his personal knowledge of being a black man in America, Kee understands why black people created gospel music; because Kee's "folks" are connected culturally to Africa, he understands how to create acceptable black gospel music.

The unique characteristics of Kee's musical sound are evident in a com-position entitled "Let Us Not Be Weary" from his choral recording *Lily in the Valley*. As with most of Kee's recordings, "Let Us Not Be Weary" opens with the entire VIP (or Victory in Praise) choir (including the New Life Community Choir) singing the refrain. The refrain is made up of two parts, primary and secondary, and it is sung twice. After each of the two verses, which includes a male solo voice and male combo, the secondary refrain section is sung by the entire choir. While Kee is not the lead singer, it is clear that he is in charge, actively directing the choir by providing verbal prompts to cue sectional intros. It is also not unusual to hear Kee name the persons who are singing solos in the composition. If nothing else, this exemplifies the kind of community that is present within black gospel choirs.

Another unique facet of Kee's choral compositions is his creation of "vo-cal riffs" for each of the three sections (or vocal parts) of his choir—so-prano, alto, and tenor. Worked out into two phrases, four measures each, the sections are heard separately. Each section repeats its individual phrases twice, then the phrases are layered and sung together twice. The first line of each vocal part (or section) is different for each part, but the second line is common to all parts and is sung in unison (or all together). As each section sings its respective lines, Kee acts as the leader reciting the words then smoothly moving into scat singing.

After this variation on the opening refrain, Kee modulates one-half step into the vamp section of the composition. The vamp section is a common device of Classic Gospel, and it usually occurs near the close of a compo-sition. Within it, the VIP Choir sings a refrain consisting of a four-measure phrase followed by seven repetitions of it, over which Kee sings a free melodic line combined with parts of a sermonette intensifying the message of the refrain. With each repetition of the line "Ye Shall Receive Your Just Reward," there is a half-step modulation up to the conclusion. This com-position alone exhibits Kee's ease with combining jazz and rhythm and blues/funk elements into a Classic/Contemporary Gospel style of choral arranging.

KEE'S THEOLOGY

John P. Kee's relatively short life—he was born in 1962—is interesting to say the least. His sojourn—beginning in the church under the tutelage of his father, mother, and maternal grandmother, out into the world play-ing in secular bands, and then returning to the church composing and di-recting gospel choirs—can best be described as that of the biblical "Prodigal Son." If anyone can speak to the concerns and problems facing young people today, it appears no person is better equipped than Kee. Simply put, Kee has taken the commission and life of Jesus Christ seriously. In doing so, Kee is expressing a theology that is his own, developed from his personal experiences in life and his personal encounters with God.

Just as Classic Gospel composers wrote lyrics that portrayed "Jesus as Everything," so do the lyrics of Kee. I found that Kee's songs generally fall into two categories: those that focus on the "everythingness" of God and Jesus and those that focus on the struggle of human beings through the testimony narrative. Within this rubric of "Jesus as Everything," Kee's compositions can be divided into the following three areas: (1) Jesus as Friend and Protector, (2) Jesus as Liberator, and (3) Jesus as Reconciler. Within the paradigm of testimonies of human struggle, compositions can be described as focusing on perserverance, determination, and steadfastness.

"Jesus as Friend and Protector" has a long history within African American culture. Indeed, one of the unique elements of African American theology and religion is the down-to-earth conversational relationship African Americans have established with Jesus seen in the way he is spoken of and addressed. Yes, "Jesus is a friend indeed, In the time of need," but he is also recognized for his divine position as the Son of God. The essence of gospel is to spread the good news about Jesus to all people and that first requires a relationship that is almost as common as friendships between human beings.

Liberation is a central theme in African American culture in general. The residuals of oppression and discrimination have also caused this concept to be a significant discourse in African American cultural productions. The exception with Kee's music, as well as with most gospel music, is that liberation is requested for relief from sin, not relief from societal oppression. Therefore, Jesus is asked by John to "wash me" so that I can be made in "Your perfect way." He also speaks of being "transformed" and having a "New Life" because Jesus came and "made it right." In short, Kee was relieved of the oppression of sin.

References to "Jesus as Reconciler" are found in the title cut of Kee's *Colorblind* recording that explores racism. He wonders if we all became "colorblind, Would hatred remain," or instead "would we begin To heal the wounds inside," wounds resulting from "racism that has scarred our [lives]." Kee closes by celebrating the fact that even though people are not colorblind, on an individual basis they can humble themselves, pray to God, and be confident that God "shall heal the land."

The testimonies of human struggle accentuate the decisions made by African American gospel composers to follow Jesus, and they illustrate examples of personal counsel to listeners. These types of songs by Kee encourage followers of Christ to use the power God has given them to "wave their problems and sorrows away." These songs also instruct Christians to "walk by faith, not by sight" and to "not be weary in well doing" because in "due season [they] shall reap [their] reward" in heaven. Other songs describe satisfaction with God and aspirations to be "more like Jesus." Overall, these testimonies of human struggle are personalistic, individualistic, and highly introspective. Yet, at the same time, they are communal and collective in that they are attempting to express situations to which many African American listeners can relate.

CONCLUSION

Black Urban/Contemporary Gospel is a blend of sacred and secular musical traditions in America. It is a sacred music form that is significant for its documentation of the experiences of African Americans living in urban areas in the 1980s and 1990s. According to black gospel scholar Irene V. Jackson-Brown, gospel songs "deal with the immediate problems affecting Blacks and are specifically designed to help Black people to surmount the immediate circumstances in their lives."[91] The theologies of black Urban/Contemporary Gospel composers accomplish this psychological and cultural task for many African Americans. All in all, it is an unwavering faith and hope in God through music that has allowed African Americans (composers included) to deal with and surmount the circumstances of being black in American society. Also, it is the valuing of an African-derived aesthetic of rhythm, percussiveness, and call-and-response that has allowed these African Americans to be black in American society.

NOTES

1. Eileen Southern, *The Music of Black Americans: A History*, 2d ed. (New York: W. W. Norton, 1983), 444–45.

2. J. Jefferson Cleveland, "A Historical Account of the Hymn in the Black Worship Experience," in *Songs of Zion* (Nashville: Abingdon Press, 1981), #172.

3. Jon Michael Spencer, *Protest and Praise: Sacred Music of Black Religion* (Minneapolis: Fortress Press, 1990), 208.

4. Southern, *Music of Black Americans*, 450.

5. C. Eric Lincoln and Lawrence H. Mamiya, *The Black Church in the African American Experience* (Durham: Duke University Press, 1990), 360.

6. Spencer, *Protest and Praise*, 214.

7. Southern, *Music of Black Americans*, 453.

8. Lincoln and Mamiya, *The Black Church*, 361.

9. Bernice Johnson Reagon, ed., *"We'll Understand It Better By and By": Pioneering African American Gospel Composers* (Washington, D.C.: Smithsonian Institution Press, 1992), 14–17; 81–82.

10. Spencer, *Protest and Praise*, 214.

11. Lincoln and Mamiya, *The Black Church*, 361–62.

12. Southern, *Music of Black Americans*, 462.

13. Lincoln and Mamiya, *The Black Church*, 360–61.

14. Portia K. Maultsby, "The Impact of Gospel Music on the Secular Music Industry," in Bernice Johnson Reagon, ed., *"We'll Understand It Better By and*

By": *Pioneering African American Gospel Composers* (Washington, D.C.: Smithsonian Institution Press, 1992), 19.

15. Daniel Kingman, *American Music: A Panorama*, 2d ed. (New York: Schirmer Books, 1990), 265, 267.

16. Horace C. Boyer, "Take My Hand, Precious Lord, Lead Me On," in Bernice Johnson Reagon, ed., *"We'll Understand It Better By and By": Pioneering African American Gospel Composers* (Washington, D.C.: Smithsonian Institution Press, 1992), 142.

17. Bernice Johnson Reagon, "Kenneth Morris: 'I'll Be a Servant for the Lord,' " in Bernice Johnson Reagon, ed., *"We'll Understand It Better By and By": Pioneering African American Gospel Composers* (Washington, D.C.: Smithsonian Institution Press, 1992), 330–33, 336–37.

18. William Barlow, *"Looking Up at Down": The Emergence of Blues Culture* (Philadelphia: Temple University Press, 1989), 128–29.

19. Reagon, "Kenneth Morris," 332–33, 336–37.

20. Spencer, *Protest and Praise*, 217.

21. In fact, "Oh Happy Day" was such a success in America that in 1969, it was the only gospel single ever to reach *Billboard*'s Pop Top Ten. James Earl Hardy, "Has Gospel Lost Sight of God?" *Emerge* (October 1990): 83.

22. Maultsby, "The Impact of Gospel Music," 21.

23. Spencer, *Protest and Praise*, 217.

24. Horace C. Boyer, "A Comparative Analysis of Traditional and Contemporary Gospel Music," in Irene V. Jackson-Brown, ed., *More Than Dancing: Essays on Afro-American Music and Musicians* (Westport, Conn.: Greenwood Press, 1985), 138–39.

25. Lincoln and Mamiya, *The Black Church*, 377; and Boyer, "Take My Hand," 132.

26. Chris Willman, "Rap Gets Religion," *Los Angeles Times Calendar* (May 11, 1990): 6.

27. "Rapper Mike-E. Wants the Church 2-No: G-Rap is 4 Good," *American Gospel* (September/October 1991): 29.

28. Interview with Michael Alan Brooks, 25 June 1991.

29. "Fred Hammond Goes Solo: But He's Still Commissioned," *American Gospel* (September/October 1991): 20.

30. Tim A. Smith, "The Winans Take It to the Limit," *Contemporary Christian Music* (September 1993): 20.

31. Southern, *Music of Black Americans*, 466.

32. Interview with Brooks.

33. Lincoln and Mamiya, *The Black Church*, 362.

34. James Earl Hardy, "Fascinating Rhythms: Has Gospel Lost Sight of God?" *Emerge* (October 1990): 83.

35. B. J. Widick, *Detroit: City of Race and Class Violence*, rev. ed. (Detroit: Wayne State University Press, 1989), 26–27.

36. Lincoln and Mamiya, *The Black Church*, 363–64.

37. Ortiz M. Walton, *Music: Black, White and Blue* (New York: Wm. Morrow, 1972), 2–3.

38. See "Fred Hammond Goes Solo: But He's Still Commissioned," *American*

Gospel (September/October 1991): 20; and "Rapper Mike-E. Wants the Church 2-No: G-Rap is 4 Good," *American Gospel* (September/October 1991): 29.

39. Refer to Tricia Rose's chapter 3 entitled "Soul Sonic Forces: Technology, Orality, and Black Cultural Practice in Rap Music" in *Black Noise: Rap Music and Black Culture in Contemporary America* (Hanover, N.H.: Wesleyan/University Press of New England, 1994) for an excellent discussion of this issue in rap music production.

40. See "Rapper Mike-E. Wants the Church 2-No: G-Rap is 4 Good," *American Gospel* (September/October 1991): 29; and "Bridging the Gap: Contemporary Christian Music," *Score Magazine* (September/October 1993): 18.

41. Joy Duckett Cain, "The Gospel According to BeBe and CeCe," *Essence* (December 1992): 82.

42. See "Bridging the Gap: Contemporary Christian Music," *Score Magazine* (September/October 1993): 18; "Fred Hammond Goes Solo: But He's Still Commissioned," *American Gospel* (September/October 1991): 20; and "Rapper Mike-E. Wants the Church 2-No: G-Rap is 4 Good," *American Gospel* (September/October 1991): 29.

43. Lincoln and Mamiya, *The Black Church*, 362–63.

44. Southern, *Music of Black Americans*, 456, 472.

45. Lincoln and Mamiya, *The Black Church*, 377.

46. Willman, "Rap Gets Religion," 6, 76.

47. James T. Jones IV, "Gospel Meets Rap to Make a Joyful Modern Noise," *USA Today*, (August 7, 1990): 4D.

48. Ibid.

49. Commissioned, *Matters of the Heart* (Benson/A&M, 84418-2868-2, 1994).

50. P. J., "About People: The Winans," *Essence* (February 1988): 32.

51. Patrick MacDonald, "The Winans' Spirited Act: Pop Goes the Gospel," *Seattle (Washington) Times* (20 November 1987).

52. Southern, *Music of Black Americans*, 456, 472.

53. BeBe and CeCe Winans, *Heaven* (Sparrow/Capitol, CDP-590959, 1988).

54. Ibid. Whitney Houston on "Hold Up the Light."

55. (MC) Hammer on "The Blood" and Luther Vandross on "Searching for Love" in BeBe and CeCe Winans, *Different Lifestyles* (Sparrow/Capitol, CDP-592078, 1991).

56. Allison Samuels, "BeBe and CeCe Winans: Different Lifestyles," *Upscale* (November 1993): 31–32.

57. Ibid.

58. A simplified definition of the term "overdubbing" is adding musical material in later recording sessions.

59. E. Ann Kaplan, "Feminist Criticism and Television," in Robert C. Allen, ed., *Channels of Discourse* (Chapel Hill: University of North Carolina Press, 1987), 233, 246.

60. The term *counterpoint* used here is when the solo singer and vocal unit or units sing contrasting material simultaneously. Daniel Kingman, *American Music: A Panorama*, 2d ed. (New York: Schirmer Books, 1990), 221.

61. Hardy, "Fascinating Rhythms," 81.

62. Ibid.

63. See also Take 6's cover of Hall and Oates' "Biggest Part of Me" on *Join the Band*.

64. Jones, 4D. *Emphasis mine.*

65. Mellonee V. Burnim, "The Black Gospel Music Tradition: A Complex of Ideology, Aesthetic, and Behavior," in Irene V. Jackson-Brown, ed., *More Than Dancing: Essays on Afro-American Music and Musicians* (Westport, Conn.: Greenwood Press, 1985), 158.

66. See Chapters 2 and 3 in Angela Marie Spence Nelson, "A Theomusicological Approach to Rap: A Model for the Study of African American Popular and Folk Musics" (Ph.D. diss., Bowling Green State University, 1992).

67. Winans, "Love Has No Color," *Decisions* (Qwest, 9–25510–1, 1987).

68. Jones, "Gospel Meets Rap," 4D.

69. Spencer, *Protest and Praise*, 207.

70. Sister Souljah, "Survival Handbook vs. Global Extinction," *360 Degrees of Power* (Epic, ET48713, 1992).

71. Winans, "Love Has No Color," *Decisions* (Qwest, 9–25510–1, 1987); and James T. Jones, IV, "Gospel Meets Rap to Make a Joyful Modern Noise," *USA Today* (7 August 1990): 4D.

72. Jon Michael Spencer, *Blues and Evil* (Knoxville: The University of Tennessee Press, 1993), 68; and John Hicks, *Evil and the God of Love* (San Francisco: Harper and Row, 1978), 6.

73. LeRoi Jones (Amiri Baraka), *Black Music* (New York: Morrow Quill, 1966), 183.

74. James H. Cone, "Sanctification, Liberation and Black Worship," *Journal of Religious Thought* 10–11.

75. Boogie Down Productions, "Who Protects Us From You," *Ghetto Music: The Blueprint of Hip Hop* (Jive, 1187-4-J, 1989).

76. Commissioned, "Heart of Mine," *Ordinary Just Won't Do* (Light, 7-115-73026-1, 1989).

77. Winans, "Goodness, Mercy and Grace," *Introducing the Winans* (Elektra/Light, E1-60089, 1981).

78. Commissioned, "Hold Me," *Number 7* (Benson/A&M, 75021-8527-4, 1991).

79. Ibid. "Go Tell Somebody," *Go Tell Somebody* (Elektra/Light, SPCN-7-115-71148-8, 1986).

80. BeBe and CeCe Winans, "Meantime," *Heaven* (Sparrow/Capitol, CDP-590959, 1988).

81. Winans, "Breaking of Day," *Decisions* (Qwest, 9-25510-1, 1987).

82. James H. Cone, *The Spirituals and the Blues: An Interpretation* (San Francisco: Harper and Row, 1972), 62–63.

83. Jon Michael Spencer, "God in Secular Music Culture: The Theodicy of the Blues as the Paradigm of Proof," *Black Sacred Music* 3.2 (Fall 1989): 17–18; and *Blues and Evil*, 69.

84. "Moral evil is evil that we human beings originate: cruel, unjust, vicious, perverse thoughts and deeds. Natural evil is the evil that originates independently of human actions: in disease bacilli, earthquakes, storms, droughts, tornadoes, etc." Hick, *Evil*, 12.

85. Commissioned, "Hide the Word," *Go Tell Somebody* (Elektra/Light, SPCN-7-115-71148-8, 1986).

86. Winans, "Are We Really Doing Your Will?" *Introducing the Winans* (Elektra/Light, E1–60089, 1981).

87. Teresa Hairston, "America's Love Affair with the 'Prince of Gospel': John P. Kee," *Score* (July/August 1993): 39.

88. Hilary Clay Hicks, "John P. Kee: On the Battlefield for the Lord," *American Gospel* (July/August 1991): 36.

89. Ibid.

90. See from *Lily in the Valley*, "I Love Jesus," "Lily in the Valley," from *Wash Me*, "Standing in the Need," "Sinner Man," "I Must Tell Jesus," and from *Colorblind*, "Alright."

91. Cited in Jon Michael Spencer, *Protest and Praise*, 199.

SELECT DISCOGRAPHY

Armstrong, Vanessa Bell. *Something on the Inside*. Jive/Zomba, J2–1468, 1993.

Commissioned. *I'm Going On*. Elektra/Light, LS-5861, 1985.

———. *Go Tell Somebody*. Elektra/Light, SPCN-7-115-71148-8, 1986.

———. *On the Winning Side*. Elektra/Light, 7-115-73005-9, 1987.

———. *Will You Be Ready?* Light, 7-115-73019-9, 1988.

———. *Ordinary Just Won't Do*. Light, 7-115-73026-1, 1989.

———. *State of Mind*. Benson, CO2653, 1990.

———. *Number 7*. Benson/A&M, 75021-8527-4, 1991.

———. *Matters of the Heart*. Benson/A&M, 84418-2868-2, 1994.

Hammond, Fred. *I Am Persuaded*. Benson, CD02727, 1991.

Kee, John P. *Yes, Lord*. Verity, J2-3000, 1987.

———. *Just Me This Time*. Verity, J2-3002, 1990.

———. *Colorblind*. Verity, JS-3009, 1994.

Kee, John P. and Friends. *There Is Hope*. Verity, J2-3001, 1990.

Kee, John P. and the New Life Community Choir. *We Walk By Faith*. Tyscot, 7901403144, 1992.

Kee, John P., Presents the VIP Music and Arts Seminar Mass Choir. *Lily in the Valley*. Star Song, SSD-8800, 1993.

New Life Community Choir featuring John P. Kee. *Wait On Him*. Verity, J2-3003, 1989.

———. *Wash Me*. Star Song, SSD-8295, 1990.

———. *Show Up!* Star Song, SSD-0034, 1994.

Take 6. *Join The Band*. Reprise, 9-45497-2, 1994.

Winans, Angie and Debbie. *Angie and Debbie*. Capitol, CDP595582, 1993.

Winans, BeBe and CeCe. *BeBe and CeCe Winans*. Sparrow/Capitol, CDP-546883, 1987.

———. *Heaven*. Sparrow/Capitol, CDP-590959, 1988.

———. *Different Lifestyles*. Sparrow/Capitol, CDP-592078, 1991.

———. *Relationships*. Sparrow/Capitol, 1994.

Winans, The. *Introducing the Winans*. Elektra/Light, E1-60089, 1981.

———. *Long Time Comin'*. Light, LS-5826, 1983.

———. *Tomorrow*. Light, LS-5853, 1984.

———. *Let My People Go*. Qwest, 9–25344–1, 1985.

———. *Decisions*. Qwest, 9–25510–1, 1987.

———. *Return*. Qwest, 9–26161–4, 1990.

———. *All Out*. Qwest, 9–45213–4, 1993.

5

Jazz and the Resilience of African Americans

Ferdinand Jones

The star trumpeter, Freddie Hubbard, spotted Betty Carter, the revered jazz singer, in the audience at New York's Blue Note jazz club and invited her to sit in with his group. On the stage then were six world-class jazz artists, each one a virtuoso. Carter consulted briefly with the musicians about what song she wanted to sing and in what key and tempo. In less than a minute Carter was delighting the audience with her adventurous musical exploration of the familiar song "Over the Rainbow." Inspired, her fellow musicians created new sound configurations in their solos, complements to Carter's singing and one another's playing. The looks on their faces and their body movements conveyed complete expressive fulfillment. All were soaring in artistic release, each one in turn claiming his possession of the song, while collectively transforming it into yet another musical idea. The audience smiling, sighing, rocking in its seats, was on its feet at the number's conclusion. The musicians, their eyes sparkling satisfaction, embraced Carter and signaled congratulations to one another.

North American jazz is an especially fruitful source of knowledge of African American psychology. It has the characteristic of connecting onto its musical frame, without altering it, all aspects of other African American music, as well as virtually any other music genre. In this respect, jazz is the epitome of the African American cultural identity and an on going summary of its development. Moreover, jazz illustrates subjective processes that have been crucial to the psychological survival of black Americans.

Among the properties of jazz that demonstrate these dynamics are its refined use of improvisation, the provocative interplay among its performers, and the interaction of the musicians with their audiences.

The intention here is to analyze these characteristics of jazz, focusing primarily on improvisation, for how they can instruct us about the processes by which African Americans have handled the mental stabilization tasks of being in various conditions of oppression while needing to establish and sustain competent views of themselves.

The analysis will begin with a brief overview of elements in African American culture that highlight African American coping psychology and that are paralleled in the evolution of jazz. These are the African oral and folk traditions that make up the blues and that, together with the blues, became major aspects of jazz's roots.

Crucial resistive and self-enhancing psychological mechanisms are contained in these expressive folk media. Their sustaining utility induced the synthesis of black folk music with other music genres to form jazz. Resistance to psychological destruction is therefore an intricate part of jazz's formation. The benefits of that resistance—self-efficacy and self-esteem— are fundamental resilience aspects of African American culture, and they are amply represented in jazz performance and in its consumption.

THE AFRICAN AMERICAN ORAL TRADITION

Africans gradually developed a culture in North America that counteracted their demeaned status in a society defined and dominated by whites. African American culture syncretized the memories of home in West Africa with the experience in slavery and the encounter with the Euro-American culture into which the Africans were forced. The character of African American culture existent today naturally represents all aspects of this synthesis.

North American jazz music represents a seminal feature of African heritage, the oral tradition. Rooted in the African homeland, the oral tradition was adapted to fit the North American context. Its intangibility undoubtedly allowed it to survive the destruction of slavery while most material African cultural elements could not.[1]

The oral tradition is a central vehicle of African philosophy, communication, ritual, organization, spiritual life, record keeping, and recreation, and it performed similar functions in the Africans' new world. That tradition includes animal fables, ghost tales, slave narratives, proverbs, toasts, and sermons, as well as music making. The relationship of North American jazz to oral expression in African American culture is linear. A major part of jazz's origins stem from the blues. The blues were a merger in form and sentiment of the secular and religious music of the slaves: the work songs, spirituals, lullabies, and shouts and hollers. These, in turn, were musical manifestations of the spoken-word tradition.

The Signifyin' Monkey, a traditional folk rhyme or toast, is a vivid illustration of the verbal counterpart to black music. A brief examination of
it will demonstrate the psychological dexterity of African Americans that
underlies all their expressive media including jazz. There are, of course,
many versions of this toast; an adaptation composed for this discussion
begins with the monkey instigating conflict between two of the most powerful figures in the jungle, the lion and the elephant.

> The Signifyin' Monkey said to the Lion one day,
> There's a big ole Elephant messin' with your family in a scandolous
>   way.
> Talkin' about your mama and your niece,
> Say he even ask your grandma for a piece.
> The Lion got so mad he knocked down trees,
> Brought a herd of giraffes to they knees.
> He found Mr. Elephant layin' under a tree,
> Said get your rusty butt up 'cause it's gonna be you or me.

He is successful in manipulating these animal symbols of domination to
fight one another but, the monkey gets into trouble in the process.

> Monkey laughin' and jumpin' all around,
> But his foot slipped from a limb and he fell to the ground.

The drama ends with the monkey tricking his way out of his near-fatal
predicament. He must settle for being segregated from the powerful once
again, where he presumably will use his intellectual and verbal skills to
achieve further psychological victories.

> Lion fixed to kill him.
> Monkey said, "Hold it, brother, let's fight fair."
> You stand here and I stand over there.
> Lion backed up prepared to fight.
> Monkey swung up plumb out of sight.
> Lion shook his head, said if you and your children want to remain
>   alive,
> Up in them trees is where you better stay with all your jive.
> And that's where they are to this very day,
> Lyin' and signifyin'
> And damn near always gettin' away.

Signifying means indirect talk rather than frontal pronouncement; it emphasizes verbal facility and innuendo. The monkey is a symbolic figure of
the African American survival mentality. He embodies the refined use of

wit, words, and wiles employed by African Americans when direct protest or aggression could be fatal.

The monkey is a trickster. He knows that jungle animals who possess more physical strength than he are generally ignorant of his superior intellectual resources. He is therefore able to verbally manipulate (signify) powerful animals like lions and elephants into self-destructive positions.

The literary scholar Henry Louis Gates, Jr., advances a theory of such African American oral subversion in his book *The Signifying Monkey: A Theory of African-American Literary Criticism*.[2] Included in his analysis is a discussion of the invention and variation that characterizes African Americans' adaptation of standard English language in folklore and music and that is epitomized in jazz.

There are so many examples of signifying in jazz that one could write a formal history of its development on this basis alone.[3]

Black instrumentalists and jazz singers through the ages, like African American storytellers, exercise resistance and self-definition. The blues, for instance, are stories of everyday African American life. As discussed above, jazz retains many blues elements including the life commentary function.[4]

Jazz rhythms, another defining characteristic of the music, also relate back through the blues and African American folk music to link with African drumming. Africans employed percussion instruments extensively and with sophistication in daily life. They used them to accompany rituals, as instruments of communication, and as a primary expressive medium. The use of rhythm in work, religion, and play (if not immediately with actual drums, since they were banned during slavery) was carried to North America and adapted to the conditions of the bondsmen and women.

These distinctive expressive features, cultivated over three centuries, make evident a crucial African American resistive posture. It is the readiness to perceive and operate on the basis of one's own interpretation of reality. It is vividly illustrated in language inventiveness, and it was extended and elaborated in African American music forms such as work, worship, and play songs. A direct connection is therefore apparent between traditional African American oral expression and jazz. Jazz's place at the core of African American cultural content, texture, and psychology is consequently indisputable.

THE BLUES

So much of jazz's disposition is founded in the blues that it is useful to look a bit more closely at them for further insights into jazz's foundations and cultural meaning. (Peter R. Aschoff, in this volume, discusses extensively what can only be touched on here.)

The ironies in blues have a resistive intent, for instance. The blues singer laments a loss or comments on an event or a social circumstance employing lyrics that accentuate personal autonomy and philosophical mastery over what might otherwise be total tragedy.

> Hard times and trouble took the red from my heart,
> turned it blue.
> Hard times and trouble took the red from my heart,
> turned it blue.
> But every sunny day's gonna' be mine again too!

The singer may be vulnerable to a cheating lover, but he sings about action he can take to hold on to his integrity.

> I'm movin' you to the outskirts of town,
> Pretty Mama.
> I'm movin' you to the outskirts of town.
> Don't want to have to worry 'bout you foolin' around.

The blues articulate and normalize the universal black American experience. By their continuous appeal in African American history, they signal their pivotal value. Paul Oliver writes of this dimension of the blues in his study *Blues Fell This Morning*.

In the sharply defined images of life that the blues reflects are mirrored the minutiae of experience of the ordinary black person. The words that the singer uttered, the thoughts, the passions, and reactions to which he gave voice were those that were shared by countless thousands of others. An unemployed laborer found comfort in the blues of a man who had suffered the despair of the penniless, the "cold-in-hand"; the forsaken lover shared the bitterness of one who has been "mistreated" and the would-be philanderer swaggered along the sidewalk with the bragging blues of the "high-brown sheik." When the blues singer told of his escape from disaster, when he addressed the absent woman that he loved, when he sang of the train that would take him to a "better land," he sang to himself, but he was aware that others whom he did not know would sing the blues in like circumstances.[5]

While occurring in many other cultures, communication devices in folk music, such as employing double meanings, turning the tables, indirect assertion, metaphorical reference—often occurring spontaneously—underscore blues origins in African American folklore and therefore identify them as typical of African American oral expressiveness. The blues are a vehicle for affirming and demonstrating self-efficacy, as asserted above. The psychological significance of these resistive modes cannot be overemphasized, since so much of the historical African American condition contains elements that threatened positive self-identities.

Jazz players are educated in the blues tradition. They are urged to tell their own "story" playing in the blues idiom itself or referring to the blues sensibility in the jazz repertory. There is more to jazz music than blues, since jazz is a complex art form employing diverse structures and musical possibilities. But its sharing of the same cultural tradition as the blues is a fundamental identifying characteristic.

JAZZ IMPROVISATION AND THE AFRICAN AMERICAN CHALLENGE ATTITUDE

Improvisation in jazz is a combination of variation and invention. The jazz solo is a unique one-time composition that has a structure made of the musical properties of a preexisting composition. The musician develops his or her musical ideas onto this frame. In many instances, the musicians will remember how they previously treated this or similar pieces and also what they may have liked in other players' renditions. The musician's mood, technical facility, and the performance setting will also influence the approach. And hearing the treatment given the piece by the other band members will additionally determine the individual's contribution to the ensemble's ultimate goal: a collectively rendered fresh composition.

The mental set of the individual musician guides him or her in soloing and also as a participant in the group enterprise. This disposition directs the musician to approach his or her contribution to a given musical piece with the expectation that the whole is to be an interpretation. Its playing is to be an "on the spot" recomposition, a spontaneous invention or variation. The agreed on music to be "played with" may be a popular song or it may be an original composition in song or suite form. Both conditions, each for its own reasons, are meant to simulate the creativity of the musicians who will perform the piece.

Today, young musicians learning to play jazz will have formally studied its language, including improvising, much like having studied a foreign language. For example, they will have learned to apply customary jazz treatments to the harmony, melody, texture, and rhythm of a piece to express their own ideas and feelings. They will also have been taught the traditions and the sensibility associated with jazz playing and performance. Along with learning the language of jazz, they will strive for technical proficiency in playing their instruments.

In the earlier days of jazz's history, these lessons would have been taught and practiced in an informal apprentice and mentoring system and by intensive study of famous recorded solos.

Mentoring and learning from recorded solos is still considered important to jazz education today, because so much of what jazz playing is about is understanding the intangibles of the jazz approach to music and the subtleties of how to develop one's personalized style. As in any craft, learning one's own way can often start with mastering that of an admired senior artist.

The parallel of jazz improvisation to the everyday mental processes of African American individuals is the stance that given reality is not a constant but is to be interpreted. This kind of "playing" is guided by an attitude of resistance to set ways of perceiving, thinking, and behaving. The mental improvisational mode evolved over the time of the African presence in North America. It is a psychological posture that will be referred to here as the *challenge attitude*.

The challenge attitude in African American culture is expecting that there is another, perhaps opposite, meaning to what white authority presents as truth, especially as it pertains to the challenger's self-identity. It prepares black Americans to screen stimuli for their potential threat. The individual interprets others' words, norms, and givens from a skeptical position. The others' "truth" can therefore be either redefined or accepted unaltered. The action of interpretation is the key element in the interchange. It affirms the interpreter's subjective autonomy and therefore spares the individual from psychological dominance even when he or she cannot control the physical circumstance.

The challenge attitude is also called "realistic skepticism" by many observers and "down to earth realism" by others. The psychologist Adelbert H. Jenkins presents a well-developed theory of a related phenomenon that he calls *dialectic*.[6] Gates uses the term *counternarrative* in referring to the same interpretive attitude in African American culture.[7] Extreme dimensions of this posture have been labeled in various places as pathological and sometimes mislabeled as "black paranoia."[8]

This challenge attitude was a part of African American culture from its beginning. It was the means for retaining humanity within the inhumane system of slavery. Ever since then, African Americans have employed the well-tested challenge stance to hold on to their own sense of how things are. Its sustaining uses ranged from surreptitiously keeping one's name while being given another one by the slaveholder in the early phases of American slavery to the more intricate mental gyrations in later times that enabled the black person to dismiss a white person's assignations when they were interpreted to be threatening.

The challenge attitude is taught directly and indirectly in African American communities. It is a major contributor to the mental health of its members. It has enabled them to develop competence and high self-esteem in the midst of a dominant society that constantly denied and therefore always threatened to undermine this potential.

For example, the slaveholder might have believed his slaves were inherently lazy and therefore needed to be goaded or forced to work. To the slave, the reasons for not being an enthusiastic worker had nothing to do with his or her inherent dispositions. He or she ignored the attribution of laziness, recognizing that this view was opposite to his or her own. After emancipation, white landowners might have expressed their belief to black sharecroppers that they were not smart enough to exist independent from their exploitative systems. For black sharecroppers, the holding of their own beliefs that it was power and dishonesty that locked them into those situations was the action of the challenging and self-affirming interpretation. The general white populace believes African-descendent people are intellectually inferior to whites. They therefore have often not supported the construction of equal educational systems for black children. African American teachers, parents, and pupils, socialized to challenge white assumptions about them, have relied on the ample proof of their equal potential from witnessing what many of them achieved despite their disadvantaged position in the society.

The African American individual is routinely prepared to fashion an alternative interpretation of the reality he or she is presented by the dominant society. This interpretive process is like jazz improvisation in that it requires the *action* or *agency* of the interpreter. It highlights the resilience of the interpretive mind-set, and it relies on the healthy confidence that the outcome of the process will be a personally satisfying or even beautiful rendition of African American style expression.

The challenge posture parallels jazz in yet another way. Both use language to assert the agency of the individual African American. Jazz is transposed language in an African American arts medium. Jazz, among other black American music forms, gives a voice to people who historically have been denied the freedom to be openly assertive. By its refined use of communications inventiveness and its construction of safe expressive settings, it embodies the psychological utility of the African American oral tradition discussed earlier. As LeRoi Jones, in a passage from his classic study *Blues People*,[9] instructs:

And just as the lyrics of the African songs were usually as important or *more* important than the music, the lyrics of the work songs and the later blues were equally important to the Negro's concept of music. In fact the "shouts" and "field hollars" were little more than highly rhythmical lyrics. Even the purely instrumental music of the American Negro contains the constant reference to vocal music. Blues playing is the closest imitation of the human voice of any music I've heard; the vocal effects that jazz musicians have delighted in from Bunk Johnson to Ornette Coleman are evidence of this.

Psychologists have recently begun to recognize both the significance and the effectiveness of an oppressed peoples' ability to fashion distinctive, self-assertive language forms. They describe the process of reshaping words and their definitions, as well as other oral communications media, to serve self-esteem purposes. Their theories resonate with the observations of African American oral innovation carried over into jazz that is offered in this chapter.

Edward E. Sampson[10] for instance, is impressed with the political implications of having and not having a voice in majority-minority relationships. In his description of "a discursive framework" of psychological analysis, he asserts a position that lends support to the thesis that jazz is an expression of significant psychological survival mechanisms among African Americans.

At this point, it should be clear why identity movements are seeking a *voice* for themselves in their own terms and why they challenge the uncritical understandings developed by traditional psychological and social science. Without their own voice, whenever they speak, they would do so in a manner that keeps their positioned disadvantage vis-à-vis the dominant groups who have constructed them for this purpose. The form of domination that these identity movements challenge, then, is built into *the very order of things* . . . As long as members of such groups use the voice of those who have constructed them, they will continue to be complicit in their own domination. Only by finding, declaring, and effectively using their own voice can they hope to break from the trap.

Another social scientist, Shulamit Reinharz, also writes about the power of naming one's own experience, especially for otherwise disenfranchised groups: "Voice, in particular, has become a kind of megametaphor representing presence, power, participation, protest, and identity. Other metaphors for power have been based on images of vision and writing, but I believe that these are less potent than the metaphor of voice."[11]

Linda Goss and Marian E. Barnes's *Talk That Talk: An Anthology of African-American Storytelling*[12] is an example of these affirmations. In introducing their book they state that

Since the beginning of time folks have always wanted to spread the word. The ones who can spread the word most effectively have the ability to "talk dat talk" and "walk dat walk." In other words they grab the imagination of the listener and hold on to it for as long as they like, conjuring up images of the good and the bad, the weak and the strong, and the trickster and the fool. They have the ability to make you laugh until you cry, cry until you laugh, stand up and shout, or stare in amazement at their gestures and characterizations.

In the African-American culture, past and present, these folks have gone by many names. Today they are called preachers, healers, teachers, comedians, blues singers, poets, dancers, rappers, liars, painters, and historians. In a performance, all storytellers will use whatever it takes to get the story across. To hear them is to hear the drum, the heartbeat of Africa. To see them tell the story is to experience highlights of African ritual, at its best, a total theatrical performance.

In so many words then, jazz *playing is saying*. The music is but one of the several media of African American voice that preserves and transmits cultural values and teaches psychological resilience.

The process of interpretation for the African American individual ideally begins with the expectation that certain, if not all, words have ironic meaning and therefore need not be taken at face value. The activity of discovering or inventing the other meanings affirms the interpreting individual as a purposeful actor—one who is psychologically free and competent. Like the jazz soloist, the everyday black interpreter of perceptual phenomena has been socialized to be assured that his or her creation of "the story" is potentially compelling. There is the conviction on the interpreter's part that "truth" is a construction. Sometimes the jazz musician plays the tune as it is written; but the individualized touch will nevertheless be apparent through all of the subtle ways he or she decides to render it. The African American individual in everyday life need not always radically reconstruct incoming stimuli. What is most crucial is maintaining the attitude that radical interpretation is an available option.

The jazz performance is similar to and also different from what takes place under "ordinary" circumstances. The difference is readily comprehensible in considering the singular experience of the jazz player. Songs, or musical compositions roughly defined, are any musician's facts, data, or words. They are configured in notes and other features of musical communication. Unlike facts, however, they are generally not meant to be considered in a static way, not even by their composers. The jazz musician is the consummate song innovator. He or she recomposes songs as a matter of course.

However, to grasp the similarity of this routine to the mental processing of the historical nonmusic playing African American, one needs to think about it somewhat less concretely. Under many developmental circumstances, the average African American learns that general reality may or may not have any more fixed quality to it than the jazz player's song. They are taught to look for its multiple meanings and thereby to exercise their capacity to redefine their condition. In the process, the psychologically vital function of self-affirmation is served. Its satisfaction stimulates its repetition. Repetition prompts its refinement, and further satisfaction and reinforcement are produced.

Another dimension of this self-defining mechanism explains the need African Americans often have had to communicate with one another in code. This was an obvious necessity during slavery when personal survival was attached to the practice of forbidden African customs. For example, non-Christian religious observance relied on secret communication. Arthur C. Jones describes such subversive activity in his analysis of the spirituals in his book *Wade in the Water: The Wisdom of the Spirituals*[13] and in his chapter in this volume. The use of verbal inflection, differential word emphasis, oblique references, metaphor, and allegory to encode the speaker's intent is very much the way African Americans have effectively adapted language to their purposes over time. The consequence is that they love to play with language, and they find deep gratification in verbal invention.[14]

The African-American world view therefore includes both the preparedness to screen incoming stimuli and to guard outgoing communication when dealing with white authorities. The origins of this stance are readily understandable. Blacks have had continuous reasons to doubt that whites have their best interests at heart. Through institutionalized and personal practices, Europeans and their descendants in America have accentuated their difference from and superiority to people of color. Africans, in particular, typify that difference. Whites, possessing the power in American society, named the tune to be played, so to speak. Blacks had to invent self-protective communication and interpretive strategies; a process of improvising on that tune thereby evolved. These strategies are in the foundation of African American culture.

The historian Rhett S. Jones[15] writes that structural isolation was the impetus for the development of African American culture. Slaves largely lived apart from whites and interacted with them only under cautious circumstances. And they were denied entry into whites' socialization environments. These conditions impelled an already existing momentum to forge metaphysical principles and behavioral standards of their own. African American culture therefore consists of a unique combination of elements remembered, borrowed, and conceived. Jones argues that this construction became comprehensive and efficient because the rigid racial separation in North America required it to be so. The system of legal racial segregation that succeeded slavery perpetuated the same necessity. And since the enactment of the Voting Rights Act in 1965, which removed the last legal barrier to equality for black Americans, the society seems to be moving toward a new, more elastic configuration of race relations, however problematic that process appears to be at the time of this writing.

A part of psychology's past "documentation" of African Americans' unequal human status has been based in the theory that slavery and its aftermath destroyed blacks' beliefs in themselves, and not having positive self-esteem prevented the full development of their sense of general competence.[16] This theory, along with others and attendant studies that persist to this day,[17] has been deconstructed in the last three decades.[18] Jenkins revisits the negative professional literature on the subject of the nature and origins of black Americans' self-esteem He states: "This revised view of the Black family states that the Black family has long had a structure that would enable it to nurture the personal aspects of self-esteem and self-concept. What Black families seem to have done historically is engender a sense of personal worth in their children by separating the personal sense of themselves from the negative perceptions a racist society has attached to racial group membership."[19]

Jenkins and other present-day theorists of African American psychology help us to appreciate and understand the complexities of African Americans' self-esteem development. Starting with elaborating the obvious: The majority of African Americans acquire and maintain positive perceptions of themselves, they note that all individuals develop their knowledge and evaluation of who they are from the influences of their families and then from concentrically broader social circles. Families and immediate communities usually provide developing individuals with the basis for their positive value. As African American children come under the influence of the larger American society, they are increasingly exposed to manifestations of the white supremacy myth. This threatens to undermine the positive sense of themselves that they attained at home. Therefore, the lessons built into African American folklore, language, religion, and music aid the developing black individual in negotiating these contrasting influences. The challenge attitude guides individuals to disbelieve the destructive white supremacy assumption and to hold on to the positive attributions received from those who are most important in their lives. The challenge instructions are no less than life-preserving in their psychological necessity.

Considering musical improvisation again, while it can be found in all sorts of music, it is essential to the definition of jazz, attesting to its importance in the culture from which it has evolved. Jazz improvisation encourages the individual artist's assertiveness and hones the performance groups' intercommunication in the process of reaching a common goal. Being able to assert one's competent wholeness as a human being and to emphasize community ties and interdependent modes of thought and action have been tenacious psychological stances for African Americans.

African American psychological adaptability is dramatic and unique in its forms and in its cultural consequences—but not in its humanity. Evidence of the adaptive capacities of all people can be seen in this persistently disparaged human group. African Americans have demonstrated a most effective example of how a people can resist the worst psychological destruction and even create beauty out of their adversity. The African American story is an ironic, ongoing demonstration of the humanity of all people.

THE INTERPLAY AMONG JAZZ PERFORMERS

Jazz musicians are generally engaged in a collaborative enterprise. This is not a rule, nor is solo jazz playing a rare occurrence. By one of its signature definitions, jazz seeks innovation, and this has led some individual jazz artists to explore musical expression without accompaniment, sometimes with stellar results. But in the usual jazz performance, the musicians produce a group composition while simultaneously making personal statements. Playing this music well requires maximum skill and preparation and optimal communication among the players. The jazz performance in these respects reflects many of the sustaining features of traditional African American communities, as discussed earlier.

In the early days of New Orleans jazz, musicians performed what is known as collective improvisation. Each player simultaneously improvised on a tune with the aim of creating one spontaneously unified recomposition. This was group composing in its most vivid sense. Pure collective improvisation is now almost absent from jazz except in a few New Orleans ensembles. Many brass bands in New Orleans today play the closest thing to the old style (see Michael G. White's chapter in this volume). Without diverging into too much jazz history, it is interesting to note that the change came about after the entrance into jazz of the spectacular soloing talent of Louis Armstrong. Ever since Armstrong, the jazz solo has become a prominent feature of jazz music making.

The psychologist Wade Nobles theorizes that West African worldviews undergird African American psychology. He asserts that a collectivistic (tribal) outlook more accurately defines the core of African American self-concepts than the individualistic perspective that characterizes the broader North American society.[20] According to this thesis, the African American individual must regularly negotiate between these different existential realities.

The fact that the modern day African American person develops in two cultures and is therefore instilled with both collectivistic and individualistic sources of identity is not as daunting a condition to manage as it may seem. Everyone's self-concept is composed of many parts, some of which may be conflicting, and all are in constant refinement and development. For African Americans, the developmental task includes locating the means for experiencing an aspect of themselves that is in interdependent relation with other aspects. This is a need that is deeply embedded in African American culture because it was a psychological sustaining force throughout the difficult periods of its evolution.

A way to begin to analyze the African American jazz musicians' performance interactions is to perceive them as exercising this kind of mental negotiation. On one hand, like all African American individuals, there is the view of oneself as one part of the whole, in this case, the band. On the other hand, the individual is also aware of a singular personal identity. (Complicating this process is another, parallel identity duality that will be stated here without elaboration since it is another vast subject in itself: The black American is aware that he or she is perceived as inferior by whites while at the same time he or she holds the opposite self-view. This dichotomous self-perception, although potentially troublesome to some African Americans, is not unlike several psychological demands on them as they develop and function within a broader society that perceives and treats them ambivalently.)

The jazz ensemble symbolizes the successful resolution of the African American dualistic self-appraisal. The players are united to create an integrated musical rendition while providing each player with optimal creative stimulation. The musician is attuned to his or her own artistic response to the music influenced by a stream of personal associations. At the same time, these reactions are stimulated by the other artists' playing. This dynamic recalls the call-and-response process that characterized the secular and religious songs of early African American history and that are pertinent parts of jazz's origins.

The perspective that the jazz ensemble is a microcosm of the African American community includes other dimensions. The musicians employ a commonly shared tradition within which there are customary understandings of how one behaves and of what experience means. Members of the community feel a bond that carries with it certain responsibilities. Elders instruct developing younger players. Mutually beneficial information is shared. The integrity of artistic exploration is respected even when there is competition or "family" feuds. Subgroupings of individuals form around similar artistic interests, particular life styles, friendships, or business arrangements.

By the time a group of professional musicians are on the bandstand to perform, most assumptions about what will take place are understood. Someone has assembled compatible individuals together. There are at least verbal business agreements regarding pay, time, and so forth. A common level of technical facility and general musicianship is expected. The music has usually been rehearsed.

These preconditions set the stage for the interplay of the musicians. The treatment they will give the compositions is therefore not impromptu, as some uninformed listeners believe. A foundation of skill, previous experience, values, beliefs, customs, traditions, and practice undergirds it. Under optimal circumstances, the artists assert their individuality in the security of that multidetermined context. They feel free to draw on the full range of their sensations and cognitions. Their listening and responding to fellow band members are mutually inspirational because of shared outlooks and assumptions. Even though there may be personal rivalries, or even animosities in their nonmusical relationships, individual satisfaction will generally coalesce into collective satisfaction in the music-making moments. Even under less than optimal circumstances, these are the standards the musicians hold themselves to.

North American racial realities are also mirrored in jazz musicians' intergroup relations. Jazz has two separate histories, black and white, albeit with chronologically increasing overlap. North American culture and African American culture are intertwined in so many respects that to speak of them separately can seem absurd, at least on the surface. The separation stems, of course, from historical differential power discrepancies that were justified in the white American mind and built into North American social institutions.

African American culture includes, among other features, phenomena developed to subversively preserve its members' from accepting and believing the white view of them as lesser human beings. Jazz contains these phenomena in abundance, as has been argued in this chapter. White Americans obviously do not need the sustaining phenomena that jazz embodies. The white American jazz musician therefore has related to the music from a different psychological perspective, whether mainly personal or aesthetic. These motivations can be nonetheless strong, of course. Expressively rich African American style and spirit were magnetic to early white musicians who lived racially segregated from black people. White musicians played jazz with their friends. It appealed to succeeding generations of musicians who sometimes did not identify it as other than the music they had learned from their white mentors. Because of this situation, and the general pervasiveness of the white supremacy myth, jazz's black origins were historically ignored, minimized, or denied by some white jazz players.[21] However, the seminal advances in jazz have been made by African American artists with a few notable exceptions.

The white jazz musician learns to express himself or herself through an artistic medium that originated in black culture. A musician from any background can certainly become fluent in this style of expression. A musician makes highly personalized statements regardless of cultural group membership. However, African American culture naturally influences the sensibility of jazz playing. The white American jazz player must learn what the black American player usually has already had to learn about African American expressive style, since, as discussed earlier, it is a part of all aspects of African American culture.

The cultural aspects of racial identity are necessarily different for the white American jazz artist. They are no less complicated, but they are less pivotal to his or her self-concept. Some writers have attempted to represent the white musicians who are interested in jazz as rebellious outsiders.[22] Others account for the substantial history of white players in jazz by denying jazz's African American definition and, therefore, its consequence in African American culture.[23]

Racially integrated jazz bands are common now, of course. Integrated workplaces and neighborhoods characterize much of present American society too. However, jazz musicians, who unself-consciously share an African American–dominated music vocabulary may be further along in establishing unguarded relationships than most others in interracial situations. Jazz playing may also illuminate a constructive direction for cross-cultural relations in America in general.

It has been but a short time in history since numerous spaces existed in which African Americans could feel truly safe and relaxed. Until recently, these have been available to African Americans mainly within the bound-aries of their set-apart communities. The art that evolved in these pre-serves, like jazz, exhibits that spirit of refuge. It was in black communities and their institutions that black Americans could be safely bold and asser-tive. Jazz players made music with the same free attitude. Out of these preconditions for creativity, they established the art form that remains astoundingly inspirational to American musicians and audiences and their counterparts all over the world.

THE INTERACTION BETWEEN JAZZ PERFORMERS AND THEIR AUDIENCES

People in jazz audiences are not merely consumers. If they allow it, they can become aware that the music's appealing aurality, palpable rhythms, exciting spontaneity, and artistic virtuosity make up a cultural ritual of which they are also a part. Wittingly or not, their presence contributes to a vital cultural process. The musicians play for themselves individually and collectively, but their artistry is also strongly affected by the audience's response.

Some African Americans, especially those who did not grow up in the age when jazz was popular music, believe jazz has become similar to Eu-ropean concert music and is therefore detached from everyday black life. Jazz has certainly evolved into a "serious" art form. This means that to fully appreciate it, you have to attend to it. What jazz artists do to compose beautiful musical statements is so varied and intricate that the casual lis-tener will not hear it. As discussed earlier however, jazz's folk and utilitar-ian origins are nevertheless present. The call-and-response dynamic, for example, that is one aspect of the spectrum of black music, is sometimes more subtle in today's jazz playing, but it is nonetheless a part of it. The blues sensibility is almost always evident in jazz music making too. And although the primary function of jazz music is no longer to stimulate danc-ing, its rhythms still entertain us. In fact, jazz has developed to contain even more enjoyable features. The informed listener can marvel at the mu-sicianship. He or she can delight in the musical inventiveness and in the way it is fostered by the communication among the musicians. The nuances of creativity in progress before them can be an additional source of delight. Those who follow the development of the music can also take pleasure from the vitality of the tradition in which it is located, appreciating all the history it still evokes as well as its new developments.

Most jazz performers seek a connection with their audiences. Jazz au-diences are also happiest when that connection with the musicians has been made. The musicians know when their listeners are excited, moved, bored, or distracted, and they respond accordingly. In disappointing instances they may withdraw into themselves, shutting out an unresponsive audience. In the best moments, they are inspired by listeners who react to their emotional expression and to the subtleties of their invention.

Once again the representation of African American cultural elements in the jazz performance is to be seen. Jazz audiences come to experience the atmosphere of live music-making as well as hearing it. The music contains infectious elements: free individual expression in the context of extraordinary team play, musical virtuosity and invention, multiple moods, intriguing combinations of artistic statements, challenging assertions of truth. The listeners are invited into celebrations of black American psychological strengths. These are pleasing, unguarded, moments of cultural connection and standards of effective human relations.

Ethnographer Paul F. Berliner, in his book *Thinking in Jazz*, discusses the comments of several jazz artists on this subject:

As implied above, various aspects of the experience shared by improvisers and audience within the realm of jazz are reminiscent of intense qualities of human relationship experienced "in real life," that is, off the stage. Tommy Turrentine, who generally enjoys joking and making other people laugh, says that "it's the same thing when I play. I feel good when I get a response." From Charlie Persip's perspective, "there are divine moments when you receive feed-back from audiences which make you feel sure that you're on the right road. The thrill of being liked and the pure adoration of fans is like falling in love."[24]

A further word about jazz's folk origins should be included here. The thesis of jazz in black American culture presented in this discussion does not turn on whether it remains a folk art or whether it is the "fine art" of specific individuals.[25] Such an argument sets up an artificial dichotomy in what is, in actuality, an evolutionary process.

All art forms began in folk traditions within which individual virtuosity flourished. What it means when writers describe "folk art" as different from "fine art" is that collective origins are prominent in one instance and individual virtuosity is emphasized in the other. Folk art, it should be noted, however, does not preclude individual artistry. "Folk artists" are artists who generally have not been celebrated beyond their immediate locales and times. It is ultimately the accumulated work itself rather than the individual contributors to it that receives our appreciation. But we should not forget that there were always creative individual contributors. African American culture grew out of a collective experience. The contribution of individuals to all the parts of that process is largely undocumented. The same can be said, of course, of the origins of any culture.

An art tradition requires more than individuals with talent, however. It must serve sustaining societal purposes as well, whether they are mainly concrete or mainly abstract. Artists work within cultures to make their singular statements. Their productions certainly express who they are as individuals, but their art also represents commonly shared needs and values. When extraordinarily creative artists come along, their influence is sometimes so powerful that they alone move their medium in uncharted directions. They are nevertheless, and at first, still working from premises laid out before them. One therefore appreciates, for example, the enormous, even courageous creativity of a Charles Ives or an Aaron Copeland, while at the same time recognizing their effect on and reflection of the European-American symphonic repertory. After a certain time in African American history, one can similarly begin to distinguish the marks of its geniuses, like Muddy Waters and Charlie Parker.

Some theorists in psychology have written about the ways African Americans maintain an individual identity along with a sense of themselves that is indistinguishable from the group identity of African Americans. Nobles, cited earlier for instance, enunciates the concept of "we-ness," and "the survival of the tribe" in his model of African American psychology.[26] To crudely summarize this thesis, the black American individual retains a self-view that he or she brought from West Africa. This is a sense of self that is intricately bound with the sense of *belonging to a tribe*. African Americans, according to this viewpoint, are collectivistic in their conceptions of themselves, at least partially. When slaves were removed from their tribes in Africa, their lingering need for a sense of aggregated existence directed them to transfer a "tribal" mentality to their new circumstances. Over time, the *tribe* was defined as all of those who were fellow slaves. The theory elaborates this basic supposition by indicating all the ways African Americans will invent familial cohesion. Such designations as "play" brother and sister, or the appointment of close friends to "family" status, or the designation of another as "my homey" are illustrations.

One can apply this existential constructing to the experience of African American jazz musicians with their audiences. In the optimal jazz event, they become a coalesced whole. Out of a deeply ingrained predilection, all parties are transformed into interdependent entities. In this sense, jazz artists and audiences are in rituals of free-flowing exchange. They celebrate bold confidence and uninhibited creativity. Everyone is affirmed in moments of excitement and fulfillment.

A logical question, then, is what can be said in this regard about the relationship between the musicians who make their music in a recording studio and the listeners of recorded jazz? The relationship is obviously a removed one. Memory and imagination, however, allow the individuals to have a measure of what might be experienced in the live situation. The musicians may have memories of live performances that expand their conceptions of who is or will be hearing them. In their efforts to produce the quality music to which they aspire, they may welcome the possibilities for alterations the technology of the recording studio provides. The listener to a jazz recording can imagine being present and therefore a part of the performance she or he hears. Her or his experience of the music by recording is more likely, however, to involve memories of the various settings in which this and other recordings were heard. The music may therefore be associated with any number of actual or symbolic interpersonal connections. Alternatively, it may be enjoyed in private, thus satisfying individualistic expressive needs. And, obviously, the recordings may mean different things to a person at different times.

Jazz is now heard in concert halls, night clubs, outdoor venues, restaurants, museums, at dances, on television commercials, in films, and on recordings everywhere—in all parts of the world. People are drawn to it as they are, incidentally, to other African American expressive media. The phenomenon of its widespread popularity signals the richness of African Americans' contributions to the world and perhaps models a standard of unguarded human relations.

Thinking of the jazz performance as a ritualistic representation of those psychological phenomena that have sustained African Americans highlights the essential nature of those phenomena and, therefore, of jazz music. As the African American culture developed to become as complex as it is, so has jazz music and its place within it. Jazz holds the important values and defining characteristics of African America in its artistic essence. That is its most remarkable everyday utility.

JAZZ AND DIVERSITY AMONG AFRICAN AMERICANS

It is almost needless to say, and perhaps it should have been clearly acknowledged earlier in this discussion, that the intricacies and intertwinings of race, culture, and social class certainly make generalizations about African Americans hazardous. A universally applicable thesis about psychological phenomena in African American culture, therefore, is admittedly somewhat risky. However the prevalence of the challenge-improvisational attitude, the collectivistic-individualistic synthesis, and the dual identity process, in such ubiquitous cultural phenomena as African American folklore, music, religion, and language, supports the view of their cultural centrality and therefore their meaning for the spectrum of African American individuals.

The significance of these mental processes in African American society with all of its diversity is indeed striking. As such, it is the key to understanding why under protractedly arduous circumstances African Americans have on the whole been competent and creative rather than passively defeated.

Individual differences in development, in personality and in constitution, however, obviously influence the particular reactions of African American persons. To acknowledge only one dimension of the complex interaction of these variables, it is instructive to consider the theories of psychologists

William E. Cross, Jr., Janet E. Helms, and Thomas A. Parham. They postulate separate but overlapping models of the development of racial identity in African Americans.[27] They suggest that although all African Americans must acquire individually utilitarian responses to racism, the responses vary in their mental health implications for each individual. The stages of racial identity development these theorists explicate are junctures in an ascending process. The African American individual gradually acquires optimal competence in dealing with his or her socially precarious position in the society. Cross summarizes the end or "internalization" stage of this process in his book *Shades of Black*, while also, incidentally, indicating his conviction regarding the value of the challenge mind-set.

At the internalization stage, *the defensive function of Black identity becomes much more sophisticated and flexible. Instead of the iron shield of Immersion-Emersion, it becomes a translucent filter that is often "invisible," undetectable, which allows non-threatening information and experiences to be processed without distortion.* The structure of the protective function seems to involve (1) an awareness that racism is part of the American experience; (2) an anticipatory set—regardless of one's station in American society, one can well be a target of racism; (3) well-developed ego defenses that can be employed when confronted with racism; (4) a system blame and personal efficacy orientation in which one is predisposed to find fault in the circumstances, not the self; and (5) a religious orientation that prevents the development of a sense of bitterness or the need to demonize whites. (Emphasis added)[28]

Skeptics of African descendent peoples' capacity for constructive self-definition and actions have proclaimed their disbelief ever since the earliest encounters of Europeans with Africans. These attitudes were given authority by theories based in either religion or science. They were used to justify the system of slavery in North America. They were the basis for the legal subjugation of black Americans after emancipation. They are cited today in policy decisions and in scholarly discussions to explain poverty and disillusionment among poor African Americans. African American individuals who escape the negative assignations of the powerful majority are still seen as the exception to the rule of white supremacy. Black achievement on white terms, therefore, does not ensure protection from racist thinking and perceiving and the behavior that may result.

The depressing statistics of social system decay among some segments of African American society are no more the fault of its victims today than they have ever been.[29] The existence of these problems does not define African Americans. Nor do they off-set the phenomenal record of African Americans' achievement. Rather, these problems say more about the convergence of changing economic and social forces, North American politics, and racism than they do about anything inherent in the psychology of African Americans. In spite of racially driven institutional obstacles that are tenacious in the society, African Americans *who are not poor* are no more prone to mental illness than white Americans, to cite one revealing example.[30] Indeed, the wholehearted participation of most black Americans in the so-called American way of life could be the prototypical American success story.

The cultural critic Michael E. Dyson, commenting on the disturbing conditions of increasing numbers of poor black Americans, similarly urges that we analyze them from a perspective based on informed memory.

These harsh and bitter circumstances for most Africans in America have tested our moral resolve, our spiritual resources, and most acutely, our communal memories. But we must remember that even under the most inhumane assaults of slavery and racism, black identity, although severely challenged, was maintained. This remembering can fuel the engines of desire to reconstruct the infrastructure of black communities and redesign coping mechanisms to fit our present circumstances.[31]

Successful black psychological adaptation to adverse circumstances is, of course, not synonymous with needed progressive social change. Some African American individuals may be unable to defend themselves from "the harsh and bitter" effects of hostile politics and powerful economic fluctuations. However, like all psychologically sound persons, their inner lives can continue to prosper in spite of poverty and neglect and attitudes that paradoxically blame them for their condition. Indeed, the thesis asserted here particularly notes that creativity has always existed in black communities despite, and often in the midst of, severe hardship.

In every power-subordinate relationship, the unheard persons will seek a way to accurately articulate their own perception of existence. Jazz musicians practice a highly developed and refined art that manifests a tradition of psychological survival processes in African American culture. It grew out of the existentially critical needs of a denigrated and oppressed people who created oral-based genres of self-definition and efficacy. The action of invention in spoken, sung, and instrumental language enabled them to escape the trap of "utter psychological domination."

Jazz is a dynamic art that in ever more musically intricate ways tells the increasingly complex story of African Americans' experience. It is a precise and powerful metaphor for the African American psychological condition. Jazz music resounds with the echoes of its past sources in black folk songs, blues, and ragtime even as it incorporates Latin and other cultural styles. The African American cultural identity is likewise a fluid construction of past and present elements of experience.

African Americans have come to the point in their development of needing to detail the foundation of their cultural definition. Their present status, whatever its socioeconomic difference, has no true meaning without the grounding their history provides. While this longitudinal self-definition is celebrated by most African Americans, many of their historical subjugators have difficulty extricating their associations of black Americans from the negative and the inferior. The consequence in the political sense is the penchant to translate that perception into policies and behaviors that retard progress toward a true culturally balanced society. In relationship to jazz, these intransigent perspectives have spanned from outright rejection to total appropriation of the music to impatience with efforts to fully establish its place in African American culture.[32]

To emphasize by repeating it, African Americans are not a monolith. Their adaptations to whatever racially motivated adversity they encounter is an individual matter. The status of African Americans as a group in North American society is nonetheless precarious. There is therefore little doubt that the psychological protective mechanisms discussed here remain vital. Jazz, along with other African American expressive genres, will continue to represent the most significant of these: the self-esteem preservation effects of the challenge attitude, the constructive support of interdependent communication and cooperation, and the resolution of dualistic self-appraisals necessitated by living in an ambivalently positioned dominant society.

Jazz activity throughout the world is vibrant. The interest in the music extends to many kinds of audiences. Many young people aspire to learn to play jazz too. Some veteran jazz artists complain today about the irony that, in order to attract the attention of record producers and club and concert producers, you have to be not only young and talented but also unseasoned. Still, the numbers of truly gifted jazz musicians who have appeared lately is encouraging because it is the evidence that the music remains vital and is always expanding its cultural utility and its creative boundaries.[33]

None of the musicians on stage with Wynton Marsalis at the 1996 New Orleans Jazz Fest looked more than 15 years old, with the exception of the very grown-up New Orleans saxophonist Wessel "Warm Daddy" Anderson. I know that I didn't recognize any of their names when Wynton introduced them; and I doubted that many others in the enormous audience did either. I remember the youngsters in the band were two trumpeters, two saxophonists, a vibraphonist, a piano player, a bass player and drummer. One of the trumpet players was white, the other musicians were black. They were all carefully groomed and impeccably dressed in suits and ties. After greeting the crowd in the joyful spirit of homecoming, Wynton announced they would play a segment John Coltrane's, "A Love Supreme" suite. I sensed an air of curious anticipation around me. The band's sound was bright and tight; they were obviously well rehearsed. I realized it couldn't be that these young men were entirely unknown. They came from some jazz program, school and/or community. But when each one took his first solo at this granddaddy of jazz festivals, playing with the foremost spokesperson for jazz, it literally felt as if he were making his world debut.

The gasps that came from me seemed echoed throughout the huge tent we were in as astounding talent issued forth from every single one of the young musicians. Indeed, the last to play an initial solo, the vibraphonist, was visually and audibly so dazzling, the audience seemed to roar for them all. "Where does Wynton find these kids?" a person sitting near me said. Thank God they are out there, and that he finds them, I thought.[34]

NOTES

The following musicians and other knowledgeable individuals generously provided enlightenment about the jazz community and jazz music-making while the author was a Scholar-in-Residence at the Schomburg Center for Research in Black Culture in 1987: Chris Anderson, Eddie Bonnemere, John Blake, Marion Brown, Dr. George Butler, Lester Cobb, Katherine Cox, Charles Davis, Percy France, Jimmy Heath, Eddie Henderson, Luther Henderson, Clifford Jordon, Junior Manse, Jackie McClean, Mulgrew Miller, Khalid Moss, Albert Murray, Jamil Nasser, Rigmor Newman, Rufus Reid, Max Roach, Andy Simkins, Arthur Taylor, Dr. Billy Taylor, Bobby Thomas, Leon Thomas, Ed Williams, and James Williams.

1. R. Bastide, *African Civilizations in the New World* (New York: Harper & Row, 1971). See also J. S. Blassingame, *The Slave Community: Plantation Life in the Antebellum South*, 2nd ed. (New York: Oxford University Press, 1979); H. A. Baker, *Blues, Ideology, and Afro-American Literature: A Vernacular Theory* (Chicago: University of Chicago Press, 1984); M. C. Gridley and W. Rave, "Towards Identification of African Traits in Early Jazz," *Black Perspectives in Music* 12 no. 1 (1984): 45–56; P. K. Maultsby, "Africanism in African-American Music," in Joseph E. Holloway, ed., *Africanism in American Culture* (Bloomington, Ind.: Indiana University Press, 1990), 185–210.

2. H. L. Gates, Jr., *The Signifying Monkey: A Theory of African-American Literary Criticism* (New York: Oxford University Press, 1988).

3. Gates, *The Signifying Monkey*.

4. L. Jones, *Blues People: The Negro Experience in White America and the Music that Developed from It* (New York: William Morrow, 1963). See also A. Murray, *Stomping the Blues* (New York: McGraw-Hill, 1976).

5. P. Oliver, *Blues Fell This Morning: Meaning in the Blues*, 2nd ed. (Cambridge: Cambridge University Press, 1990).

6. A. H. Jenkins, *Psychology and African-Americans: A Humanistic Approach*, 2nd ed. (Boston: Allyn & Bacon, 1995), 42–43.

7. H. L. Gates, Jr., "Thirteen Ways of Looking at a Black Man," *The New Yorker*, October 23, 1995, 56–65.

8. W. H. Grier and P. M. Cobbs, *Black Rage* (New York: Basic Books, 1968).

9. L. Jones, *Blues People: The Negro Experience in White America and the Music that Developed from It* (New York: William Morrow, 1963).

10. E. E. Sampson, "Identity Politics: Challenges to Psychology's Understanding," *American Psychologist* 48, no. 12 (1993): 1219–30.

11. S. Reinharz, "Toward an Ethnography of 'Voice' and 'Silence,' " in E. J. Trickett, R. J. Watts and D. Birman, eds., *Human Diversity: Perspectives on People in Context* (San Francisco: Jossey-Bass, 1991), 178–200.

12. L. Goss and M. E. Barnes, *Talk That Talk: An Anthology of African-American Storytelling* (New York: Simon & Schuster, 1989).

13. A. C. Jones, *Wade in the Water: The Wisdom of the Spirituals* (Maryknoll, N.Y.: Orbis, 1993).

14. M. S. Harper and R. B. Steptoe, *Chant of Saints: A Gathering of Afro-American Literature* (Chicago: University of Illinois Press, 1979). See also Gates, "Thirteen Ways of Looking"; M. E. Dyson, *Reflecting Black: African-American Cultural Criticism* (Minneapolis: University of Minnesota Press, 1993).

15. R. S. Jones, "Structural Isolation and the Genesis of Black Nationalism in North America," *Colby Library Quarterly* 15, no. 4 (1979): 252–266.

16. T. Thomas and S. Sillin, *Racism and Psychiatry* (New York: Brunner/Mazel, 1972). See also G. N. Grob, *Mental Illness and American Society, 1875–1940* (Princeton, N.J.: Princeton University Press, 1983).

17. R. J. Hernnstein and C. Murray, *The Bell Curve: Intelligence and Class Structure in American Life* (New York: The Free Press, 1994).

18. W. H. Tucker, *The Science and Politics of Racial Research* (Champaign: University of Illinois Press, 1994). See also "Focus: The Bell Curve Controversy" (1995, Dec.). *Notes From the Society for the Psychological Study of Ethnic Minority Issues*, 9(2). American Psychological Association; E. W. Gordon, "Putting Them in Their Place," *Readings: A Journal of Reviews and Commentary in Mental Health* 10 no. 1 (1995): 8–14.

19. Jenkins, *Psychology and African-Americans*, 42–43.

20. W. Nobles, "Extended Self: Rethinking the So-Called Negro Self-Concept," *Journal of Black Psychology* 2 no. 2, (1976): 15–24.

21. For various discussions of this issue see A. P. Merriam and R. W. Mack, "The Jazz Community," *Social Forces* 3 no. 38 (1960): 211–220. See also G. Schuller, *Early Jazz: Its Roots and Musical Development* (New York: Oxford University Press, 1968); C. Gerard, *Jazz in Black and White: Race, Culture and Identity in the Jazz Community* (Westport, Conn.: Praeger, 1998).

22. N. Leonard, "Some Further Thoughts on Jazzmen as Romantic Outsiders," *Journal of Jazz Studies* 2 no. 2 (1975): 42–52. See also J. L. Collier, *The Reception of Jazz in America, A New View*. Monograph No. 27. Brooklyn, New York: Conservatory of Music, Institute For Studies in American Music; C. L. Lastrucci, "The Professional Dance Musician," *Journal of Musicology* 3 no. 4 (1941): 168–172.

23. H. O. Brown, *The Story of the Original Dixieland Jazz Band* (Baton Rouge: Louisiana State University Press, 1960). See also L. Feather, *The Jazz Years: Earwitness to an Era* (New York: Da Capo, 1987): 116.

24. P. F. Berliner, *Thinking in Jazz: The Infinite Art of Improvisation* (Chicago: University of Chicago Press, 1994).

25. P. Patton, "Who Owns the Blues?" *New York Times*, 26 November 1995, p. 1, 35.

26. Nobles, "Extended Self," 15–24.

27. J. E. Helms, *Black and White Racial Identity: Theory, Research, and Practice* (Westport, Conn.: Greenwood Press, 1990). See also W. E. Cross, Jr., *Shades of Black: Diversity in African-American Identity* (Philadelphia: Temple University Press, 1991); W. E. Cross, Jr., T. A. Parham, and J. E. Helms, "The Stages

of Black Identity Development: Nigrescence Models," in R. L. Jones, ed., *Black Psychology* (Berkeley: Cobb & Henry, 1991), 319–38.

28. Cross, *Shades of Black*.

29. J. W. Wilson, *The Truly Disadvantaged: The Inner City, the Underclass, and Public Policy* (Chicago: University of Chicago Press, 1987). See also J. T. Gibbs, ed., *Young, Black and Male in America: An Endangered Species* (Dover, Mass.: Auburn House, 1988); A. Hacker, *Two Nations, Black, White, Separate, Hostile, Unequal* (New York: Scribner, 1992).

30. V. M. Mays and G. Albee, "Psychotherapy With Ethnic Minorities," in D. K. Freedheim, ed., *History of Psychotherapy, A Century of Change* (Washington: American Psychological Association, 1992), 552–570.

31. Dyson, *Reflecting Black*. See also Cross, *Shades of Black*.

32. F. Conroy, "Stop Nitpicking a Genius," *New York Times Magazine*, 26 June 1995, 28–31, 48, 54, 70.

33. T. Piazza, "Keepers of the Flame, And Hot," *New York Times*, 12 March 1995, 332, 40.

34. F. Jones, personal account.

6

The Meaning of Rap Music in Contemporary Black Culture

Cheryl L. Keyes

Rap music evolved among black inner city youth of New York City during the 1970s as a quasi-song with rhyme and rhythmic speech, which draws on black street language and is recited over a musical soundtrack. By the late 1970s, rap music began attracting the attention of many, including music entrepreneurs, who were enchanted with its rhyme, speech-song qualities, rhythmic aspects, and its financial potential. Among the first successful promoters and record producers of rap were Sylvia and Joe Robinson, cofounders of Sugarhill Records (of Englewood, New Jersey), who popularized this form to the masses with the group Sugarhill Gang. The Gang's initial recording, "Rapper's Delight," skyrocketed in the charts in 1979, making it the first successful commercial rap recording.[1] By 1986, this nascent form entered the popular music mainstream by way of Run-DMC's fusion of rap with rock, as best illustrated in their rendition of Aerosmith's 1977 hit "Walk This Way."

With its growing popularity, rap music expanded regionally, producing artists from Los Angeles, Oakland, Houston, Miami, Atlanta, Chicago, Detroit, and Seattle. In addition, the audience and performers of this music began to include a non-black constituency as best represented with artist and groups like Mellow Man Ace, the Beastie Boys, Cypress Hill, and House of Pain. Black youth continue to remain, however, major creative forces of the rap tradition in defining its musical direction. Furthermore, this musical genre remains firmly entrenched in the black cultural aesthetic, where it unfolds as a complex form that is deeply rooted in the aesthetic, philosophy, ideology, and tradition of urban black street culture.

This chapter explores the social dynamism of the street milieu and how this context gives life, shape, and meaning to the rap music tradition. As such, the discussion is two-fold. First, it surveys common misconceptions surrounding the definition of rap music; second this chapter positions rap as an expression reflective of street life and culture of inner-city America via the voices of black youth.

THE RAP ATTACK

Although rap music is becoming more and more popular in the musical mainstream, it is also the subject of heated controversy. Critics posit that rap music is a lewd form of expression associated with the urban under-class, while others believe that it is too coarse, thus causing youth to act violently.[2] Those who describe rap as a "lower-class, street-oriented phe-nomenon"[3] believe that it is in conflict with conservative middle-class values. As music critic Lisa Robinson notes in an interview with Steve Fox: "It's (rap music) not something they [middle-class America] really understand. It is very black and very urban, and people are scared of that."[4]

Elaborating further on the above observation, music journalist critic Nel-son George finds that negative responses to this music are concluded from the hardcore or tough posture conveyed by its artists, who are black for the most part. For example: "They [rappers] speak in a very aggressive style. They stand aggressively; they dress in an assertive manner, in a way that is not seemingly acceptable to whites in the mainstream. . . . this turns off a lot of middle-class black folks as well. It's not racial; it's more of a class thing."[5]

Moreover, rap music is central to films that address street gangs or ju-venile delinquency, similar to rock 'n' roll's filmic association during the 1950s.[6] *Colors* (1988), *Boyz N the Hood* (1991), *Juice* (1992), and *Menace II Society* (1993) represent those films in which rap dominates these films' soundtracks. Moreover, mainstream media further fuel the demonization of rap via reports of violence at rap music concerts as well. Some writers contend that rap's beat and other aesthetic qualities are conducive to vio-lent behavior: "Hence, the rap today is anger and the so-called background music or scratching is so intense that it beckons you to act violent."[7]

Commonly expressed themes by rap artists are "the desire to be number one" and sociopolitical commentary. But by late 1988, rap's themes ad-vanced tales about street gang life, and for this reason it acquired the name "gangsta" rap by the music industry. Because of the graphic lyrical content, including gendered epithets, rap was the center of several censorship de-bates. The most publicized of the censorship debates involved the Miami-based trio 2 Live Crew. Their album, *As Nasty as They Wanna Be* (1989), whose song titles included "Me So Horny" and "Bad Ass Bitch," was con-demned by segments of the black community, Parents' Music Resource

Center (PMRC) and the government. The Crew was accused of polluting the minds of American youth and aestheticizing violence against women. As a result of the controversy, 2 Live Crew's album "was the first in the United States to be banned by a federal judge; members of the group were arrested at a live performance in Florida, and the controversy surrounding the Crew became all the rage in the 1990s."[8] Censorship in the form of "civil responsibility"[9] emerged with record executives and the 1994 congressional hearings on Capital Hill. William Bennett, former U.S. Education Secretary and "drug czar," and C. Delores Tucker, chairwoman of the National Political Congress of Black Women, began meeting with record executives at Time-Warner, which at the time was a distributing arm for the gangsta rap label Death Row Records. Among those testifying against gangsta rap at these hearings were Tucker and singer Dionne Warwick.

Other anti-gang sentiments erupted as well: Reverend Calvin Butts III, minister of the Abyssinian Baptist Church in Harlem, destroyed gangsta rap CDs and cassettes with a steamroller; anti–gangsta rap factions convinced record companies to use warning labels on CDs containing explicit lyrics. These groups also demanded that major record companies halt their manufacture of gangsta rap and that they terminate relationships with rap artists whose music is deemed too risqué, racist, sexist, or too poignant in tone.

Among those with different opinions about gangsta rap were rap artist Yo-Yo, music entrepreneur Ernie Singleton, state of California Congresswoman Maxine Waters, and Reverend Jesse Jackson, who saw the anti–gangsta rap crusade as an attempt to marginalize black youth. They used the hearings to try to convince the public that the problem was not with the lyrics but with the devastating realities and consequences of ghetto life. Jackson said, "So many of us are removed from the [inner city] environment and have become insensitive to the issues affecting the youth there. Rap music deals with the kids' reality of living with high unemployment, a high crime rate, and the devastating drug problem."[10]

Finally, rap music has been scrutinized on other fronts. Musicians of nonpopular traditions argue that this music is merely noise and is depleted of aesthetic appeal and musical elements that constitute the "serious" music of the West. Jazz classical trumpeter Wynton Marsalis summarizes popular opinion when commenting: "When you get to rap music, you can't reduce anymore. When you get past that, it's not music anymore."[11]

Controversial forms that threaten mainstream tastes, like rap music, may always be subjected to intense scrutiny by parent watchdogs and powerful political forces in the same way rock 'n' roll was during its early years. Perhaps those who are rather ambivalent about rap music can move beyond essentializing it as a decadent form and, more important, come to realize that this expression is not an aberration of black culture but rather a part of a continuum of black expressive culture.

An objective analysis of rap music must involve the artist's perspective. Only then can one engage in a thorough and critical assessment of this tradition and adequately interpret its aesthetic qualities and performance practices. Central to this discussion is viewing rap music as a part of a continuum of African-derived expressive forms.

Foundation of Rap Music

The roots of rap can be traced from African bardic traditions to rural Southern expressions of African Americans—toasts, sermons, blues, game songs—all of which are recited in a chanted rhyme or poetic fashion. Salient features of these forms include metaphor, braggadocio, mimicry, formulaic expressions, double entendre, repetition, rhyme and "signifyin'" (that is, indirect references and allusions). Between the 1920s and 1950s, southern folk forms were transported by southern African American migrants to the urban North. These traditions were, then, transformed and modified in the new environment to reflect urban life. For example, southern rural contexts where blacks assembled to hear performances of neighborhood blues artists in juke joints were now re-created in urban contexts such as local street corner taverns or speakeasies. These new gathering places—parks, taverns or street corners—now considered remote from the home and religious centers, comprise what urban blacks call "the streets."

Sociologist Eugene Perkins recognizes the streets as an institution very similar to the way that the church, school, and family are conceived as institutions. Yet unlike the other three institutions, the streets emerge as the primary survival center when other institutions fail to provide the essential tools needed for survival in what Perkins refers to as "the ghetto colony."[12] It is here where one learns about the intricate yet ominous nature of the *hood* (ghetto) and, more important, how to survive in it and how to combat economical, political, and sociological oppression in the inner city.

A major prerequisite for survival in the streets is learning how to communicate effectively. For instance, the 1960's black nationalist figure H. "Rap" Brown credits street education for his verbal skills in his reputed memoir *Die Nigger Die*: "I learned how to talk in the streets, not from reading about Dick and Jane going to the zoo and all that simple shit. Sometimes I wonder why I ever bothered to go to school. Practically everything I know I learned on the corner."[13] Thus, the streets become the crucible out of which African American urban expressive traditions are forged. More important, it is in this context from which the forerunner of Brown's style emerged, "jive."

"Jive" is a variation of the English word *jibe*. Dan Burley, a noted scholar of jive talk, dates the appearance of the word *jive* to the streets of Chicago during the 1920s: "In the sense in which it came into use among Negroes in Chicago about the year 1921, it meant to taunt, to scoff, to sneer—an expression of sarcastic comment."[14] Hence, jive is described as a highly effective way of talking about someone's ancestors and hereditary traits through colorful and metaphoric terms, later referred to simply as jiving someone.[15] Jiving is employed in several social contexts, including intimate ones where a man woos a woman or vice versa; however, it is more commonly used as a competitive tool—a way of establishing one's "rep" (reputation) in the streets. Speakers determine the effectiveness of jive talk by how it is used in the proper context, which is knowing what to say, how to say it, and when to say it. What differentiates jive from its southern verbal counterparts is the use of a vocabulary derived exclusively from the urban experience. Hence, the urban term for street becomes "stroll," boy becomes "cat," girl becomes "chic," and house becomes "crib."

The art of jive talk, therefore, lies in its originality; it is, nonetheless, continuous. "When [its] freshness wears out, when a word no longer holds any spark of spirited energy, it is discarded as useless to the process of . . . life."[16] For instance, prior to the 1970s, "to understand" entered into urban street culture as "dig," but by the 1980s, "dig" became "word-up."

During the post-World War II years, jive talk had proliferated on all levels in the urban milieu—from the church to the street corner. English scholar Clyde Taylor notes that the source of jive comes from jazz "hipster" culture.[17] Jazz musicians created idiomatic expressions from jive, and it was exclusively used to communicate with other jazz colleagues. Such words as "jam"/having a good time; "blow"/to play well; "cat"/jazz colleague; "bad"/good, and "shed"/to practice[18] are just a few of the many words that are commonplace in the jazz vernacular. Even prominent jazz bandleaders such as Cab Calloway, Count Basie, and jazz-turned-rhythm and blues extraordinaire Louis Jordan have occasionally interspersed quasi-sung narrative sections of jive talk into their performances as a means of creating rapport with African American audiences.

Black comedians also laced their monologues with street jive. Many of these comedians flourished during the 1940s in Harlem, where they often served as hosts of talent shows at theaters like the famous Apollo. Early popularizers of jive humor included Jackie "Moms" Mabley, Redd Foxx, Godfrey Cambridge, Pigmeat Markham, and Rudy Ray Moore, the man known for popularizing "Dolemite" and "The Signifying Monkey" toast narratives via audio recordings.

The art of "jiving" to music in rhyme over radio airwaves was introduced in the late 1940s by African American radio disc jockeys later dubbed as personality jocks.[19] As jazz great Dizzy Gillespie recollects, "We [jazz musicians] added some colorful and creative concepts to the English language, but . . . Daddy-O Daylie, a disc jockey in Chicago, originated much more of the hip language during our era than I did."[20] Holmes "Daddy-O" Day-lie and colleague Al Benson, also of Chicago, were pioneers of radio jive. The late Norman Spaulding notes that

the language and style of Benson [for instance], had an enormous impact upon the cultural world of the Chicago black community. He gave public visibility and legitimacy in the community to the culture of "the street" and to the styles and perspectives of southern blacks. . . . The intermixture of Benson's southern style with the northern middle-class style resulted in a hybrid black style that evolved into a black urban language.[21]

Although personality jocks achieved a certain power in the black community because of their jive talk abilities, they also ushered in record spinning techniques—"talking through" and "riding gain"—which rap music disc jockeys further modified. The former involves lowering the volume of music and continuing to talk as it plays while the latter occurs when the disc jockey boosts or lowers the volume on the audio board in order to accent various parts of a record.[22] Furthermore, "talking through" resembles the concept of rappin[23] over music and "riding gain" is similar to phasing, aptly called cutting, as popularized by rap mixer pioneer Grandmaster Flash.

By the 1960s, jive talk was redefined and given a newer meaning by black nationalist H. "Rap" Brown, who embellished his political speeches with signifyin', rhyme, and metaphor. Brown's style of speaking inaugurated the shift from jive to rap and soon gained popular acceptance among young urban admirers as rappin. Brown explains how he acquired the name "Rap":

What [I] try to do is totally destroy somebody else with words. It's that whole competition thing again, fighting each other. There'd be sometimes forty or fifty dudes standing around and the winner was determined by the way they [crowd/audience] responded to what was said. If you fell all over each other laughing, then you knew you'd scored. It was a bad scene for the dude that was getting humiliated. I seldom was. That's why they called me Rap, 'cause I could rap.[24]

By the mid-1960s, Brown's style of speaking was set to a musical accompaniment by black nationalist poets—the Last Poets of Harlem, Watts Prophets of Los Angeles, and singer-pianist poet Gil Scott-Heron, who recited rhyming couplets over African percussion instruments.

In the late 1960s and the 1970s, rappin to music emerged as two distinct song styles: the soul rap and the funk-style rap. The soul rap, a rappin monologue celebrating the feats and woes of love, was popularized by Isaac Hayes and further developed by Barry White and Millie Jackson. The funk-style rap, introduced by George Clinton and his group Parliament, consisted of rappin monologues on topics about partying. Unlike the music of the political poets, the love and funk-style raps were not in rhyme but rather loosely chanted over a repetitive instrumental accompaniment. These artists, nonetheless, laid the foundation for a type of musical poetry begun primarily by African American youth of the Bronx called rap music.

There are basically several factors that gave rise to rap as a contemporary form of popular music. With the ushering in of postindustrial conditions, information service corporations replaced industrial factories, changes in the federal government policies reshaped the economy albeit effecting the redistribution of monies from working-class of color to the white dominant class, and the reduction of monetary support for public school system music programs in cities like New York during the 1970s.[25] Additionally, with the overcommercialization of popular dance forms including disco, and the ongoing club gang violence, African American youth left the indoor scene and created in neighborhood city parks outdoor discotheques, featuring a disc jockey (DJ) and an emcee (MC). Rap artist The Real Roxanne observed that "People used to do jams [parties] outside in the school yard or handball court. Someone used to bring their two turntables out and plug it into the lamp post outside and that's how they got their power. People would listen and dance to the music out in the streets."[26]

Music performed in neighborhood outdoor areas was provided by an itinerant DJ, the mobile or street DJs. Street DJs were evaluated by the type of music they played as well as by the size of their sound systems. Similar to radio jockeys, street DJs occasionally spoke to their audiences in rhyme while simultaneously dovetailing one record after the other facilitated by two turntables. Popular jockeys included Pete "DJ" Jones of the Bronx and Grandmaster Flowers and Maboya of Brooklyn. The most innovative of street DJs, whose mixing technique immensely influenced the future sound direction and production of rap music, was Jamaican-born Clive Campbell, known as Kool "DJ" Herc. He tailored his disc jockeying style after the dub music jockeys of Jamaica, like Duke Reid and U Roy, by mixing collages of musical fragments, referred to as "break beats," from various recordings in order to create an entire new soundtrack.

Contemporaries of Kool Herc included Grand Wizard Theodore, Grandmaster Flash, and Afrika Bambaataa. For example, Grand Wizard Theodore popularized a mixing technique called "scratching": moving a record back and forth in a rhythmic manner while the tone arm's needle remains in the groove of the record, producing a scratch-like sound.[27] Grandmaster Flash pioneered the turntable techniques backspinning and "phasing" (also known as "punch phrasing"). The former, which requires having a copy of the same record on two turntables, is executed by rotating one record counterclockwise to the desired beat then rotating the second record counterclockwise to the same location, creating a loop-like effect. In "phasing," the DJ accents a short phrase of a recording during the playing of a second record by manipulating the turntable's cross-fader.

Grandmaster Flash eventually added MCs to his performance known as The Furious Five (Melle Mel, Kid Creole, Cowboy, Raheim, and Mr. Ness). They are credited as precursors for rappin in rhythm to music by exchanging rhyming couplets or phrases between MCs in a percussive, witty fashion, and in synchrony with the DJ's music.

Bambaataa, on the other hand, perfected Herc's style of mixing, by extending his break beats to include a variety of musical styles ranging from soul, funk, and disco to commercial jingles and television themes. But more important, he is credited as starting a nonviolent organization called the Zulu Nation—a youth organization comprised of local inner city artists of breakdancing, graffiti, and DJs, and eventually rhymin' MCs—which laid the foundation for a youth mass arts movement known as hip-hop.

Hip-hop not only encompasses street art forms but it denotes an attitude, rendered in the form of dress, gestures, and language associated with street culture. However, this arts movement is no longer confined to the streets of New York City. By the late 1980s, the music industry witnessed the proliferation of rap in other areas including Los Angeles, Oakland, and Houston, and the evolution of a hip-hop culture diaspora, as apparent with its global expansion.[28] Nevertheless, the South Bronx is recognized by hip-hop adherents as the birthplace of hip-hop culture and music. Hence, the merging of MCs and DJs set the precedent for this urban musical form in which DJs provide the soundtrack/beat over which MCs recite rhymes. The following sections examine rap's social context and its performative qualities as understood by its artists.

KEEPIN' IT DOWN WITH THE STREETS

Germane to interpreting rap music is viewing it through the lens of street culture and aesthetics. Rap artists affirm that one has to come from the streets or understand street culture in order to properly interpret and perform this music. Succinctly stated by veteran/old school rap producer disc jockey Marley Marl: "You've got to be from the streets to know what rap is about, or at least be out there to know what's going on."[29] In agreement, the veteran rap-producing team Full Force contends: "Rap is from the streets. If you don't know what's going on out there, you can't do rap. You can live in Beverly Hills, but your heart has to be in the streets."[30]

This aesthetic also informs the production of rap music videos as well. Filmmaker Hype Williams posits that all the classroom theory about filmmaking is not going to help when it comes to directing and making rap music videos; one has to go the streets in order to make hip-hop rap music videos. In validating the authenticity of his videos, Williams asserts that he comes from the streets and "this reflects in all that I do; the camera [lens] is an extension of that."[31]

While adherents of rap constantly acknowledge the importance of street culture, outsiders, on the other hand, regard the street aesthetic as repulsive and too raw in tone. During my fieldwork of rap music, I discovered that persons who react negatively to this music often are unable to decode its verbal and musical language. This language, however, is meaningful and intelligible to members of the rap community. Rap's verbal language style is derived from a nonstandard dialect that thrives within African American street culture, properly called street speech.

According to linguist John Baugh, street speech is derived from a nonstandard dialect that thrives within black street culture.[32] The term *nonstandard* does not suggest here that rap language or street speech is grammatically incorrect when compared with mainstream English, but instead the term defines the constant reinvention of and variation in new terminologies associated with street speech. What differentiates street talk from its standardized counterpart is the use of a vocabulary derived exclusively from the urban experience. For example, black street speakers of the 1960s used the word *bad* to mean that is good or that is excellent. One can determine the meaning of bad as something atrocious or something good solely by the speaker's vocal tone level, stress, facial expression, and the context in which *bad* is used.[33] In the 1980s, rap/hip-hop music speakers began replacing *bad* with the words *def* and *phat* (pronounced fat) to describe something good or great.

Manifestations of a street tradition in rap music is further accentuated by what its artists commonly refer to as a "hip-hop attitude." This attitude conveys how rap artists wish to be perceived by others. The rapper's use of street speech, dress, and body gestures authenticates one's association with a street aesthetic. Veteran DJ Jam Master Jay of Run-DMC attributes the group's success to this type of street attitude. He explains: "That's part of what makes us so good. We're aggressive. We walk with a strut. We wear our hats a certain way. We've got the feeling. Street feeling."[34]

Rap artists also adopt various street persona, which they portray via their performances as a way to salute those, who, in some cases, impacted their lives while growing up in the *hood*. The late Tupac Shakur once stated in an interview: "I spent a lot of my times in the street. Because the words I say [don't] come from a mother's mouth or a father's mouth, they're words that come from a pimp's mouth, a ho's mouth, or a prostitute's, or a hustler's, or a drug dealer's. . . . These were my role models."[35]

Sociologist Eugene Perkins identifies five personalities typical to street culture: pimp (mack/player), hustler (drug dealer), street man, working-class man, and militant (black nationalist). Perkins, however, limits his examination to males. Rap artists add, nevertheless, other street archetypes that are not always gender-specific yet appear most commonly in rap performer's personae: prostitute (ho), gangsta, or thug. For example, Big Daddy Kane, Snoop Doggy Dogg,[36] and Too Short depict the mack image, while Ice-T takes on roles as an O.G. (veteran or original gangsta) and street hustler/pimp; MC Eiht and the Geto Boys represent gangsta lifestyles. Public Enemy, Sister Souljah, Paris, and X-Clan bring to their performances a black nationalist stance with their lyrics as well as clothing—army fatigues and African apparel. Rap artists' portrayals of street characters make statements about *being down* (connected) or *keepin it real* with the streets, which, in turn, are packaged as images by which audiences recognize them. The social structure of the inner-city gang translates in the rap music tradition as a *crew* (also referred to as a *posse*). A crew denotes support members of a rap group (for example, Doug E. Fresh and The Get Fresh Crew or The World Class Wreckin' Cru). Sal Abbatiello, rap music club owner and founder of Fever Records, defines a crew as "a group of people that are down [connected] with a particular rapper. The crew sounds like a gang which is a gang but it's an organization of rappers and their followers."[37]

The crew, in many ways, parallels the amen corner, the responsorial comments from the congregation, which characterizes African American worship services. It also delivers essential parts of the rapper's text and helps focus attention on important lines to which rappers wish their audiences to respond.

Every rapper tried to recruit and the crews wanted to be with them cause they were popular. If a rapper would say, "What's that word when you're bustin' loose?" The crew knew to yell out, "Juice, Juice!" The rapper would say a line and they [the crew] would just say the answer after that. So everybody [rappers] had to have their own crew or then they didn't look like they had any clout.[38]

The number of members in a crew signifies the leader's power, status, and merit as a rapper. On more contemporary fronts "being down" or associated with an artists is like being "hooked-up" or being a link on a chain, suggests rap critic Russell Potter. "Record companies for their own motives are receptive to these chains [because] this structure gives them a free connection to other potential successes."[39] For instance, C-Murder, Mia X, Mystikal, Silkk the Shocker, and Snoop Dogg are associated with producer-rapper Master P and have all recorded on P's No Limit record label. In advancing the concept of posse, they refer to themselves as Soldiers, No Limit Soldiers.

One's *rep*, or reputation, is highly revered in the rap community. The individual's ability to develop a distinctive style forms the criterion for such achievement. Style constitutes an attitude that pervades every aspect of life among African Americans, from how one is born to how one is buried[40] and everything in between.[41] Geneva Gay observes that

style has to do with that unique, individualistic ambience with which a person invests his or her presence and being; the appropriate combination of timing, tempo, rhythm, words, and sounds for an established context; and the aesthetic finesse with which any kind of statement, attitude, or value is delivered. It is carriage and persona! It is poetry in motion—life, living, exuberance, and energy.[42]

But if someone *bites* (uses) another rapper's rhymes or lacks originality, rap artists call the offender a "sucker," "perpetrator," or *wack*. In this regard, Run-DMC is credited as the first to popularly define sucker in the recording "Sucker M.C.'s":

> you're a sucker m.c. and you're my fan . . . you try to bite
> lines, your rhymes are mine. You's the sucker M.C.[43]

Rappers underscore their self-styled *rep* through self-appointed praise names or earned praise names, which indicate merit or distinction. Kool Moe Dee is cool; Doug E. Fresh offers something new (fresh); Ice-T is a cold-blooded player; Heavy D defines himself as an overweight lover; Queen Pen writes or "pens" her own lyrics;[44] Grandmaster Flash exhibits extraordinary speed (flash) at mixing; and H. "Rap" Brown demonstrates verbal dexterity. While many of the aforementioned praise names may seem self-aggrandizing, other stage names are loaded with meanings, hence, "re-code mainstream values by employing so-called 'negative images' to attack mainstream values or to communicate very powerful messages about issues of self-respect."[45] Among these are Intelligent Hoodlum (also known as Tragedy), Public Enemy, Special Ed, Bytches with Problems, Capone-N-Noreaga, Outkast, and Niggas With Attitude, to name but a few.

The conceptual framework of rap music is rooted in a street style. An artist's use of street speech, characters, attitude, and crews asserts that one is "down" with the street. Rap artists measure the success of their performances by signals, cues, and expressions from the audience—verbal exclamations, handclapping, and dancing. An excellent performance is defined, however, by poetic logic, rhythm and timing, articulation, lyrical fluidity, quality, stage presence, and above all, "freshness." These qualities will be examined under the broad categories of black language and rhetorical style, music-making practices, and paramusical-lingual features.

Black Language and Rhetorical Style

Rap music predominantly uses the artifice and art of African American oral performance to communicate effectively to its listeners. As one critic of this tradition observes: "The rap artists combine the potent tradition in black culture: the preacher and singer. [They] appeal to the rhetorical practices eloquently honed in African American religious practices, and the cultural potency of singing/musical tradition to produce an engaging hybrid."[46]

Inherent in rap, as in its musical and verbal antecedents, "still remains the concept of black rhetoric, folk expressions, bodily movement, charismatic energy, cadence, tonal range and timbre" as manifested through the overall performance.[47] Peculiar to rap are black language and rhetorical style, music-making practices, and paramusical-lingual features. An initial discussion of rap in this manner begins with its language component, which, interestingly, is the most controversial yet misunderstood aspect of this genre.

There have been many arguments concerning the musicality of rap music among musicians of written traditions. Some have maintained that rap is the antithesis of music because it has no discernible melody or pitches, but rather "verbosity."[48] In contrast to conventional definitions of music, rap widens the parameters of music to encompass elements of both speech and song. Ethnomusicologist George List states in his seminal study, "The Boundaries of Speech and Song," that "both speech and song are (1) vocally produced, (2) linguistically meaningful, and (3) melodic."[49] Because of the manner in which meaning and melody are achieved in rap, one can add to List's traits rhythmic. Hence, it is not surprising that MCs interpret their art as "talking but . . . [creating] a melody in itself,"[50] "a rhythm in itself,"[51] and "rhythmic chanting."[52] What performers define as melodic qualities in rap, scholars refer to as tonal semantics. Concomitant to the melodic tones is the accenting of certain words. The synchrony of lyrics, melody, and rhythm creates a fluidity known as *flow* among MCs.[53] MC Dynasty asserts that "the rhythm of the beat and music . . . got to be there for the lyrics like [to] join into one."[54] In this sense, the rhythm track functions as a time organizer around which the rhymed couplet unit weaves. The interlocking of text and accompaniment creates the fitting together of parts to form an entire rhythmic idea. Furthermore, MCs exhibit their ability to flow by interweaving rhymes not only to the beat of the music but sometimes to an internalized beat, as rendered in an a cappella format or during improvised performances, as in *freestylin*.

MCs exploit other language devices to manipulate meaning through metaphor, allusions, and imagery broadly classified as signification. In his groundbreaking study *The Signifying Monkey: A Theory of African-American Criticism*, Henry Louis Gates, Jr. explores the relationship between African and African American vernacular tradition through the art of signification, or "signifyin(g)," which defines its usage among African Americans. Linguist Geneva Smitherman further lists specific characteristics of signifyin(g) in the following manner: indirection, circumlocution, metaphorical-imagistic (but [with] images rooted in the everyday, real word), humorous, ironic rhythmic fluency and sound; teachy but not preachy, directed at person or persons usually present in the situational context, punning, play on words, and introduction of the semantically or logically unexpected.[55]

A striking feature of signifyin(g) found in the rap text is "metaphorical-imagistic . . . rooted in the everyday real . . . world" of ghetto America. As one interviewee contends, rap artists use their texts to create "lyrical movies."[56] The artist most celebrated for his talent in metaphorical imagery is Melle Mel. Rap music producer Larry Smith praises him highly: "Melle Mel has a voice and . . . is the Langston Hughes of the music. Yeah, I'm saying when he paints [raps], he paints a picture. He describes with words and you see everything Mel tells you. Everything! Everything!"[57]

In "The Message," (1982)[58] Melle Mel alludes to the ghetto as "a jungle" thereby creating for his listeners an illusion through metaphor. "The Message" unfolds through vivid imagery about the grim realities of ghetto life. Here, the average inner-city youth grows up "livin' second rate" as stated earlier. Several years after the release of "The Message," similar rap songs abound recounting ghetto lore from "Ghetto Bastard" (1991) by Naughty By Nature, "The Ghetto" (1990) by Too Short, and "Hard Knock Life (Ghetto Anthem)" (1998) by Jay-Z to the most poignant controversial "gangsta" raps—"A Gangsta's Fairytale" (1990), "The Drive-By" (1990) by Ice Cube, and "Niggas Bleed" (1997) by Notorious B.I.G., all depict the ongoing afflictions of inner city youth, who feel politically, economically, and socially marginalized in mainstream America.

Drawing on the seminal work of linguist-anthropologist Claudia Mitchell-Kernan, Gates agrees that "the black concept of signifying incorporates essentially a folk notion that dictionary entries for words are not always sufficient for interpreting meaning or messages, or that meaning goes beyond such interpretations."[59] Mitchell-Kernan also observes that

Complimentary remarks may be delivered in a left-handed fashion. A particular utterance may be an insult in one context and not another. What pretends to be informative may intend to be persuasive. The hearer is thus constrained to attend to all potential meaning carrying symbolic systems in speech events—the total universe.[60]

In this regard, certain terms used by rappers may be perceived as negative or an insult by mainstream English speakers; however, their actual meaning depends on the context. Idiosyncratic to signifin(g) in this manner is the use of gendered labels and expletives in the lyrics. While some auditors perceive such words to be, as Mitchell-Kernan has previously informed us, "an insult in one context," they are considered to be nonoffensive in another context, although it depends on who uses the terms. When referring to females, male rappers like male street speakers, commonly use "bitch" and "ho" to refer to nonkindred females, explains street-educated journalist Nathan McCall. He recollects: "According to street wisdom, there were two types of females: There were women, such as your mother, sister, and teacher, and there were bitches and 'hos [whores]. . . . Bitches and 'hos were good for one thing—boning [sexual intercourse]."[61] While the above notion about women does not differ from the way a number of other men position women as sexual objects, the majority of male rappers this author interviewed concur with street conventional meanings of these words.

There are alternative uses on "bitch" and "ho" in the rap community. Layla Turkkan, a Bronx-born rap music entrepreneur, has observed that males sometimes refer to each other as bitches albeit as a form of play.

They'll [men] call each other a bitch. . . . It's really a linguistic thing. It's just [used in] a bunch of boast raps and exaggerated tales. It's just kind of like flexing their muscles, and kind of how they talk when they're hanging out together, but it's not to be taken literally.[62]

The use of bitch in this case parallels that of "ho," as when some male MCs use the word to refer to a sexually promiscuous man rather than a woman, as in Whodini's "I'm a Ho" (1986).[63]

While McCall, Turkkan, and Whodini are among those who express how males commonly refer to both women and men as bitches or hoes, other women, like rapper Queen Latifah, adamantly feel that some rappers are "gettin' a little carried away with that" [bitch-ho references to women].[64]

Regardless of the above, other female rappers have reclaimed the words "bitch" and "ho" in the names of their groups: Bytches with Problems (BWP) and Hoes With Attitude (HWA). Rapper Yo-Yo founded Intelligent Black Women's Coalition in response to the vilification of black women in rap music. Male rapper Too Short reports that using the word "bitch" in his music pays: "Long time ago I couldn't use the word Bitch without being looked down upon by the community . . . but now I can use the term and get paid."[65]

But in spite of the various contexts and ways these words are used, gendered terms can be powerful, especially when "bitch" is used to refer to a physically, emotionally, or sexually frail male as Turkkan's discussion alludes to. Furthermore, some vernacular speakers argue that while "bitch" and "ho" function as humor for some within specific social contexts, their use frequently reinforces patterns of social power while giving men "privileges to perpetuate misogynistic humor [namely] against black women."[66]

MCs use the words *muthafucka* and *nigga*. Commonly used to refer to a low-life, vulgar person or as a racial epithet, these words are reclaimed from their negative associations by hip-hop speakers. For example, "muthafucka" can describe a person of distinction. LL Cool J uses "muthafucka" to say that he has not met anyone who can out-rhyme him.[67]

In both street speech and hip-hop argot "fuck" or "fuckin" is used as a superlative or grammatical intensifier. Doug E. Fresh explains the manner in which it is used as a superlative: "Sometimes you know . . . when they're (rappers) cussin, [they're] getting across a point even stronger sometimes.

You know how somebody say, 'Hey don't do that.' Or if somebody say, 'Hey don't fuck with that.' The effect is much stronger. You know what I mean."[68]

Eventually the superlative and nominal versions of "fuck" are used simultaneously, as observed by this author while attending the Battle of MCs/Deejays Competition held at the Seventh Annual New Music Seminar in New York City in July 1986. In the midst of a finalist's performance, a few rappers from the audience loudly blurted that they wanted to challenge MC Melle Mel, one of the honored judges of the competition. Infuriated by this interruption, the finalist Grandmaster Caz stated to Melle Mel's contenders: "If someone like me don't want to challenge him [Melle Mel], and all these muthafuckas that got the caliber to challenge him don't, y'all bums just stay where the fuck you're at. . . . This is my show, he's [Melle Mel] judgin' my shit and you back the fuck off until this is over with." Caz's words were most effective, for the competition resumed without further delay.

When used in a positive sense, "nigga" enters as a term of endearment for one's buddy or neighborhood friend, and if spoken by a female MC, a male lover. However, the use of this term is solely determined by the word when an adjective or possessive precedes it: *my* nigga, *main* nigga, *real* nigga, or its acronymic rendering as in 2Pac's song "Strictly 4 My N.I.G.G.A.Z."[69] More negative associations of this word as heard by this author include, "two-minute motherfucka" (a sexually inept man)[70] "house niggaz,"[71] "fake nigga," and "bitch nigga."

Rappers highlight their lyrical dexterity through braggadocio. As boasting and exaggerated language escalates, it evolves into a form of signifyin(g) known to the rap community as "dissin," the act of *dis*respecting or downplaying someone else's attributes while praising one's self. During the formative years of rap music, it was not unusual for an MC to verbally challenge an opponent through freestylin. Famous battles (contests) included KRS-One of BDP and MC Shan of the Juice Crew and Busy Bee and Kool Moe Dee. Many of these contests were live, unrehearsed performances, but as rap music grew into a commercial music industry, verbal battles ensued on record. A memorable recording was the battle between veteran Kool Moe Dee and his then younger challenger LL Cool J in the late 1980s—"Let's Go" (1988) and "Jack The Ripper" (1988), for example.

Music Making Practices

Rap artists will forthrightly admit that

> . . . rap groups don't need no band.
> All we need in order to achieve,

is some help from the master [disc jockey] you better
believe . . .
The deejay will give you one-hundred percent.[72]

Each rap group has a DJ whose sole responsibility is to provide the musical
soundtrack by which MCs construct rhyming couplets and to which the
dancers rock. The DJ who supplies "one-hundred percent" possesses an
excellent sense of timing and a mastery of turntable techniques.

The soundtrack is composed of what DJs call "breaks" or "break-
beats"—collages of musical fragments from prerecorded songs. Break-beats
are created via various turntable techniques. Several of these were
previously introduced—scratching, backspinning, and phasing. DJs of the
turntable, dubbed turntabalists, also use additional techniques, "cutting"
and "blending." In cutting, the DJ repeats a word or musical phrase
through editing. In blending, the DJ combines music or text from two different disks to create a "new" piece of music.[73] Ethnomusicologist Miles
White, who conducted a study of the turntable, divided mixing techniques
into those using a single turntable and those using dual turntables. He
found that while backspinning, scratching, and cutting can all be executed
on a single turntable, mixing, blending, and punch-phrasing (phasing) require two turntables. Furthermore, with the use of two turntables, DJs can
fuse break-beats or collages of sound from prerecorded disks into one cohesive unit.

Since mixing requires precision and a good sense of inner timing, DJs
use a headphone during performances in order to precisely determine
break-beats as well as to cue-up records. Developing an acuity for break-
beats requires knowledge of dance favorites, from percussion-oriented
songs such as "Apache" by Incredible Bongo Band and "It's Just Begun"
by Jimmy Castor, to heavy funk beats like "Funky Drummer" by James
Brown, "Flashlight" by Parliament-Funkadelic, or the mellow sounds of
"Between the Sheets" by the Isley Brothers. Although the success of a DJ
is based on his or her repertory of break-beats, uncovering them and then
protecting one's "trade secret" can be quite tedious. During the 1970s, DJs
like Afrika Bambaataa and Kool Herc were known to soak off record labels
so other DJs would not know the names of the break-beats. According to
Jazzy Jay, a protégé of Afrika Bambaataa, "[w]e'd find these beats, these
heavy percussive beats . . . a lot of times it would be a two-second spot, a
drum beat, a drum break, and we'd mix that back and forth, extend it,
make it 20 minutes long."[74]

In the 1980s, shopping for break-beats presented few problems because
of existing compilations. Record collector Lenny Roberts compiled more
than twenty volumes of break-beats in *Ultimate Breaks and Beats* (n.d.).
Roberts's series was distributed by the late Stanley Platzer, a well-known
hip-hop record dealer at the famous Music Factory in New York City.[75]

Following in a similar vein, some of the most sampled artists in rap music have decided to release compilations of their music. For example, funkster George Clinton, progenitor of the group Parliament-Funkadelic, has a two-volume set compilation, *Parliament: Tear the Roof Off, 1974–1980*, in response to those DJs who need access to his music. But by the 1990s, with the growing value placed on originality, DJs shifted from compilations to searching out their own beat material. For example, Bronx DJ Diamond, who owns thousands of old recordings, believes that there is an art to finding a break that somebody else does not know about: "It makes people go, 'Oh shit, where'd he get that from?' That's part of the mystique."[76]

By the mid-1980s, DJs supplemented the manual process of mixing music with digital sampling and the use of synthesizers, including drum machines. Sampling allows DJs to mix and mingle bits and pieces of breaks from records into musical collages of sounds.[77] Because of their raw sound quality, the most popular samplers used are the Akai S900 and the sampling drum machine, the Emu Sp1200 and the Roland TR-808. Mixes with the heavy "kick" characteristic of the Roland TR-808 quality are appropriately termed "boom-bap."

Hence, rap DJs experiment with, yet bend, the Western norms of timbre and texture homogeneity to create a new aesthetic. Ethnomusicologist Portia K. Maultsby observes that

the unique sound associated with black music results from the manipulation of timbre, texture and shaping in ways uncommon to Western practice. Musicians bring intensity to their performance by alternating lyrical, percussive, and raspy timbres; juxtaposing vocal and instrumental textures; changing pitch at dynamic levels; alternating straight with vibrato tones and weaving moans, shouts, grunts, hollers, and screams into the melody.[78]

Through digital sampling, rap DJs fuse various timbres and textures: voluminous bass sounds (that is, bass guitar and drum), strident piercing sounds (for example, high glissandi), static "noise," harmonic dissonance, and a battery of vocal ornamentations from James Brown's yells, grunts, moans, and shouts to speech excerpts. According to Cedric Singleton of Black Market Records, the music of Public Enemy (PE) represents quintessence of the fusing aesthetic because of the group's use of "a whole lot of sampling. They get a groove going and build on top of that groove, and build on top of that groove; they just build on top of grooves. They are like an enigma too."[79] PE's concept, the mastermind of the Bomb Squad (a production team composed of Hank Shocklee, Eric Sadler, and others), employs dissonant sonorities, booming bass guitar and kick bass drum sounds, interlocking speech and music rhythms, and a boisterous-aggressive rap style, best exemplified in "Fight the Power."[80]

Texture and timbre qualities are distinct to geographical regions as well.

For example, in areas where a car culture reigns, like Miami and Los Angeles, the booming bass and closed-kick (short delay in sound) created on the Roland TR-808 tend to dominate in mixes, as DJs create soundtracks for cars rather than home stereo systems. Thus, rap musicians coined the term "jeep beats" when referring to booming bass soundtracks. Rap producer Marley Marl contends that rap is music "made for steering (cruising)," as in volumes 1 and 2 of his album *Steering Pleasure*. Marl states that he made his album "for people who wanna have som'n cool playing in their rides. You won't get the same effect if you play the tracks through a regular system; you need a hype car system. The beats are programmed to make the speakers howl."[81]

Paramusical-lingual Factors

Rap music is undoubtedly an amalgam of street language coding, style, and raw beats. But on a paramusical-lingual level, particular posturing, dress, jewelry, and hairstyles underscore the message of the music. One veteran rapper discusses the importance of bringing a hip-hop posture to the stage via basic gestures.

It's like a performance. You've got to give them [audience] a good performance. It has a lot of acting to do with it. You have to act it out. You've got to make the audience feel what you're saying and understand it as well . . . sort of like a hip hop thing in the street. The young kids relate to the hand movements when they're talking . . . and when they see you doing that on stage, they could really relate to that.[82]

Gestures are further used to accentuate the messages rap artists are trying to convey to their audiences. For example, facial expressions are particularly important when rappin in the hardcore style. In many cases, rap artists prefer not to smile on stage during a performance. As rapper Sparky Dee states: "You have to come hard . . . If you come soft, you get booed off the stage; and you can't smile."[83] Additionally, the libation gesture as seen in gangsta rap videos during the 1990s finds its roots in a ceremony derived from African rituals. Following that tradition, rap artists occasionally pour a bottle of beer onto the ground in recognition of dead *homies* (neighborhood peers) who have been stricken by gang-related violence.

Rap artists regard clothing also as "a way to make the most powerful statement about themselves."[84] Attire visually conveys the message, image, and style of a rap artist. For example, Flavor Flav of Public Enemy wears a huge clock strung around his neck to signify black social consciousness time; the group members also dress in army fatigues to represent their militant stance. West Coast gangsta rappers appropriate the Chicano *cholo* style with the wearing of bandannas, oversized pants with shirt tails worn outside. The duo Kris Kross popularized baggy jeans worn backwards, while others, including Arrested Development and Nefertiti, ushered in the wearing of traditional African clothes—kente hats, fezzes, or kufi (crowns) with the Kemetic ankh emblem and African dress. Particular to the shapely woman, fly girl or attractive female stylists of rap such as Salt'N'Pepa and Yo-Yo, is the wearing of tight-fitting shorts called pum-pums, specific to reggae dancehall culture. In response to the street style, fashion designers created hip-hop clothing lines that are advertised in rapzines and stage performances or modeled by hip-hop artists in their music videos. Noted designers of these fashions are Phat Farm, Karl Kani, Enyce, Fubu, Tommy Hilfiger, and Davoucci, to name but a few.

Articles of jewelry also signify political statements. Gold chains, brace-lets, and earrings are considered trademarks of most rappers. Male rappers are known for wearing large, seemingly heavy gold necklaces, whereas fe-males place more emphasis on large, seemingly heavy gold earrings. In addition, hairstyles, from elaborate braiding, blonde hairdo's, finger waves, dreadlocks, Afros, to baldness are consistent with the rapper's personal attitude. Other dress paraphernalia is the wearing of sunglasses, which con-veys an air of "coolness." Often characterized as a street-derived pose adopted by black males, Richard Majors contends that the purpose of "be-ing cool" is to enhance social competence, pride, dignity, self-esteem, and respect.[85] Artists who have traditionally expressed the posture of coolness in performances by wearing sunglasses include Kool Moe Dee and Profes-sor X of X-Clan.[86]

CONCLUSION

Rap music is a musical form that encapsulates urban African American street aesthetics and traditions, and expresses the every day realities of ur-ban African Americans' lives in contemporary society. Central to under-standing this form is viewing it as part of a continuum of African American expressive culture. Antecedents of rap include the African bardic tradition, blues, toasts, jive, black radio DJs, and funk/soul style jive.

The effectiveness of a performance involves the careful rendering of all the above concepts: black language and rhetorical style, music-making practices, and paramusical-lingual features. All these aspects of perfor-mance are important in the interpretation of the rap tradition. Through performance, rap artists display aspects of urban street culture as exhibited through language dress, gestures, and, above all, style. Despite its over-whelming success in the musical mainstream, rap remains very street-oriented. Rap unfolds as a complex form that is rooted in the aesthetic philosophy, ideology, and tradition of urban black street culture. Hence, the social dynamics of the street milieu give shape, depth, meaning, and essence to this musical tradition.

NOTES

1. Although Sugarhill Gang is credited as the initial rap group to receive national exposure, members of the New York rap community credit the Fatback Band, a New York-based funk group, as recording the first and authentic rap song "King Tim III" (1979). "King Tim III" was released several months before "Rapper's Delight."

2. See Juan Williams, "Fighting Words," *Washington Post*, 15 October 1989, secs. G1 and G8–9; Jerry Adler, Jennifer Foote and Ray Sawhill, "Rap Rage." *Newsweek*, March 19, 1990, 56–59; Phyllis Stark, "Gangsta Rap Under the Gun," *Billboard*, December 18, 1993, 1, 103; and John M. Broder, "Dole Indicts Hollywood for Debasing Culture," *Los Angeles Times*, 1 June 1995, secs. A1, A15.

3. David Nathan, "Major Labels are Suddenly Singing a Different Tune While Indies Grow Stronger as Rap Emerges as The Most Popular Vital New Music Form of the '80s," *Billboard*, December 24, 1988, sec. R10.

4. Steve Fox, interview with Lisa Robinson, "Rappin' to the Beat," *20/20* transcript, (July 9, 1981), p. 13.

5. *Positively Black*—a New York City–based television program feature segment on rap music (December 7, 1987).

6. Many of the 1950's films in which one finds rock 'n' roll music include *The Wild One* (1954), *Rebel Without a Cause* (1955), and *Blackboard Jungle* (1955), for example.

7. Don Thomas, "Puttin' the Rap on 'Rap Attacks,' " *Big Red*, July 26, 1986, p. 20.

8. Houston Baker, *Black Studies, Rap, and The Academy* (Chicago: University of Chicago Press, 1993), 63. 2 Live Crew won all of their court cases through testimonies of expert witnesses hired by their lawyer. Among the expert witnesses was Henry Louis Gates, Jr., a scholar of black culture and literature. Gates testified that 2 Live Crew were simply utilizing the art of signifying, which he describes as "one of the most venerated forms of art" in African American vernacular speech. For further information about the details and comments of Gates's testimony, see Sara Rimer, "Rap Band Members Found Not Guilty in Obscenity Trial," *New York Times*, 19 October 1990, secs. A1, A30.

9. Michael Eric Dyson, *Between God and Gangsta Rap: Bearing Witness to Black Culture* (New York: Oxford University Press, 1996), 103.

10. Craig Rosen et al. "House Panel to Examine Rap," *Billboard*, February 19, 1994, 103.

11. n.a. "Marsalis Rips Rap and Heavy Metal Musicians," *Jet*, (November 6, 1989), p. 22. See also Richard Ahrens, "Rap: Music? Not!," *Los Angeles Times*, 24 June 1995, sec. F6.

12. Eugene Perkins, *Home Is a Dirty Street: The Social Oppression of Black Children* (Chicago: Third World Press, 1975), 26.

13. Quoted in Alan Dundes's *Mother Wit From the Laughing Barrel: Readings in the Interpretation of Afro-American Folklore* (New York: Garland, 1981), 354.

14. Dan Burley, "The Technique of Jive," in *Mother Wit from the Laughing Barrel: Readings in the Interpretation of Afro-American Folklore*, ed. Alan Dundes (1973; reprint, New York: Garland, 1981), 207.

15. Ibid.

16. Clyde Taylor, "The Language of Hip: From Africa To What's Happening Now" *First World* (January/February 1977): 31.

17. Ibid., 30.

18. Rising diagonal mark indicates the common word/phrase equivalent.

19. Nelson George, *The Death of Rhythm & Blues* (New York: Plume, 1988), 42, 116–118.

20. Dizzy Gillespie with Al Fraser, *To Be or No . . . To Bop* (New York: Doubleday 1979), 281.

21. Norman W. Spaulding, "History of Black Oriented Radio in Chicago, 1920–1963" (Ph.D. diss., University of Illinois, 1981), 123–124.

22. Gilbert A. Williams, "The Black Disc Jockey As A Cultural Hero." *Popular Music and Society* 10 no. 3 (October): p. 81.

23. Similar to Henry Louis Gates's (1986) rationale for the respelling of signifying as signifyin(g) to account for black speakers' pronunciation, I have chosen to spell rapping throughout my text without the g. This spelling also captured the way the word is pronounced by hip-hop speakers as well.

24. H. Rap Brown, "Street Smarts," in *Mother With from the Laughing Barrel: Readings in the Interpretation of Afro-American Folklore*, 1973. Reprint. edited by Alan Dundes (New York: Garland, 1981), 354.

25. For further information regarding postindustrial changes and their effects on cities like New York, see Kenneth Jackson, *Crabgrass Frontier: The Suburbanization of the United States* (New York: Oxford University Press, 1985); John Mollenkopf and Manuel Castells, eds. *Dual City: Restructuring New York* (Princeton: Princeton University Press, 1991); Jim Rooney, *Organizing the South Bronx* (Albany: State University of New York, 1995). In assessing the effects of these changes on the musical landscape of New York City, see Steven Hager, *Hip Hop: The Illustrated History of Break Dancing, Rap Music, and Graffiti* (New York: St. Martin's Press, 1984); Tricia Rose, *Black Noise: Rap Music and Black Culture in Contemporary America* (Hanover: Wesleyan/New England, 1994); and Cheryl L. Keyes, "At The Crossroads: Rap Music and Its African Nexus," *Ethnomusicology*, 40, no. 2 (Spring/Summer, 1996): 223–248.

26. Telephone interview with The Real Roxanne, Brooklyn, New York, July 30, 1986.

27. Since Theodore's innovation, the art of "scratching" has been advanced by contemporary hip-hop DJs. For further information, see *Rap Pages* article by Doc Rice, "The Language of Scratching" (September 1998): 30.

28. Although popular rapzines—*The Source, Rap Pages, Vibe, Blaze,* and England's *Hip-Hop Connection*—spotlight rap music in various parts of the world, specific studies or featured stories have also addressed the dispersal of hip-hop culture and rap music. See, for example, James Bernard, "A Newcomer Abroad, Rap Speaks Up," and Steven Erlanger, et al.,"The Many Accents of Rap Around the World," *New York Times*, 23 August 1992, Sec. 2, pp. 1, 22–23; Brian Cross, *It's Not About a Salary . . . : Rap, Race, and Resistance in Los Angeles* (New York: Verso Press, 1993); André J. M. Prévos, "The Evolution of French Rap and Hip Hop Culture in the 1980s and 1990s," *French Review* 69, no. 5, (April 1996): 713–725.

29. Debi Fee, "Rap Producers: Taking on the Challenge of Creating a Sense of Longevity Amid Change," *Billboard* (December 24, 1988): R8.

30. Ibid., Sec. R21.

31. *Yo! MTV Raps*, hosted by Fab 5 Freddy (February 11, 1995).

32. See John Baugh, *Black Street Speech: Its History, Structure and Survival* (Texas Linguistics Series. Austin: University of Texas Press, 1983), p 5.

33. Also refer to Fab 5 Freddy, *Words & Phrases of the Hip-Hop Generation* (Stamford: Longmeadow Press, 1992); and Clarence Major, *Juba to Jive: A Dictionary of African-American Slang* (New York: Penguin, 1994).

34. David Hinckley, "You Can 'Run,' But You Can't Hide," *Daily News*, 16 July 1986, p. 21.

35. Tupac Shakur, *Conversation with Ed Gordon*, Washington, DC: Black Entertainment Television (BET) (aired September 21, 1994).

36. When Calvin Broadus was recording under the Death Row label, his stage name was Snoop Doggy Dogg. However, when he left Death Row in 1998 to join Master P's No Limits Records, he dropped Doggy and currently goes by the stage name Snoop Dogg.

37. Interview with Sal Abbatiello, Bronx, New York, June 3, 1986.

38. Ibid.

39. Russell A. Potter, *Spectacular Vernaculars: Hip-Hop and the Politics of Postmodernism* (Albany: State University of New York, 1995), 115.

40. Thomas Kochman, *Black and White: Styles in Conflict* (Chicago: University of Chicago Press, 1981), 130.

41. Geneva Gay, "Expressive Ethos of Afro-American Culture," in *Expressively Black: the Cultural Basis of Ethnic Identity*, edited by Geneva Gay and Willie L. Baber (New York: Praeger, 1987), 9.

42. Ibid., 8–9.

43. Run-DMC, "Sucker M.C.'s." *Run DMC* (Profile PRO-1202A, 1984).

44. There is the belief that women MCs cannot write excellent rhymes like their male counterparts. As such, some manager-producers invite male MCs to write the lyrics for their female clients. In refuting this stereotype, Queen Pen uses her name to indicate that she "pens" her own lyrics.

45. Tommy Lott, "Marooned in America: Black Urban Youth Culture and Social Pathology." In *The Underclass Question*, edited by Bill E. Lawson (Philadelphia: Temple University Press, 1992), 84, 89(N54).

46. Michael Dyson, "Culture of Hip-Hop." *Zeta* (June 1989): 50.

47. Pearl Williams-Jones, "Afro-American Gospel Music: A Crystallization of the Black Aesthetic." *Ethnomusicology* 19, no. 3 (September 1975): 381.

48. Richard Ahrens, "Rap: Music? Not!," *Los Angeles Times*, 24 June 1995, sec. F6.

49. George List, "The Boundaries of Speech and Song." *Ethnomusicology*, 7, no. 1 (1963): 253.

50. Interview with Afrika Bambaataa, Manhattan, New York, June 10, 1986.

51. Interview with Marc Blake, Long Island, New York, August 24, 1986.

52. Interview with Melle Mel, Manhattan, New York, June 7, 1986.

53. In examining this concept as an overarching aesthetic common to all hip-hop arts, see Tricia Rose, *Black Noise: Rap Music and Black Culture in Contemporary America* (Hanover: Wesleyan/New England Press, 1994), 38–39.

54. Interview with *Dynasty*, Manhattan, New York, May 23, 1986.

55. Geneva Smitherman, *Talkin and Testifyin: The Language of Black America* (Detroit: Wayne State University Press, 1986), 121.

56. Interview with Cedric Singleton, Manhattan, New York, October 12, 1992.

57. Telephone interview with Larry Smith, Brooklyn, New York, July 12, 1986.

58. "The Message" ranks as the first politically toned rap in the annals of popular music history. According to Sugar Hill Records cofounder Joe Robinson, it was written and performed by Melle Mel and Duke Bootee, a percussionist in the house band of Sugar Hill Records. The following lyrics, however, are performed by Melle Mel.

59. Henry Louis Gates, Jr., *The Signifying Monkey: A Theory of African-American Literary Criticism* (New York: Oxford University Press, 1988), 81.

60. Claudia Mitchell-Kernan, "Signifying As a Form of Verbal Art," in *Mother Wit From the Laughing Barrel: Readings in the Interpretation of Afro-American Folklore*, ed. Alan Dundes (1973; reprint, Garland Press, 1981), 325.

61. Nathan McCall, *Makes Me Wanna Holler: A Young Black Man in America* (New York: Vintage Books, 1994), 40, 42.

62. Interview with Layla Turkkan, Manhattan, New York, November 23, 1992.

63. Whodini, "I'm a Ho." *Back in Black* (Jive/Arista JC8-8407, 1986).

64. Interview with Queen Latifah, Jersey City, New Jersey, July 8, 1993.

65. *Rap City Rhapsody*. 1990. Produced by Akili Buchanan, KQED, Inc.

66. Kimberle Crenshaw, "Beyond Racism and Misogyny: Black Feminism and 2 Live Crew," *Boston Review*, 16, no. 6 (December 1991), 32.

67. LL Cool J., "I'm Bad." *Bigger and Deffer*. [12-inch LP] (Jive 1178-4-JS, 1989).

68. Interview with Doug E. Fresh, Manhattan, New York, August 19, 1986.

69. The late 2Pac used this phrase for the title cut from his sophomore album *Strictly 4 My N.I.G.G.A.Z* (1993). On his debut album *2Pocalypse Now* (1991), 2Pac decodes each letter of N.I.G.G.A.Z—Never Ignorant Getting Goals Accomplished—in the sociopolitical song "Words of Wisdom."

70. "Two-minute motherfucker" is a phrase used in the song "Two Minute Brother" by Bytches with Problems (BWP), which depicts a man who is unable to sustain lovemaking past two minutes.

71. "House Nigga," defined by African Americans as a black person who reports to whites or outsiders about the intimate business of his or her people. This term is also the name of a song by KRS-One (1991).

72. Whodini, "Funky Beat." *Back In Black* (Jive/Arista JCB-8407, 1986).

73. See Miles White, "The Phonograph Turntable and Performance Practice in Hip-Hop Music: Classifactory, Analytic and Applied Aspects of Organological Inquiry." Paper presented at the 41st Annual Meeting of the Society for Ethnomusicology, Toronto, Canada, (October 31–November 3, 1996).

74. John Leland and Steve Stein. "What It Is," *The Village Voice: Hip Hop Nation* (January 19, 1988), 26.

75. Ibid., 26–28.

76. S. H. Fernando, "Spinning Isn't Everything," *The Source: the Magazine of Hip-Hop Music, Culture & Politics* (September 1995), 54.

77. Mar Kemp. "Name That Tune: Sampling—Whose Music Is It Anyway?" *Option* (May–June, 1989), 26.

78. Portia K. Maultsby, "Africanisms in African-American Music," in *Africanisms in American Culture*, ed. Joseph E. Holloway (Bloomington: University of Indiana Press, 1990), 191–192.

79. Interview with Cedric Singleton, Manhattan, New York, October 12, 1992.

80. See Keyes, "At the Crossroads" (1996).

81. Quoted in Havelock Nelson, "Marley Marl: Soul Controller, Sole Survivor," *The Source: The Magazine of Hip-Hop Music, Culture, & Politics* (October 1991), 39.

82. Telephone interview with The Real Roxanne, Brooklyn, New York, July 30, 1986.

83. Jill Pearlman, "Girls Rappin' Round Table," *The Paper* (Summer 1988), 27.

84. Thomas Kochman, *Black and White: Styles in Conflict* (Chicago: University of Chicago Press, 1981), 132.

85. Richard Majors and Janet Mancini Billson, *Cool Pose: The Dilemmas of Black Manhood in America* (New York: Lexington Books, 1992), 105.

86. For further information on rap artists and the aesthetic of "coolness," see Keyes, "At the Crossroads."

BIBLIOGRAPHY

Abbatiello, Sal. Interview with the author. Bronx, New York. June 3, 1986.

Adler, Jerry, Jennifer Foote, and Ray Sawhill. "Rap Rage." *Newsweek*, 19 March 1990, 56–63.

Baker, Houston A. *Black Studies, Rap, and The Academy*. Chicago: University of Chicago Press, 1993.

Bambaataa, Afrika. Interview with the author. Manhattan, New York. June 10, 1986.

Baugh, John. *Black Street Speech: Its History, Structure and Survival*. Texas Linguistics Series. Austin: University of Texas Press, 1983.

Bernard, James, et al. "A Newcomer Abroad, Rap Speaks Up," and "The Many Accents of Rap Around the World." *New York Times*, 23 August 1992, sec. 2: 1, 22–23.

Blake, Marc. Interview with the author. Long Island, New York. August 24, 1986.

Braxton, Greg and Jerry Crowe. "Black Leaders Weighing In on Rap Debate." *Los Angeles Times* (June 14, 1995), pp. F1; F8.

Brown, H. Rap. "Street Smarts." In *Mother Wit from the Laughing Barrel: Readings in the Interpretation of Afro-American Folklore*. 1973. Reprint, edited by Alan Dundes, New York: Garland Press, 1981.

Burley, Dan. "The Technique of Jive." In *Mother Wit from The Laughing Barrel: Readings in the Interpretation of Afro-American Folklore*, 1973. Reprint, edited by Alan Dundes, New York: Garland Press, 1981.

Crenshaw, Kimberle. "Beyond Racism and Misogyny: Black Feminism and 2 Live Crew." *Boston Review* 16, no. 6 (December 1991): 6, 30–33.

Cross, Brian. *It's Not About a Salary . . . : Rap, Race, and Resistance in Los Angeles*. New York: Verso, 1993.

Cut Master D.C. Interview with the author. Brooklyn, New York. June 21, 1986.

Doug E. Fresh. Interview with the author. Manhattan, New York. August 19, 1986.

Dynasty. Interview with the author, Manhattan, New York. August 18, 1986.

Dyson, Michael. "Culture of Hip-Hop." *Zeta* (June 1989): 44–50.

———. *Between God and Gangsta Rap: Bearing Witness to Black Culture*. New York: Oxford, 1996.

Fab 5 Freddy. *Words & Phrases of the Hip-Hop Generation*. Stamford, Conn.: Longmeadow Press, 1992.

Fee, Debi. "Rap Producers: Taking on the Challenge of Creating a Sense Longevity Amid Change." *Billboard* (December 24, 1988): R-8, 21.

Fernando, S. H. "Spinning Isn't Everthing." *The Source: The Magazine of Hip-Hop Music, Culture, and Politics* (September 1994): 54–56.

Fox, Steve. "Rappin' to the Beat." 20/20 transcript (July 9, 1981): 11–14.

Gates, Henry Louis Jr. *The Signifying Monkey: A Theory of African-American Literary Criticism*. New York: Oxford University Press, 1988.

Gay, Geneva. "Expressive Ethos of Afro-American Culture." In *Expressively Black: The Cultural Basis of Ethnic Identity*. Edited by Geneva Gay and Willie L. Baber. New York: Praeger, 1987.

George, Nelson. *The Death of Rhythm and Blues*. New York: Plume, 1988.

Gillespie, Dizzy with Al Fraser. *To Be or No . . . To Bop*. New York: Doubleday, 1979.

Glasgow, Douglas. *The Black Underclass: Poverty, Unemployment, and Entrapment of Ghetto Youth*. San Francisco: Jossey-Bass, 1980.

Hager, Steven. *Hip-Hop: The Illustrated History of Break Dancing, Rap Music, and Graffiti*. New York: St. Martin's Press, 1984.

Jackson, Kenneth. *Crabgrass Frontier: The Suburbanization of the United States*. New York: Oxford University Press, 1985.

Kemp, Mar. "Name That Tune: Sampling—Whose Music Is It Anyway?" *Option* (May–June 1989): 66–69, 129.

Keyes, Cheryl L. "At the Crossroads: Rap Music and Its African Nexus." *Ethnomusicology* 40, no. 2 (Spring/Summer 1996): 223–248.

Kochman, Thomas. *Black and White: Styles in Conflict*. Chicago: University of Chicago Press, 1981.

Leland, John and Steve Stein. "What It Is," *The Village Voice*, Hip Hop Nation Special Section (January 19, 1988): 26–30.

List, George. "The Boundaries of Speech and Song." *Ethnomusicology*, no. 71 (1963): 252–268.

Lott, Tommy. "Marooned in America: Black Urban Youth Culture and Social Pathology." In *The Underclass Question*. Edited by Bill E. Lawson. Philadelphia: Temple University Press, 1992.

Major, Clarence. *Juba to Jive: A Dictionary of African-American Slang*. New York: Penguin, 1994.

Majors, Richard and Janet Mancini Billson. *Cool Pose: The Dilemmas of Black Manhood in America*. New York: Touchstone/Simon & Schuster, 1992.

"Marsalis Rips Rap and Heavy Metal Musicians." *Jet* (November 6, 1989), p. 22.

Maultsby, Portia K. "Africanisms in African-American Music." In *Africanisms in American Culture*. Edited by Joseph E. Holloway. Bloomington: University of Indiana Press, 1990.

McCall, Nathan. *Makes You Wanna Holler: A Young Black Man in America*. New York: Vintage Books, 1994.

Melle Mel. Interview with the author. Manhattan, New York. June 7, 1986.

Mitchell-Kernan, Claudia. "Signifying as a Form of Verbal Art." In *Mother Wit from the Laughing Barrel: Readings in the Interpretation of Afro-American Folklore*. Edited by Alan Dundes, 1973. Reprint, edited by Alan Dundes, New York: Garland Press, 1981.

Mollenkopf, John and Manuel Castells, eds. *Dual City: Restructuring New York.* New York: Russell Sage Foundation, 1991.

Moon, Tom. 1991. "Public Enemy's Bomb Squad." *Musician* (October): 69–72, 76.

Nathan, David. "The Majors: Marketing Campaign Yield Spectacular Results as Activated Labels Gear Up for Record Year." *Billboard* (June 18, 1988): B3, B14, B22.

Nelson, Havelock. "Marley Marl: Soul Controller, Sole Survivor." *The Source: The Magazine of Hip-Hop Music, Culture & Politics* (October 1991): 36–39.

Pearlman, Jill. "Girls Rappin' Round Table." *The Paper* (Summer 1988): 25–27.

Perkins, Eugene. *Home Is a Dirty Street: The Social Oppression of Black Children.* Chicago: Third World Press, 1975.

Positively Black (aired December 7, 1987).

Potter, Russell A. *Spectacular Vernaculars: Hip-Hop and the Politics of Postmodernism,* 1995.

Prevos, Andre J. M. "The Evolution of French Rap and Hip Hop Culture in the 1980s and 1990s." *French Review* 69, no. 5 (April 1996): 713–725.

Queen Latifah. Interview with the author, Jersey City, New Jersey. July 8, 1993.

Rap City Rhapsody. 1990. Produced by Akili Buchanan, KQED, Inc.

Rappin (July 1990): 24, 31.

The Real Roxanne. Telephone interview with the author. Brooklyn, New York. July 30, 1986.

Rice, Doc. "The Language of Scratching." *Rap Pages: The Survival Guide for Hip-Hop Culture, Lifestyles, and Music.* (September 1998): 30.

Rooney, Jim. *Organizing the South Bronx.* Albany: State University of New York, 1995.

Rose, Tricia. *Black Noise: Rap Music and Black Culture in Contemporary America.* Hanover: Wesleyan/New England, 1994.

Rosen, Craig. "House Panel to Examine Rap." *Billboard* (February 19, 1994): 1, 103.

Shakur, Tupac. *Conversation with Ed Gordon.* Washington, DC: Black Entertainment Television (BET) (aired September 21, 1994).

Singleton, Cedric. Interview with the author. Manhattan, New York. October 12, 1992.

Smith, Larry. Telephone interview with the author. Brooklyn, New York. July 12, 1986.

Smitherman, Geneva. *Talkin and Testifyin: The Language of Black America.* 1977 Reprint. Detroit: Wayne State University, 1986.

Spaulding, Norman W. "History of Black Oriented Radio in Chicago, 1929–1963." Ph.D. diss., University of Illinois, 1981.

Stark, Phyllis, "Gangsta Rap Under the Gun." *Billboard* (December 18, 1993): 1, 103.

Taylor, Clyde. "The Language of Hip: From Africa To What's Happening Now." *First World* (January/February): 25–32.

Thomas, Don. "Puttin' the Rap on Rap Attacks." *Big Red* (July 1986): 2–21.

Toop, David. *Rap Attack 2: African Rap to Global Hip Hop.* Revised and Expanded Edition. New York: Serpent's Tail, 1991.

Turkkan, Layla. Interview with the author. Manhattan, New York, November 23, 1992.

White, Miles. "The Phonograph Turntable and Performance Practice in Hip-Hop Music: Classifactory, Analytic and Applied Aspects of Organological Inquiry." Paper presented at the 41st Annual Meeting of the Society of Ethnomusicology, Toronto, Canada, (October 31–November 3, 1996).

Williams, Gilbert A. "The Black Disc Jockey as a Cultural Hero." *Popular Music and Society* Vol. 10, no. 3 (October 1986): 79–90.

Williams-Jones, Pearl. "Afro-American Gospel Music: A Crystallization of the Black Aesthetic." *Ethnomusicology* 19, no. 3 (September 1975): pp. 373–385.

Wilson, Olly. "The Significance of the Relationship Between Afro-American Music and West African Music." *Black Perspective in Music* 2 (Spring 1974): 3–22.

Yo! MTV Raps, hosted by Fab Five Freddy (February 11, 1995 segment).

DISCOGRAPHY

Boogie Down Productions. "My Philosophy." *By All Means Necessary*. Jive/RCA 10934-3, 1988.

———. "House Nigga's." *Edutainment*. Jive 1358, 1990.

Bytches With Problems (BWP). "Two-Minute Brother." *The Bytches*. No Face/RAL CT 47068, 1991.

Lady B. "To the Beat Y'All." *Great Rap Hits*. Sugar Hill SH-246A, 1980.

LL Cool J. "I'm Bad." *Bigger and Deffer*. Def Jam CT40793, 1987.

Melle Mel and Duke Bootee. *The Message* [12-inch disk]. Sugar Hill SH-582, 1982.

Public Enemy. *Fight the Power* [EP]. 1989. Motown MOTC, 1972.

Queen Latifah. "U.N.I.T.Y." *Black Reign*. Motown 37463-6370-4, 1993.

Run-DMC. "Sucker M. C's." *Run-DMC*. Profile PRO-120A, 1984.

2Pac. *Strictly 4 My N.I.G.G.A.Z*. Interscope 7 92209-2, 1993.

Whodini. "I'm a Ho" and "Funky Beat." *Back in Black*. Jive/Arista JC8-8407, 1986.

7

Paying Dues Toward an African American Aesthetic: An Autobiographical Essay

William C. Lowe

In science fiction, the creation of enchained texts bridges political opinion, aesthetic preferences, commitments to hardware or software, and spans all degrees of literary merit.[1] What follows in this chapter is probably not science fiction, but this offering of enchained texts is informed by this author's love for and commitment to the science fiction genre, especially the works of Samuel Delany. It is informed by said love because said love for Delany's and other science fiction writers' work is an integral and self-conscious part of this author's sense of personal and community aesthetic. The enchained and intertwined texts, as well as references to scores and tapes that make up this chapter, certainly bridge political opinion, and they form a political opinion, aesthetically defined.

In the spirit of Delany's *American Shore*, this chapter consists of texts about texts; and these texts about texts become new texts in their own right. Or not.

The major texts are references to and descriptions of scores and recordings of the author's compositions, compositions that were begun and/or completed during, and as planned parts of, the author's study of composition from 1980 through 1989 with Professors William Barron, Charles Garner, Paul DiMarinis, Roger Solie and T. Ranganathan. This study took place within the context of the World Music Program at Wesleyan University, Middletown, Connecticut. As such, the graduate seminar in Ethnomusicology, with Professor David McAllester, is equally relevant. So, who is this author of the chapter, this enchainer of texts and nontexts?

I am a performer (bass trombone and tuba) and a composer, primarily in the jazz tradition, with an undergraduate degree and several years of graduate work in American Studies; since 1970, I have chosen, because I love it, to teach full-time on the college-level in English departments and music departments, to undergraduates and graduate students, for remedial programs and elite northeastern establishments; I have organized day care centers, international jazz festivals, junior high school curricula, and big bands; mostly, I'm at home with music in the theater.

As autobiography, this chapter is the continuation of an older project. As a composer's diary, this chapter is very incomplete because it is limited to the time frame and focus of the older project. The author's work with the late Bill Barron—mentor, teacher, and colleague—is the core of another major and is not included here. Also missing from this chapter are the ongoing collaborations and lessons and gigs and struggles over the years with a host of excellent musicians, including Frank Foster, Jaki Byard, James Jabbo Ware, Bill Russo, Sinclair Acey, Frank Wilkins, Sa Davis, Keith Copeland, David Bindman, Ray Copeland, Leonard Brown . . . to name a very few. The more recent compositional developments, including the Song Cycle "Signifyin' Natives" and involvements with African Diaspora musicians and poets in Cuba and the British Isles, are the results of the aesthetics described in this chapter. The common thread uniting all these efforts is the belief in the necessity of a creative aesthetic informed by human involvement in an ever-shifting and always vital African American cultural context. This chapter is offered as a story about one person's development of such an aesthetic within an environment shaped by the dynamics of living both inside and outside of the education academy.

On one level, this chapter is presented as a piece of music, a composition informed by and in conversation with an African American rhythmic tradition. On another level, this chapter is about music, about the act of composing within an African American rhythmic tradition.

Like most texts, this chapter is also about other texts, other essays. It is about these others in very direct ways (as exemplified by the opening epigraph) and in very, very indirect ways. This chapter is about other texts by professional musicians, such as Marion Brown[2] and Bill Dixon[3] and George Russell[4], who share or have shared "dual" citizenship within and without the academic arena. This chapter is not an attempt to copy these others nor is it necessarily a critique of these others; this chapter simply recognizes its community of discourse, its family.

"REB!" "NIAMBI'S DANCE," "MIBHAW," and "TJBJ": These chapter headings from the author's master's thesis in Composition and Aesthetics[5] are also the titles of the compositions under discussion in this chapter. The compositions speak for themselves: The texts and scores that appear in the master's thesis speak to and for themselves—texts do that, a lot. The commentaries presented in this chapter are not meant to be definitive, exhaustive critiques or explications or analyses of the compositions. The commentaries are in conversation with the scores and the music and are a part of the scores and music, especially considering that the same enchaining mind gave birth to the lot and litter. The commentaries do not attempt to totally explain the compositions, but/and the commentaries, of necessity and design, *do* contain information about the music and the composer and/or the process. Which is really all about trying to define and develop an African American aesthetic: A way of conducting creative business.

Aesthetics in this chapter refers not only to concepts of beauty, but also implies and points to ways and methods and motivations and strategies for getting stuff done; that is, an aesthetic must include a theory for process and for judgment. These theories may not always be stated directly; they may change shape and definition and direction and intensity, but they exist and, therefore, require the intense attention of the developing and developed artist.

A developing African American aesthetic within the context of a World Music university environment must be in conversation with that environment. The aesthetic under consideration in this chapter recognizes its responsibility to not only craft and creativity (narrowly defined), but also welcomes the responsibilities inherent in the teaching process. The old epigram about people who can't do something wind up teaching that something is not considered wisdom in the aesthetic under consideration in this chapter: Teaching *is* a doing, a doing with incredible potential as source and context for the creative enterprise.

Issues of race and class and gender inform and form the cultural conversation known as the African American tradition. This tradition is not only a subject matter of texts and poems and plays and dances and music, it *is* these texts and poems and plays and dances and music. Recognition of and identification with the enslaved and the descendants of the enslaved do not create the African American aesthetic. Conversing with and through and because of and in spite of these recognitions and identifications is the beginning of the creation of an African American aesthetic: a never-ending story, too often told to an idiot, with sound and fury signifying or, rather, SIGNIFYIN'. Monkeys need not apply.

And the craft is of utmost importance. What does the music sound like? Where and how is it going? With the exception of REB!, each of the large ensemble scores and recordings is matched by at least one other recording of a small ensemble version of the scored composition. The movement from small to large is more often than not the regularly working situation, where the big band (unless you are Ellington or Basie or Jabbo Ware or Sun Ra) is a special, every-so-often treat. Much is learned in the small group setting that's then transferred or conversed with in the large band versions of the compositions. In the case of NIAMBI'S DANCE, MIBHAW and TJBJ, the small group version preceded the big band version.

REB!

Originally conceived as the centerpiece of the master's thesis, REB! was the specific focus of much of the author's compositional development at that time: On one level, it is about his journey as a composer. The gathering of many kinds and sizes and textures of ensembles into one is a statement directed to the inherent eclectic reality of the general African American musical environment. This eclectic reality serves as both form and content for the piece.

Juxtapositions abound, but juxtapositioning is not the point. Rather, the manipulations (it is hoped skillfully) of chosen juxtapositions create a rhythm, a rhythm that must then *swing*. Juxtapositioning becomes not the point, but the point of departure. Indeed, in jazz (and other blues-based music) syncopation abounds, but is not really the point; rather, the blues-based swing is the successfully skillful manipulation of syncopations within a context of personalized composition in the moment. Swing is a way of doing rhythmic business. Swing is an attitude, a compositional and performative expectation. Swing is a matter of interpretation and articulation. After the fact, swing can be analyzed as the simultaneous manifestations of duple and triple meters and/or inflections during a sustained performance. The juxtaposition of the duples and the triples inherent to successfully swung music is the stylistic device—the living trope—that is signified in the varied levels of music and meaning of the composition called REB!

Improvisation, like swing, is a requirement of the successful performance of blues-based music. Improvisation is here defined as "composition in the moment." The improviser brings to the improvisational moment more "stuff" than he/she needs; the improvising technique, then, becomes the choosing of which stuff to proclaim or declaim or use or shout or silence at any point in time. These choices occur within the context of many simultaneous conversations: conversations among ensemble members, conversations with the form of the composition, conversations with the history and stylistic integrity/imperatives of the musical genres at hand, conversations with the improviser's own wealth of memory and technique and creative motion. This "stuff" is personal and person specific: my stuff is not necessarily your stuff. And there is no correct amount of "stuff." "Stuff" can include musical ideas and chords and scales and instrumental technique and technical innovations and cultural histories. "Practice" is the space where "stuff" is identified, created, honed, polished, discarded and, ultimately, owned. "Stuff" brought to the improvisational moment is ready to go, hot to trot, and available on immediate demand. And it may never get used! Silence is one of the most effective choices available to the composer and/or improviser: Without silence, music looses its definition. The choice of silence in music creates space. Without space, the improvised line or the composed piece approaches noise: Without space, the improvised line or the composed piece fails to swing.

Which is to say that REB! is supposed to swing on several levels—of meaning and music. The composition manipulates the juxtapositions of symphony orchestra, gospel choir, truncated big band, jazz soloists and Hammond organ to create a rhythm of confused performance practice signals. The manipulation of these apparently disparate performance ensembles into a cohesive, flowing "new" ensemble is the swing of the thing.

Which is not to imply that REB! is the first instance of such amalgamations. On the contrary, the mixing of choir and orchestra and jazz band is as old as the primal conversation between and among African American and Euro-American musical forms/practices. The very development of an African American aesthetic, in time and over time, is the chronicle of the aforementioned conversation. African American aesthetics tend to be about this inherent dualism vis-à-vis the Euro-American "mainstream": The African American modes of expression are both inside and outside the Euro-American mainstream. And, confusingly, the African American aesthetic and/or its conversation with the Euro-American creates or re-creates the mainstream aesthetic. This dualistic aesthetic environment is the context within which REB!'s juxtapositions gain and create meaning. Or ought to, if the piece is/was/will be successful or correct or beautiful or otherwise "good." The development of the African American composer takes place within a cultural arena informed by but not totally controlled by this dualistic aesthetic environment. A part of my response to and participation in and collaboration with this aesthetic dualism is the creation and presentation of the composition called REB!

Which seems like an awful lot of baggage for one twenty-minute oratorio based on/motivated by my belated response to the death of my Grandfather. And it is!

In an honest effort to "de-baggage" the discourse, the reader/audience might be directed to the music itself: Listen to the music![6] Hear the rhythm of form created by the juxtapositioning of jazz/blues-based improvisation within the "confines" of a full symphony orchestra. Notice what happens when the initial dream of a sweet gospel choir is deferred by that initial shout of "REB!," to be followed by the amassed choir reading from my Grandfather's favorite New Testament text (I Corinthians, Chapter 13) while the orchestra and the jazz soloist with rhythm section engage in convers(ion)ation. That's an example of the swing of juxtapositions, not to mention the inherent demand to swing in the "naked blues–based" sense foisted on the solo trumpet, just because he is the solo trumpet and his part calls for jazz improvisation. These many-leveled calls to swing continue throughout the piece. Or not.

And for the composer, REB! is not just about the music. The choice of story line and detail must also be informed by an African American aesthetic and historic sensibility. Maybe it's not the composer's "Great American Novel," but certainly the choice of oratorio hints at a "Great African American Short Story." Listen—and read!

> The fictions of the old men
> are their final fecundity.[7]

REB! was nine months in the making. The overall shape of the piece came early on. (This is not always the case: Some compositions' form/shape remain a mystery unfolding until the end!) An immediate challenge was to consider a number of different ways to utilize the strings: I had never written for strings before; now I had an entire orchestra to write for. Strings could carry melody, of course, and I also wanted to explore the possibilities of the strings as "big organ": harmonic devices that carried chordal information. Jazz phrasing in the string sections would have to be a matter of instruction on my part. A key to the success of the piece was the availability of an orchestra with which to try certain things. Roger Solie and the Wesleyan University Orchestra graciously provided that access.

For the last four months of birthing, REB! was developed as a work in progress in a workshop format: The composer worked out some things, copied parts for a few dozen measures (or less, often), and brought same to an orchestra rehearsal. The combination of composing and arranging and teaching activities made the constructing of REB! very relevant to the composer's aesthetic ideology, which refuses to separate the teaching function from the creative one. When the time/energy spent in the creative process coexists with the time/energy spent in the process of teaching, then the academic environment is transformed into an arena very hospitable to the author's definition of a developing African American aesthetic. When teaching and creating are perceived as necessarily in opposition, then the creator who teaches suffers on both accounts. One must work at creating this environment of mutual creativity. One must negotiate mutual networks of trust and accountability: networks that must include students and student performing groups, academic colleagues from many disciplines, and musical colleagues both inside and outside the academy. Such work is a very important aspect of a living aesthetic. One result of such work is REB! One result of such work is growth as a composer *and* growth as a teacher. "As their flesh once labored to bring forth flesh, so the minds of the elders labor, with a like passion, to bring forth a mind . . . By this they would insure that the race endure as a race of men (sic) [as opposed to animals?]"[8]

REB! is a collage of styles and textures. After the opening declaration of tuba/voices/tutti, the English horn and tuba duet introduces a study in contrasts between a pentatonic scale and its diatonic complement.[9] The solo trumpet improvises over the pentatonic held in the strings, while the choir reads the sacred text. This triple chant of saints is rudely interrupted by a very energetic, rhythmic exploration of melodic material based on the diatonic complement of the original pentatonic. This conversation between pentatonic and diatonic continues, with textual reading for the entirety of the first movement. A punning cry of Mammy, begins near the end of the first movement and becomes the linking motif for the second movement. "Mammy," by the way, caused no small amount of grief for some of the members of the student gospel choir known as the Ebony Singers, in that the cry of "Mammy" in 1984 conjured images of Al Jolson and Aunt Jemima for these youngsters who had never really, personally experienced either of these negative and pervasive icons of African American image assault—but that's another story about the interconnectedness of music making and the teaching of cultural literacy.

The second movement, which is mostly a waltz, is a rendering of an old slave lullaby, which the composer learned from his Grandmother, the wife of the real Reb of REB![10] (The signifying ironies produced by skillful manipulations of self-referentiality are the malleable cornerstones of much African American folklore and its contemporary transformations as blues and hip-hop—so the composer was in the briar patch, doin' his work, with a vengeful passion, punnin' and what not.) The climax of this movement finds a solo violin, improvising in a minor blues form, with the orchestra operating like a BIG big band: more juxtapositioning and exchanged and changed roles.

An electrified "folk, old time" fiddler comments on a slave lullaby with a minor blues, enhanced by a symphony orchestra, while a nonroving band of Ebony Singers concludes its cry for "Mammy" with a stylized shout and lament for a deceased Southern Baptist preacher: This is the second movement of REB!, which may or may not be some signifying in the general direction of poet/novelist Ishmael Reed and *his* signifying on the beauty and excesses of a self-conscious and historic African American aesthetic and aesthetic theory.[11]

REB! the composition is dramatic in intent. Consider the Interlude. Right after the blues and before the gospel hymn, there is nothing except the choir: voices lifted, not in song or praise, but in whispered utterances of confusion—literally, a vamp, a riff on the main theme, "Reb!": a prelude, a fitting, historically precise transition to a gospel icon, a true trope, the venerable "Precious Lord." A most fitting quiet before the sacred storm. "The Baptist preacher is clearly tuned in to the spirit force that solidifies the community; so is James Brown, as was Bird, and now the new generation poets.[12]

Dowling, Dorsey, and "Precious Lord" have got their NOMMO workin'. The Reverend C. D. Dowling, a short, strong black Southern Baptist minister, was known to friend, foe, and family (including his four-eyed firstborn grandson) as Reb. A preacher/scholar/carpenter who was also a musician, Reb's favorite of favorite "church" songs was "Precious Lord": which is one reason why it was sung at his funeral. Thomas A. Dorsey, a short, strong black southern blues pianist of world renown (he was an accompanist and arranger and composer for many blues singers, including Ma Rainey), left the secular life to become the undisputed "Father of Gospel Music."[13] Talent scout (he "discovered" and then championed the careers of both Mother Willie Mae Ford Smith and Sallie Martin) and a very prolific gospel composer, Dorsey is most widely known as the composer of "Precious Lord." This now-classic composition was inspired by Dorsey's musings over the tragic and totally unexpected death of his first wife and their young child while he (Dorsey) was on the road spreading the gospel.[14] "Precious Lord" is truly a blues-based gospel hymn.

Dowling, Dorsey, and "Precious Lord," with NOMMO working, are a gathering of power, of force, of magic. In the hands of the composer, these three undergo the aesthetic transformation. The historic/cultural events of Dowling, Dorsey, and "Precious Lord" are transformed into a stylistic device: in this case, the "Precious Lord Fantasy" in the composition called REB!. Cultural events are transformed into stylistic devices, which have lives of their own. Stylistic devices can be shared, they can be stolen, they can be manipulated, they can be transformed, they can become cultural events of their own. How and why and when and where these transformations occur is the stuff of aesthetic definition, the content of the creative/critical process. All this, and improvisation, too.

In *Bedouin Hornbook*[15] (which, like Jean Toomer's *Cane*, may or may not be a novel), Nathaniel Mackey invents a fictional musical ensemble, the "East Bay Dread Ensemble," whose sound/music he invokes by reference to actual recordings of known jazz/First World artists (Bill Dixon's solo on such and such recording from 19 so and so). Thus, recordings are used as referents so that the narrative can have detail and, therefore, believable meaning. In the last movement of REB!, a partial transcription of a Charlie Parker recorded improvisation is used as melodic material for the strings as a way of invoking a believable sense of historic time flow in the musical narrative. This improvisation, which was recorded and then transcribed is both partner to and victim (?) of a series of transformations as a stylistic device becomes a cultural event—the ending of REB!, and this ending recalls the beginning and lies straight ahead. Listen to the music.

Narrative, gospel hymn, song for my Grandfather, slave lullaby transformed into a violin-inspired minor blues, transcribed be-bop, explorations of pentatonic scales, improvisations collated within very composed structures for large ensembles, explorations of voice and voicings for choir, new music and old referents: these are what REB! was/is. What REB! has become is something else again.

This something else was described by the composer in the following request for collaboration with the Rites and Reasons Theater at Brown University.

INTERLUDE: RITES AND REASONS

I said, RITES AND REASON makes so much sense to me. A research theater is exactly the kind of collaborative environment within which and through which I can realize REB'S LAST FUNERAL: RESOLUTION OF INVISIBLE WHIPS. This will be my project during my year's residency: to compose music; seek/collaborate with a librettist; look for the appropriate "voice" of mood, setting, and history; investigate drama as both a stylistic device and a cultural artifact/weapon/image within the African American world of the 1920s, 1930s, and 1940s. All of this research with an eye on the proper development of my opera or musical play or whatever we decide to finally name it.

REB'S LAST FUNERAL: RESOLUTION OF INVISIBLE WHIPS is a stretch that grows out of my work and interpretation of African American musical traditions. It is also a focus, or rather has become *the* focus of my interests and expertise in not only music but cultural history and criticism, literature, mass media study, theology, and teaching: You know, stuff.

Specifically, the opera grew from the seed for a large piece for orchestra, jazz band, and gospel choir, which I composed and premiered in 1984. This piece was called simply REB!

The dramatic core of the opera is the same as the thread that binds the earlier piece, REB; that is, the funeral of the Reverend C. D. Dowling, a Baptist preacher of long-standing in rural South Carolina. Reverend Dowling was/is my maternal grandfather. Now, Reb, the reverend, has presided at many funerals, as well as births, marriages, and other gatherings. By living and being himself, he has produced both physically and symbolically a diverse web of family (extended and not), friends and situations: These are the invisible whips whose resolutions are brought about by the death of this great and small man of the African American persuasion. As the story/stories/myths unfold on stage, the styles of dress and voice and movement and attitude and theology and survival are the content of this drama in the making. These styles, when expressed through music, become the form of the opera. At once a flashback drama (akin, perhaps, to *A Soldier's Story*) and a study of the mythical nature of folks and folklore (akin perhaps, to the work of Ishmael Reed or Toni Morrison or Ntozake Shange), the "opera" will proceed as a presentation of the mixtures of blues and gospel and jazz and other specific musical styles or genres. The chorus is to be a gospel choir. The orchestra will be a big jazz band augmented with strings and additional winds, and always informed by the jazz/blues performance practices.

This is what the opera started out to be, and this is the idea (along with score and recording of REB!) for which I was awarded an Individual Artist's Grant from the Connecticut Commission on the Arts in 1985. By February 1986, I was able to mount a small scene from the work in progress in which Whips appears as a three-personed being who confronts Reb at Reb's funeral and "they" all exchange theological dogma. Whips and the mobile, dead Reb are invisible to the very energetic on-stage choir, so that the audience is confronted with serious doubts and questions about the nature of reality in this play.

Which is to say that my project at Rites and Reason is to be the creative/research/presentations collaboration that I've come to know is absolutely necessary for this opera's development—and mine. I know for certain that I cannot create this work in a room alone, but rather it must be done in a workshop, but a workshop of a special kind. Turning ideas into dramatic situations that live and breathe is part of the craft of theater: I must learn/research/experience this craft.

The complex intertwining of the minstrel traditions and performance practices and images with the development of ragtime and classic blues and vaudeville and TOBA Tent Shows and American popular music from non–African American sources are made even more complex when discussed and/or lived within the context of sacred African American music (spirituals, hymns, gospels, and others). What and how all of this music means to each other and to the development of, say, a jazz tradition and an "Art Music" tradition during the Harlem Renaissance are very important and dramatic matters for the characters in an opera whose main character resists "the call" to preach in 1926 in favor of "the street," only to relent a few years later. And they are important matters for the actors who make the characters come alive (in song!) on stage; and they are important matters for the composer and librettist who may or may not have ever heard the sounds before; and they are important matters for the audience who must decide what and how and if these things mean anything.

Which is why RITES AND REASON makes so much sense to me. Research facilities and willing colleagues make my queries into the critical posture of the Harlem Renaissance intellectuals vis-à-vis jazz music and blues music and "American Art Music" have focus and result. Collected artifacts and documents of the minstrel tradition will become sources for both the "music creative" impulse and the "scholarly critical" impulse: how the music sounded and how the music meant are equally important questions for me and my opera.

So, an experiment in large ensembles, an extension of teaching/creating, a "stretch" has become the kernel (colonel?) for a much larger work, an opera. The form and efforts are/will be new, but/and the motivations are grounded in a more clearly understood and more readily articulated aesthetic.

TJBJ

TJ is, of course, Thad Jones. BJ is Big Jack, Big Jack Lowe, father of Bill Lowe. TJBJ is for progenitors. BJ, now deceased, was a living father who used to be a musician (guitar) in Chicago and Pittsburgh; leader—as Jack Spruce—of the Pittsburgh Cotton Pickers (some of the band was from Pittsburgh and nobody picked cotton, except from ladies' navels, but that's another sexist story). Members of his band included, at one time or another, Billie Eckstine, Danny Barker, Quentin "Butter" Jackson, Eddie Barefield, and Eddie Durham, to name-drop a few World War II, family, and responsibilities ended BJ's professional career.

Death ended Thad Jones's career at too early an age: This, though, is another important part of the African American aesthetic environment—the folks leave all too soon. TJBJ was written before Thad Jones died. It's not like his music, and yet it is. Another duad piece: two parts, two related colors that match/work after you've thought about it for a while.

Thad Jones and his orchestra and his writing were, and still are, living metaphors for that very sophisticated and tasty kind of big band elegance and excellence that is sometimes referred to as "controlled confusion." Thad's music was simple, until you thought about it, or tried to sight read it on a Monday night live at the Vanguard. Thad's really "difficult" music provided surprisingly simple, groovy solutions. And he always did swing, and oh, so hard!!

Which is why (partially) Thad's example is so much a part of the NEVERS! What's a NEVERS! you ask? Well . . .

DECISIONS (A.K.A. DE NEVERS)

Ten "paid" rehearsal sessions are to become a series of pieces constructed and performed as improvised choreographies by the NEVERS quartet: Sharon Freeman (pianist, hornist, composer, actor, vocalist, dancer); Mickey Davidson (dancer, choreographer, actor, vocalist, percussionist); Cecil Bridgewater (trumpeter, composer, actor, dancer); Bill Lowe (trombonist, tubaist, composer, actor, dancer). An essential part of the pieces will be the direction of the decisions as to which combinations of voices the quartet will bring to bear on each moment: Change is always possible. As a starting point within the collaboration, each of us has agreed to design a section of "stuff" to be considered and to manifest within the totality of the group. The "stuff" can be historical gestures (for example, Cecil's pledge to the "story" of second line marching and 1920's dance bands) or concept gestures (for example, Sharon's concern with mirrors, what they see in us: how we project ourselves and how we exist as reflections of ourselves and each other). The "stuff" can be material (for example, Mickey's promise of props and hot costuming). The stuff can be about completed forms (for example, Bill's pledge to bring some poems to the first session: perhaps some Hughes and/or Shange and/or Kuminyaka). This combined stuff becomes our immediate source. *How* we do the stuff will be as important as *what* we do with it.

Our project is a process we have already begun. Our project is OUR project: not Mickey's, not Sharon's, not Cecil's, not Bill's. We are our project and our process includes recognition of who we are: four multitalented, mature, and growing practitioners of African American expressive arts who together and apart have done and do (due) the "work dance of peers and masters." We have each danced for and through and with and in spite of the masters and our traditions which precede, define, and nurture us: Now is our time, our time to come together by choice, not by the chance of his gig or her dance company or their class or your theater.

It is our time to make pieces. We will make pieces about decisions, about the NEVERS. Because we four are all composer/improvisers, we will manipulate the notes and music of lives as lived and as perceived in the varied modes of African American expression. Because Mickey has made space for us to see that we four are also dancer/singers (which we suspected all along?), our pieces will be structured and free. Our performance space(s) will be zones of stage placements and zones of energy sources. We will be free to draw on the maps and rhythms and stylistic gestures of our traditions in order to tell stories that may have no narrative; and/or create narrative as an event, without a story. Each of us is an instrument; each of us "plays" several instruments. Our pieces will be rich in varied textures of sound/movements/voice: The decisions of sound/movement/voice textures will be the points of the pieces. In these pieces, we will not be confined by the necessity to tell the old stories well: Well-told old stories will become the stuff we use to improvise/compose/dance the new piece. In these pieces, we will attempt to function as a quartet of improvising composer/dancers consciously informed by our knowledge of the traditions of African American music, dance, theater, poetry and story telling. Dancer, trumpeter, tubaist, composer must all give way without giving up what is strong and therefore necessary about each set of specific skills/modes of expression.

Sharing and redefining of roles and models are desired states of piece/peace making in this collaboration. Each member of the quartet is a vital member of the quartet. Each member's value is a function of not only skill/expertise (of which there is no shortage), but is also a function of personal power and vision: Remember, we chose each other within a working environment dominated by professional situations that bring together groups of talented but not necessarily connected people. Travel and time commitment issues necessitate that the grant budget be focused on artist fees only. We plan ten (10) paid "rehearsal" sessions in March, April, and May, culminating in a public performance at Real Art Ways in late May.[16] The grant money enables us to afford to remove ourselves from the general work arena for the ten days of collaboration/creation. Theses sessions will follow the general mode of operation described above: Each session will create a new map of decisions, a new reorganization of voices, roles, and models. Each session will create another set of NEVERS. As we proceed, the interdisciplinary nature of the effort becomes less and less THE ISSUE and more and more THE STUFF. The opportunity to make pieces that are about the shifts and changes of the African American modes of expression is at once a privilege and an aesthetic necessity.

The NEVERS! is/are a new direction, which is old stuff. Old, because we age, as humans often do. We age and assume other responsibilities. Thad's gone; it's on us. Stylistic devices are, after all, just tools of the trade: skillful implements of meaningful manipulation.

Compositions and commentary toward an African American aesthetic constitute a serious indulgence. And yet, dues are a necessity. Being able to shape your own dues is a wonderful luxury, and its what we need, now.

NIAMBI'S DANCE

NIAMBI'S DANCE is a direct response to the study of solkatu[17] with T. Ranganathan. The composition is not intended to be some "fusion" of African American and South Indian music or rhythmic theories. The student in no way "mastered" solkatu or South Indian music. What the student did was to approach Mr. Ranganathan in order to develop a language and thereby act as a bridge between Ranga and Ed Blackwell. The real goal was to create an opportunity for Blackwell and Ranga to perform together. The premier of NIAMBI'S DANCE[18] was the culmination of a very particular job of work with some very specific and particular musicians.

Student Lowe felt that a piece could be created for the two master drummers, if only some language could be developed to allow Ed and Ranga to discourse about their very different and similar approaches to rhythm. After several months of study with Ranga, Lowe spoke with Blackwell about these new conceptual tools. Ed's response was a classic: "Bill, it's all in 4/4 no matter what you say!"

Ed heard what he heard, how he heard it. There was mutual respect between the two master drummers, without any false "guru" worship. And when the two master drummers met in Lowe's composition, they just "did drums."

The link, the bridge, was of course the music itself. Ed understood NIAMBI'S DANCE in his way, Ranga dealt in his. Because the composition was created in the midst of the three conversations, it (the composition) was about the conversation. Listen to the music.[19] "Since 1971, I. (Leo Smith) have been concerned with creating alternatives for a world music, one which utilizes the fundamental laws of improvisation and composition while retaining a uniqueness of its own.[20]

NIAMBI'S DANCE is constructed around a repeating eleven-beat cycle. There are three original lines, each of which approaches the eleven-beat cycle in different ways. If the eleven is thought of as 11/2, then one line is a repeating phrase of 3/2–3/2–3/2–2/2 (this line is manifest in the first measure of the fifth trombone part on the Big Band score). Another is a syncopated eighth-note figure, that is best thought of as 6/4–6/4–6/4–4/4 (the tuba line in the opening of the score).

The final line (which first appears in the soprano saxophone part) results from a subdivision to eighth notes, and then grouping the eighth notes in a pattern of 7–7–7–7–7–9, which adds up to 44 eighth notes or 22 quarters or, as desired, 11 half notes. But, that's math: The composer heard the patterns long before he was able to articulate them to anyone else.

There is much more to the composition than counting to eleven. There is humor, there is intensity. There is the decision to have a funky, blues-based back beat à la 1960's R & B, as the prime rhythm source from the trap drummer: The old New Orleans back beat becomes the glue for an African American exploration of South Indian rhythm sense. In the Big Band and JUBA versions, other lines are added in the horns, which investigate yet further ways to manifest the eleven-beat cycle: ways which swing. Indeed, the entire composition then becomes a very direct, uncomplicated, danceable funk piece, which disguises but does not obliterate the niceties of the attempts at enslavement by European and Euro-American hegemony. Somehow, the enslaved and descendants of the enslaved have been able to give music to the enslavers and still survive culturally, if not militarily and economically. This dichotomy of interests and designs must be recognized within the aesthetic discourse: recognized but not legitimized or made to seem as nostalgia. During cultural warfare, aesthetic positions become informed political positions. Or not. When in doubt, listen to the music.

MIBHAW

From the SWEET CHILDE SUITE comes MIBHAW: a study in disguise. The ballad-like opening melody is at first disguised as a double time, Latin American rave up, which it is. In both big and small band versions, the introduction's harmonic structure is improvised.

Even the title is a disguise, an anagram. The true title is from a Bill Lowe poem of 1968.

> Listen!!
> Listen!!
> Have you heard?
> Black,
> Like Mother

Is,
But Half a Word.

So that MIBHAW is really "Mother Is But Half A Word": Many possible meanings are implied and intended. The poem was written in response to many events of a cultural/political/personal nature, events that took place in London and New York and Newark and mostly in Lowe's head. The germ-idea for the composition was first presented in a concert as part of a 1968 summer music retreat attended by all the "New Music," "Avant Guarde," "Post-Coltrane," "Young Lions" from London, including one four-eyed, not quite balding New Jersey expatriate: Of course, they all loved Lowe's piece. The retreat, which included heavy debates over transcriptions of Miles Davis's solos and a healthy polemic about the universality of the new music, took place at a technical college in Glamorgan, Wales, which is a long way from London. And London is a long way from Newark and Trenton, New Jersey.

Mother, you see, is but half a word. Even Balding Trombonists have to begin their memoirs somewhere. At long last, it begins.

Thinking about Blackside School Days/Daze in 1988[21] leads me to Newark, 1967. Stokley (but now we call him Kwame!) Story: state staff time spent to determine for sure that Kwame was at least in the air over Newark within twenty-four hours of the "riot." Long distance agitating, by a bad-ass brother.

But, I was not seriously, physically hurt (scratches on my back; bad back dragged across the street with broken glass in my shirt, dirtying my fucking seerSUCKER sport coat!!) all to protect my white Dodge Dart with red vinyl upholstery and an expired inspection sticker.

On that day(s), Niggers died. Bullets crushed bone.

Hot metal lodged in black, pink flesh: violating the flesh, the bloods.

The TRENTONIAN front page the next day ran my story, with BYLINE under a picture of another bloody/bloodied/blood, who may have died, but remained misidentified, DidRag around his head.

All I did was to misread. All I did was to be confused about my constituency. I felt stupid for several weeks. In a guilty fog waiting for everybody, everyBLOODbody to yell out loud, NIGGER, WHAT WERE YOU THINKING ABOUT!! YOU WEREN'T THINKING, ABOUT! (Umh, umh, umh, the boy done went to college and got his brain fried) I mean, I walked *towards* the fucking cops after they had already announced that they were out to kick black ass; after they had already rioted there/their way out of that police station; after they had already demonstrated that any black man or woman walking in their direction must be a bad nigger, agitated from on high by Stokley/Kwame, hell bent on revolutionary fuckery of the highest (lowest, by definition) order. I mean, me and my seerSUCKER sports coat and matching press card (in my pocket instead of ON my pocket where Tom Johnson and everybody else with a sense had theirs, noticeable—very) walking back across the street towards the station, going to check on my car, for heavens sake!

That's how I got into Tom Hayden's buck/book, *Rebellion in Newark* or whatever the hell it was/is called (more sloppy scholarship). That day I became a "tall, thin Negro reporter" on the scene, covering the "riot that didn't happen" that did; checking out the police force (black cops directed traffic while white cops kicked ass); the "roving bands of Negro Youth" (not to be confused with the "bands of roving Negro Youth"); the "looters," "rioters," and CORPSES (I didn't get to see any of these up close and personal).

That's how I got on TV. But I never got to see the TV film because *they* subpoenaed the motherfucker so that I couldn't use it to prove that I had been beaten, on TV, in my seerFuckingSUCKER sport coat: on the job, being a journalist, and "almost" an intellectual.

Editor Gil said I was *almost* an intellectual right after the Newark police department AID man left the office—after telling me and Gil that what I saw happen didn't happen; and maybe Gil should just send me to safe, quiet city council meetings and me waiting for Gil to tell this cracker cop that I'm not a bumbling BOY, but one of his (Gil's) (but he's a cracker, too) staff writers, a professional journalist whose Pulitzer bound story was run front page with a BYLINE, thereby validating professionalism, and other Spencer Tracy shit like that; me waiting for Gil to drop this professional journalism dime on this cracker mother fucker and me thinking how I'm going to be real cool when Gil drops this dime and not laugh in this cracker cop's face cause that might upset the professional relationship we would all need for the follow up story; me waitin' for Gil to drop this dime . . . waitin' . . . waitin'. . . . And then the cracker cop left, but only after he finally spoke TO me instead of about me to my cracker editor in chief, this cracker cop turns to me and says, "Well, if you still say that some of our officers beat you while you were on the ground trying to get your press card out of your back pocket, if that's what happened, what were their badge numbers, huh?!?" So I said, "My momma never told me what to do when three cops were beatin' me with their billy clubs, she never told me to check their fucking badge numbers!" (Black mothers do so little to prepare their man-childs for this world.) And I'm still waiting for Gil to drop this dime or a nickel or something. . . . Anyway, the cracker cop says, "Well why not come up to Newark, to POLICE HEADQUARTERS, down in the basement where the staff photo books are and go through and see if you recognize anybody." (Like your momma, I should have said, but didn't) Besides, I'm still waiting for Gil to drop this dime and back me the FUCK UP! i WORK FOR YOU, ASSHOLE i'M YOUR STAR ASS REPORTER, WHOSE PROFESSIONALISM IS BEING ATTACKED BY THIS SEMIRETIRED NEANDERTHAL!

<<A clear case of mistaken identity, of misreading, of>>
<<being confused about my constituency. I mean, I was>>
<<ready, willing and able to assume my role as a snob>>
<<an intellectual snob with, my buddy Gil, together>>
<<snobbing this cracker cop. Only, I had forgotten>>
<<that Gil was/is a cracker, too!! Imagine, trying to>>
<<argue for my veracity in the midst of two crackers>>
<<who were used to Niggers being whatever Niggers are>>
<<supposed to be, which sure as hell ain't got nothing>>

<<to do with the professional pride of some skinny, four>>
<<eyed black motherfucker in or out of a blue and white>>
<<seerFuckingSUCKER sport coat. There is much to learn>>
And when the cracker cop finally left, Gil, having dropped nary a dime of professional support, ran this shit about how I was *almost* an intellectual; and how
with his brains and my connections we could win a Pulitzer, and all I had to do
was go undercover in Detroit to join the Black Panthers, and then let him and the
world know if and when the revolution was coming, really, that's what he wanted
"us" to do.

Then I went home . . .

Where BJ had his linoleum knife out, sitting on the front porch looking for
somebody to cut, because his oldest son got his ass kicked being an educated fool
in the Newark Riots. But that's another story . . .

Not to mention Jackie McClean and the Black Power conference and Paul Ylv-
isaker and my meeting with the NJ Secretary of State and the NAACP Legal Defense
which wasn't.

And then I went to London.

CODA

Myth is the voyage of exploration in this metaphysical space. The point
of departure is the first meeting between the quick and the dead.[22]

Yeah, but have you met Thad Jones, Ms. Deren? What happens to a
dream deferred? Jones and Deren are/were writers of extraordinary skill
and depth and wit and wisdom. He wrote music beyond words. She wrote
words that swing like music. If there is a heaven, do they meet? They meet
in Lowe's dreams, deferred. Every time one of the musicians dies, we say
that the heavenly band just got another recruit. Just imagine, just dream,
Thad Jones is playing trumpet in Dukes' band: but, while Thad was here
and Duke wasn't, we all said that Thad had inherited Duke's way with the
music—was wearing Duke's mantle. Will Thad give Duke his mantle back?
Will Thad have to return his inheritance, just so he can play third trumpet
in the man's band? And whose band will Maya write for? or whose publishing house? Will she hang out with Joseph Campbell? Will she become
a *houngon*? Are there *houngons* in heaven? or is there a special heaven for
houngons? And when you're in heaven, do you get angry because we turn
you into stylistic devices? Will you make a film of heaven, experimentally?
Will anybody see it? Maybe in my dreams, deferred? Will Thad write the
score for the soundtrack? Will God produce?

Say, have you met Thad Jones, Ms. Deren?

Have you?

Black, like mother is, but half a word . . .

Just, listen to the music.

NOTES

1. Samuel R. Delany, *The American Shore: Meditations on a Tale of Science Fiction by Thomas M. Disch* (Elizabethtown, N.Y.: Dragon Press, 1978), 2.

2. Marion Brown, *Recollections: Essays, Drawings, Miscellanea* (Frankfurt: Juergen A. Schmitt Publikationen, 1984).

3. Bill Dixon, *L'opera: A Collection of Letters, Writings, Musical Scores, Drawings and Photographs* (North Bennington, Vt.: Metamorphosis, BMI, 1986).

4. George Russell, *The Lydian Chromatic Concept of Tonal Organization For Improvisation* (New York: Concept Publishing Company, 1959).

5. William C. Lowe, *Paying Dues: Compositions and Commentary Toward an African American Aesthetic* (MA Thesis, Wesleyan University, Middletown, Connecticut, 1989).

6. REB! and other compositions are being prepared for release as a Composer's Compilation, available as a Compact Disk format.

7. Maya Deren, *Divine Horseman: The Living Gods of Haiti* (New York: McPherson & Co.,), 23.

8. Ibid., 23.

9. When all of the "possible" notes in our system of music are laid out in one octave—from C to C—they form the "chromatic scale," which consists of twelve tones. The familiar major scale (as heard in the "do a deer" ditty from the *Sound of Music*—do, re, mi, fa, sol, la, ti, do) and other diatonic scales contain seven tones. The Oriental-sounding scale produced by playing only the black keys on a piano is called a pentatonic—five note—scale. Simple number manipulation generates the concept of a diatonic scale (seven tones) and its pentatonic complement. Thus, in one octave on the piano, C to C, the white notes produce the diatonic scale of C major, while the five remaining black keys are its pentatonic complement.

10. The late Hattie M. Dowling, who taught the author to read as a part of the gift of literacy, often sang this rather postmodernly frightening slave lullaby to her first-born grandchild: "Go to sleep/Go to sleep/Go to sleep, mammy's baby/When you wake/Find sweet cake/All the pretty little horses/Old black sheep/She had a little lamb/Left him down in the valley/The bees and the butterflies/Pick out he eyes/And the poor little thing cried/Mammy, Mammy!!"

11. See Ishmael Reed, *Mumbo Jumbo* (New York: Macmillan Publishing Company, 1972).

12. Paul Carter Harrison, *The Drama of Nommo* (New York: Grove Press, Inc., 1972), xxiii.

13. Horace Clarence Boyer, "Charles Albert Tindley Progenitor of Black-American Gospel Music," in *The Black Perspective in Music* 11, no. 2 (fall 1983): 103.

14. Anthony Heilbut, *The Gospel Sound* (New York: Limelight Editions, 1985), 30.

15. Nathaniel Mackey, *Bedouin Hornbook* (Lexington: University of Kentucky, Callaloo Fiction Series, 1986).

16. Proposed for presentation in 1988 at the Hartford, Connecticut, new music and art venue, THE NEVERS project was never funded. However, the concepts and commitments remain valid as working guides for a particular kind of work. Nearly a decade later, the members of the quartet remain in touch professionally

and personally but never as THE NEVERS. Deferred projects, like dreams, are active creative spaces from which grow other projects, other dreams, other deferrals. Often, the very formulation of an idea into a project unleashes and reforms creative energy.

17. Solkatu is a system for studying the "talas" or rhythmic patterns of South Indian temple music using a combination of hand claps and designated syllables. In a way, solkatu is analogous to the solfège—do, re, mi, fa, sol, la, ti, do—use of sung syllables as ear-training devices in Euro-American music. T. Ranganathan was a master of the mridangam, a two-headed drum of South India, and was a colleague as well a friend and teacher.

18. Premier performance of "NIAMBI'S DANCE" with T. Ranganathan, mridangam; Wes Brown, bass; Ed Blackwell, trap drum set; Leonard Brown, soprano saxophone; Bill Lowe, bass trombone, World Music Hall, Wesleyan University, December 12, 1980.

19. The first commercially available recording of "NIAMBI'S DANCE" can be heard on side one, cut two from the sound recording *Look On The Rainbow* (JRT 001) performed by JUBA, with Royal Hartigan, drums; Kevin McNeal, guitar; Wes Brown, bass; Bill Lowe, bass trombone; David Bindman, soprano saxophone, on May 22, 1986.

20. Leo Smith, liner notes to his album *Divine Love*. (ECM-1-1143), 9/23/1978.

21. The author's participation with the preproduction seminar for Blackside's film documentary "Eyes On The Prize, II," prompted this reflection. The panel's concern was the interconnections of changes in the creation and motivation of Black music during the latter 1960s and early 1970s as the mood of the Civil Rights movement shifted from accommodation to resistance. The politics of music and the music of politics are dynamic strains in the development of an African American aesthetic.

22. Deren, *Divine Horseman*, 24.

8

Sacred Music for Secular Space: In Honor of John Coltrane

Leonard L. Brown

In these first days of the twenty-first century, most of the world's societies and cultures have been impacted, to varying degrees, by the power of African American music. The global appreciation, acceptance, and emulation of such African American music styles as spirituals, blues, ragtime, gospel, jazz, swing, funk, rhythm and blues, hip-hop, and rap speak clearly to the inherent human qualities and vitality of life expressed by African American musicians in their music. Of the various types of contemporary African American music to ascend to international appreciation, acceptance and, in some cases, reverence, the music commonly known as jazz and the African American musicians who created and played it have had the greatest impact. In its brief lifetime of about one hundred years, jazz has captured the hearts and souls of untold numbers of listeners and music lovers of all races, sexes, ages, languages, and cultures. The universal embracing of this expressive and improvisational form of African American music is nothing short of phenomenal. Jazz festivals celebrating the traditions and innovations of this creative improvisational music are held throughout the world.

Of the many African American musicians who have made outstanding and lasting innovative contributions to the evolution of the creative improvisational music styles commonly known as jazz, one of the most revered is saxophonist John Coltrane. During a performance career that lasted two decades (1947 to 1967), Coltrane established himself as one of the truly great innovators and creators. Combining his advanced musical concepts, approaches, and vast depth of musical knowledge, understanding, and creativity with outstanding instrumental technique, Coltrane created unique, moving, and powerful styles of improvisational music performance that expanded jazz. His approaches to tone, timbre, form, phrasing, melody, harmony, and rhythm altered conceptions of jazz. He expanded the range of the tenor saxophone to over three octaves and pioneered new approaches to saxophone technique and performance. Coltrane was also a main contributor to the development of "free" approaches to improvisation in which the standard western concepts of meter and time become dispensable. A number of his compositions have become part of the standard jazz repertoire and, even today, some thirty years after his death, his musical legacy continues to have a dominant impact.

Possibly the most enduring and endearing aspect of Coltrane's music is his sound and its ability to express sincerity, integrity, conviction, and other deep human values. His distinctive sound stirs the feelings and stimulates the imagination of listeners. One can directly trace these aspects of Coltrane's music to his nurturing and development in the African American community of High Point, North Carolina, from the mid-1920s to the early 1940s. During these formative years, Coltrane was exposed to the essential aspects of the aesthetics of African American sacred music. At a young age, he attended worship services at the A.M.E. Zion Church in High Point, North Carolina, where his grandfather served as presiding elder. The worship services featured the religious music repertoire of the black church. This was a predominantly vocal music rooted in African performance traditions that valued group participation and freedom of expression. This music was also multicontextual in that, not only could it be used for church worship services, but it was sung outside of the "sacred" church context in many "secular" aspects of daily life in the African American community. Spirituals could be sung at birthdays, while cooking dinner, while planting or harvesting, or while sitting and rocking.

Spirituals provided African Americans a direct link with the supernatural, religious, and mystical aspects of African American life that transcended the western concepts of sacred and secular. For instance, the role and function of African American sacred music in preparing for the spirit's descent in worship services is a well-documented fact. And just as well documented are the roles and functions of spirituals in secular contexts. For example, the earliest (and contemporary) repertoire of New Orleans jazz musicians included such songs as "When The Saints Go Marching In" and "Nearer My God To Thee." These and other spirituals were always a part of the second line music and dance that happened on the way back from a burial in the cemetery. In another instance, "Swing Low, Sweet Chariot" was used as a signal song to alert the enslaved to the coming of the "Underground Railroad." One of the strongest legacies of the spirituals was their ability to help provide strength and maintain hope for over 200 years of enslavement when African Americans struggled to survive in the face of daily oppression, exploitation, and death. This musical legacy of African American strength, survival rooted in spirituality, was a fundamental part of the culture of the black community that shaped and molded Coltrane's moral beliefs, views, perspectives, opinions and convictions . . . and these became the fundamental principles of his music.

Coltrane clearly saw his music as having the purpose of elevating humanity. In a November 1966 interview conducted by Frank Kofsky, Coltrane said, "I want to be a force for real good. In other words, I know that there are bad forces, I know there are forces out here that bring suffering to others and misery to the world. But I want to be the opposite force. I want to be the force which is truly for good."[1]

Through this conviction to use his music as a force for good, much of Coltrane's music took on a sacred quality regardless of the context for performance. Most notably from 1962 onward, his recordings and live performances had an increased feeling of spirituality that was unique and captivating. Clubs and other secular performance venues were transformed (however temporarily) to sacred places because of Coltrane's intent. McCoy Tyner, pianist with the Coltrane Quartet from 1960 to 1965, spoke of his experiences while playing in what is considered the classic Coltrane quartet. (It also included Jimmy Garrison playing bass and Elvin Jones playing drums.) "It was a tremendous learning experience for me and it reached the point where it was actually a jubilant experience, being on stage with them."[2]

Tyner's use of the word *jubilant* is most significant because it provides clear insight into the sacred intent of Coltrane's music. Jubilant is synonymous with exultant, triumphant, elated, exhilarated, overjoyed, and ecstatic. These terms are often used, in a descriptive sense, in reference to sacred contexts, but most of Tyner's performances with Coltrane were in secular venues.

Coltrane performed music that was intended to influence people to change things for the betterment of all mankind. In the 1966 interview by Kofsky, when asked about whether he uses his music to express the need for social change, Coltrane had this to say: "Well, I tell you. Myself, I make a conscious attempt through music to change what I have found. In other words I've tried to say this, I feel, could be better, in my opinion. So I will try to do this to make it better. This is what I feel that we feel in any situation in our lives, when there is something that we feel should be better, we must exert effort to try and make it better. So it is the same socially, musically, politically, in any department you like."[3]

Coltrane used his music to express the need for brotherhood and harmony. When questioned about jazz being against poverty and suffering and war (speaking about Vietnam specifically), he responded: "Well in my opinion I would say yes [that jazz is opposed to poverty and suffering and war] because I believe that, to me, the music is an expression of a higher ideal. Therefore brotherhood is a part of it and I believe with brotherhood there would be no poverty and also with brotherhood there would be no war."

An examination of some of the titles of Coltrane's compositions provides additional insight into the spiritual nature and intent of this remarkable musician and human being. Consider the following: "Dear Lord," "Amen," "Prayer and Affirmation," "Four AM in the Morning Vigil," "A Love Supreme," "The Revered King," "Compassion," and "Meditations." These songs were all created and recorded during the last two years of Coltrane's life when his music took on increased religious significance and featured performances that were trance like, full of power and beauty and emotionally uplifting and, for some listeners, draining.

But his earlier music also had spiritual overtones. For example, his composition "The Spiritual" (Live at The Village Vanguard, Impulse A-10) and his version of the African American traditional "Song of the Underground Railroad" (Africa/Brass Sessions Vol. 2, Impulse Records AS9273) illustrate his knowledge of and respect for two older African American music forms that are two of the "grandparents" of jazz. The arrangement and improvisational performances on Coltrane's recording of "The Spiritual" clearly illustrate the African American performance traditions of group participation and freedom of expression found in the spirituals. Likewise, the recording of the "Song of the Underground Railroad" gives one a feeling of a freedom-bound train coming to get some passengers.

Coltrane's sound was one that was rooted in the vocal tradition of early African American music, sacred or secular. In a 1979 *Down Beat* magazine article, the saxophonist Archie Shepp pointed this out as follows: "His use of field hollers in his sound really connotes a thorough and passionate understanding of tradition."[4]

With the intention to be a force of good, Coltrane's outlook was very similar to the philosophies of the great masters of ancient times in their uses of music.

The effect of instrumental music also depends upon the evolution of the player, who expresses with the tips of his fingers upon the instrument his grade of evolution; in other words his soul speaks through the instrument. A person's state of mind can be read by his touch upon any instrument, for however great an expert he may be, he cannot produce by mere skill, without developed feeling within himself, the grace and beauty which appeal to the heart.

Wind instruments . . . express the heart quality, for they are played with the breath, which is the very life. Therefore they kindle the heart's fire.[5]

These words from the writings of the great Sufi mystic and master musician Hazrat Inayat Khan are most applicable to the spiritual legacy of John Coltrane. It was Coltrane's desire to be a force for good that helped him develop the faith, pursuance, discipline, and fortitude necessary to attain the goals he reached with his music. His incredible technique was developed through consistent hard work, and disciplined practice. The driving force behind his discipline and all his practicing and studying was his intent to be a force for good. Trane realized that to use music as a force for positive change required the highest level of instrumental mastery. He believed that by reaching this highest level of musical mastery, one could then effectively express what is in one's heart and have a positive and good effect on the listener.

Probably the best known Coltrane composition that reflected his spirituality is "A Love Supreme," a four-part suite that was released in 1964 (Impulse 77). This composition was meant as praise of and to God. From the opening notes of Acknowledgment, through the powerful and exciting Resolution, to the blues-based form of Pursuance, and finally the calming and meditative sounds of Psalm, Coltrane's intent could not be misinterpreted, dismissed, or ignored. John Sinclair's review of the recording in *Jazz* magazine (October 1965) provides more insight.

And "thank God" is what John Coltrane and group do in "A Love Supreme." Don't let the religious connection Coltrane makes bother you at all—you should rejoice in it. Coltrane has chosen to term the huge love in him "God," and he pays homage to it (Him) in this record. "A Love Supreme" is *soul* music, John Coltrane's soul (and not any of those cheap merchandisers), love music, free music, they're all the same thing. The composition moves from a religious base (*Acknowledgment*), into its resolution (*Resolution*), to the reality aspect—the blues (*Pursuance*), to abstractions of the totality ... (*Psalm*).[6]

John Coltrane was a unique soul, one who comes maybe every thousand years. Coltrane manifested the power and multifunctionality of African American music. He transcended the externally dictated and presupposed western considerations of context having to be sacred or secular. His music was and is able to transform the spaces and consciousness of the listener. And his music transcends time and stylistic definitions as illustrated on the most recent release of Coltrane's music, *Stellar Regions* on Impulse/MCA. Featuring quartet performances of his later sacred compositions and delayed from reaching the public ears for almost thirty years, this recording finds Coltrane still light years ahead of anything happening today. His music is fresh and exciting, full of integrity and sincerity of purpose.

According to the ancient scriptures (oral and written) of people worldwide, one of the main purposes of music in life is to lead to uplift and enlightenment, to establish and maintain moral consciousness and responsibility, and to assist in the continued spiritual evolution of humanity. Today, too many of us in the West (and the rest of the world) have lost sight of the real purpose of music and have relegated music to the mundane role of entertainment and marketing, rather than pursuing the higher purposes of this precious art. Perhaps reflecting on the legacy of John Coltrane will spur us to reconsider what a sacred gift we have in music and life and to rejoice in the great amount of love Coltrane gave to us through music. His gave us sacred music in secular spaces, and we should be thankful for his message.

NOTES

1. John Coltrane interview by Frank Kofsky (cassette tape), Pacifica Radio Archives (N. Hollywood, CA).

2. David Wild, "The Jubilant Experience of the Classic Quartet," *Down Beat*, 46, no. 13 (1979): 48.

3. John Coltrane interview by Frank Kofsky (cassette tape).

4. "Musicians Talk About John Coltrane," *Down Beat*, 46, no. 13 (1979): 20.

5. Hazrat Inayat Khan, *The Music of Life* (Santa Fe: Omega Press, 1983), 56.

6. John Sinclair, "A Love Supreme," *Jazz* 3, no. 4, (1965): 16–17.

Reflections and Suggestions for Further Reading

As satisfying, and even exciting as it is to write about music, it is also somewhat frustrating. Music can communicate ideas and feelings in ways that are often much more effective than words. Maybe that's why ages ago humans began to sing and why we have invented numerous instruments and musical grammars to express ourselves.

As interpreters of African American music the writers of *The Triumph of the Soul* therefore have not said anything that the music doesn't express better. We've used words, to illuminate what is beneath, around and over the melodies, rhythms, textures, and harmonies. Our aim in these "transcriptions" was to locate the music in the contexts of time and the dynamics of societal relationships. We obviously believe this is a worthwhile enterprise. It is important to acknowledge however, that if no words were ever written about African American music (or any other kind of music) its intent has, is, and will already be articulated in itself.

The authors of *The Triumph of the Soul* have instructed us to view African American music as a continuous creation. Its various forms are aspects of the on-going evolution of African American culture. The salient historical themes of cultural construction are therefore contained in the music; and African American values and styles as they have been elaborated and institutionalized are also always present.

African Americans are a people originated in oppression. Consequently they have had to construct positive self-views in order to supply their own self-esteem. This process of countering negative stereotypes is a persistent theme in their music. Self-affirmation is an inherent aspect of a distinctive cultural identity that has evolved over the generations of the African American presence in North America. Among other dimensions this identity is a synthesis of African and North American world-views, modes of thinking, expression and spirituality. Arthur Jones therefore tells us that the spirituals express a "synertistic merging of core African religious beliefs with distinctively Africanized Christianity." (p. 5) And Peter Aschoff says, "Blues religious imagery and philosophy can only be understood from an African theological perspective." (p. 39) The same ideas are elaborated by Michael White in his chapter on New Orleans brass bands when he refers to "the enslaved African's 'epic memory'." (p. 72) And in her discussion of rap music and contemporary African American street culture Cheryl Keyes makes a similar point: ". . . central [to understanding the rap music tradition] is viewing it as a part of the continuum of African-derived expressive forms." (p. 156)

All of the chapter authors have specifically related black American music to the African oral tradition. Leonard Brown in his essay, for example, makes a pertinent comment on John Coltrane when he says "Coltrane's sound was one that was rooted in the vocal tradition of early African American musics, sacred and secular." (p. 204)

The intricacies of the oral tradition plus a community versus an individualistic emphasis in self conception, and a holistic spirituality are all examples of sensibilities that contribute the West African base to the culture Africans developed in North America. The significance of documenting this fact here is to comprehend black music as part of a meaningful cultural whole that stems from a combination of past and present day experiences, including the indelibly significant but historically overlooked African heritage. The richness and vitality of the music indicates the distinctive identity and strength of African American culture and people.

Readers who want to learn more about the meaning of African American music in culture can find illuminating discussions in the following books and articles:

Barlow, William. *Looking Up at Down: The Emergence of Blues Culture*. Philadelphia: Temple University Press, 1989.

Cone, James H. *The Spirituals and the Blues: An Interpretation*. Maryknoll, N.Y.: Orbis Books, 1991 edition.

Ellison, Ralph. *Shadow and Act*. New York: Random House, 1953.

Holloway, Joseph E., ed. *Africanisms in American Culture*. Bloomington, Ind.: Indiana University Press, 1990.

Jackson-Brown, Irene V. ed. *More Than Dancing: Essays on Afro-American Music and Musicians*. Westport, Conn.: Greenwood Press, 1985.

Jones, LeRoi (Amiri Baraka). *Blues People*. New York: William Morrow, 1963.

Lomax, Alan. *The Land Where Blues Began*. New York: Pantheon Books, 1993.

Lovele, John, Jr. *Black Song, The Forge and the Flame: The Story of How the Afro-American Spiritual Was Hammered Out*. New York: Paragon House, 1986 edition.

Murray, Albert. *Stompin' The Blues*. New York: McGraw Hill, 1976.

Sidran, Ben. *Black Talk: How the Music of Black America Created a Radical Alternative to the Values of Western Literary Tradition*. New York: Holt, Rinehart & Winston, 1971.

Southern, Eileen. *The Music of Black Americans: A History* (Second edition). New York: W. W. Norton, 1983.

Walton, Ortiz M. *Music: Black, White and Blue*. New York: William Morrow, 1972.

Wilson, Olly. "The Influence of Jazz on the History and Development of Concert Music." In *New Perspectives on Jazz*. David N. Baker, ed. Washington, D.C.: Smithsonian Institution Press, 1990.

Artistic invention requires special self-confidence, or even audacity. The gifted artist knows without prior authentication that his or her productions will "work"— that she can communicate what she imagines and feels in a way that is personally gratifying and potentially also satisfying to a consumer of the art. Sufficient levels of self-confidence together with skills in dealing with life's challenges, enable most individuals, whether they are artists or not, to avoid crippling effects of trauma and hardship. The dominant American society however, has been slow to acknowledge the truth of African Americans' resilience, agency and talents. Black music is not only evidence in itself of these qualities, but it also indicates the means with which black Americans have prevailed and produced. In her chapter in *The Triumph of the Soul*, Angela Nelson explains, for example, "Having this outlet in music provides African Americans with a mechanism for dealing with life in America." (p. 116) And Ferdinand Jones explicating the *challenge* attitude that is a protective mind-set in black American culture describes how "Black instrumentalists and jazz singers . . . like African American storytellers, exercise resistance and self-definition." (p. 130) And the stance Michael White indicates as undergirding the popularity of brass band music in traditional New Orleans is the subject of his rhetorical question, "Instead of being consumed by anarchy, self-pity, and lament for one's condition, why not turn the situation around and 'celebrate' it?" (p. 81)

African American music is part of a cultural worldview that stimulates individuals to be mentally active and constructive. As Arthur Jones interprets the psychological processes involved in the creation of the spirituals for instance, they were "*in the imagination* to construct a different definition of life in the present." (p. 9, emphasis added). He also discusses the actual mental health benefits of singing black music, quoting Bernice Reagon Johnson: "Singing in the African American tradition is also effective because of the emotional and physiological changes that accompany production of sound in the body." (p. 18)

Readers can find additional discussions of African American psychological competence and resilience in the following references:

Cross, William E., Jr. *Shades of Black: Diversity in African-American Identity*. Philadelphia: Temple University Press, 1991.

Helms, Janet E. *Black and White Identity: Theory, Research and Practice*. Westport, Conn.: Greenwood Press, 1990.

Jenkins, Adelbert H. *Psychology and African-Americans, A Humanistic Approach*. Second edition. Boston: Allyn & Bacon, 1995.

Jones, Arthur C. *Wade in the Water: The Wisdom of the Spirituals*. Maryknoll, N.Y.: Orbis Books, 1993.

Levine, Lawrence. *Black Culture and Black Consciousness*. New York: Oxford University Press, 1977.

Majors, Richard, and Janet Billson Mancini. *Cool Pose: The Dilemmas of Black Manhood in America*. New York: Touchstone/Simon & Schuster, 1992.

Nobles, Wade W. "Extended Self: Rethinking the So-Called Negro Self-Concept."

In R. L. Jones, ed. *Black Psychology*, third edition. Berkeley: Cobb & Henry Publishers, 1991.

Musicians seek kinesthetic as well as aural entry into our senses. In the case of African derived music, this palpable dimension can even dominate mere listening. The spirituals, blues, ragtime, brass bands, rhythm and blues, jazz, and rap musics are therefore not only heard but also felt. Whether one is stimulated to actually move with the music or not, the kinesthetic component is central in the several elements of satisfaction its consumers receive. Indeed, one might rate the creative success of a song or instrumental rendering on the basis of how many different kinds of responses it evokes.

The authors of this book have spoken to the comprehensiveness of the various dimensions of black American music in this broadly alive sense. For instance, Leonard Brown even indicates a political aspect amidst the spiritual and aesthetic in John Coltrane's music: "Coltrane performed music that was intended to influence people to change things for the betterment of all mankind." (p. 203) Arthur Jones cites W. E. B. DuBois' tribute to the multidimensionality of the spirituals, ". . . the most beautiful expression of human experience," (p. 4) to highlight his assessment of their expressive range. Michael White notes "The brass band and related activities become a vehicle in which to express the aspirations, desires, spirit and needs of Black New Orleans." (p. 78) And Peter Aschoff also comments on the music's emotional breadth: "The blues accepts, enjoys and celebrates both the sacred and the profound sides of human nature." (p. 56)

Readers may want to also see the following discussions of how African American music expresses the range of human emotion and attitudes.

Brooks, Tilford. *America's Black Music Heritage*. Englewood Cliffs, N.J.: Prentice-Hall, 1984.

Oliver, Paul. *Blues Fell This Morning: Meaning in the Blues*. Second edition. New York: Cambridge University Press, 1990.

Reagon, Bernice Johnson. *Black American Culture and Scholarship, Contemporary Issues*. Washington, D.C.: Smithsonian Institution Press, 1985.

Spencer, Jon Michael. *Blues and Evil*. Knoxville, Tenn.: University of Tennessee Press, 1993.

———. *Protest and Praise: Sacred Music of Black Religion*. Minneapolis: Fortress Press, 1990.

The African American story is a remarkable one from many perspectives. What it documents of the psychological stamina of humans is especially impressive. It is certainly not the only historical chronicle of human resilience, of course. Through the ages survival from natural and human-made catastrophes has shown us the indomitable nature of the human spirit. African Americans have articulated their psychological survival in wondrously enduring sounds and rhythms. Their celebration of the infinite potential of the human spirit is infectious and inspirational. Ferdinand Jones in his chapter on resilience and jazz notes that "African American psychological adaptability is dramatic and unique," (p. 138) while he also asserts the universal humanity that it also indicates. And Leonard Brown states "The global appreciation, acceptance, and emulation of such African American music styles . . . speaks clearly to the inherent qualities and vitality of life expressed by African American musicians in their music." (p. 201) Michael White contributes this correlative comment on jazz: ". . . its very nature embodied and put into practice freedom of expression, unity, creativity, and competition." (p. 80) Peter Aschoff, elaborating the broad meaning of blues writes "The Blues is simultaneously a music, a traditional oral poetry, and a social and ritual experience." (p. 39)

Although there are not yet many other sources of information about African American music and what it says of the infinite potential of the human spirit, we look for future developments in the literature. These references however, touch on the subject:

Chernoff, John Miller. *African Rhythm and African Sensibility: Aesthetics and Social Action in African Idioms.* Chicago: University of Chicago Press, 1979.

Cone, James H. *The Spirituals and the Blues: An Interpretation.* Maryknoll, N.Y.: Orbis Books, 1991 edition.

Giddins, Gary. *Rhythm-A-Ning: Jazz Tradition and Innovation in the 80's.* New York: Oxford University Press, 1985.

Harding, Vincent. *There is a River: The Black Struggle for Freedom in America.* New York: Random House, 1981.

Cheryl Keyes and Angela Nelson have illustrated in their respective discourses on rap music and urban contemporary gospel in *The Triumph of the Soul*, that black American music being composed and performed today is ever innovative and increasingly influential worldwide. These genres plus blues and jazz are heard and adapted in all of the world's cultures. There is also a revival of interest in the spirituals, currently centered in the United States. And traditional New Orleans jazz is acquiring deserved appreciation and respect among contemporary American jazz musicians and their fans, matching the fascination it has always ironically had among European and Asian audiences. William Lowe's chapter in *The Triumph of the Soul* embodies many of the features of African American music that makes it unique and magnetic. For instance, he employs word play, metaphor, and other African American tropes to provide a sample of the kind of inventiveness that stimulates ever more aural inventiveness.

Many contemporary writers are struck by the way African American music has become the essence of a truly American music aesthetic. The following are examples of discussions of the African American influence in American and world music.

Baker, David N., ed. *New Perspectives on Jazz.* Washington: Smithsonian Institution Press, 1990.

Baker, Houston A. *Black Studies, Rap, and the Academy.* Chicago: University of Chicago Press, 1993.

Balliet, Whitney. *American Musicians II: Seventy-One Portraits in Jazz.* Oxford University Press, 1997.

Dyson, Michael. "Culture of Hip-Hop." *Zeta*, June 1989.

Fab 5 Freddy. *Words and Phrases of the Hip-Hop Generation*. Stamford, Conn.:
    Longmeadow Press, 1992.
Giddens, Gary. *Visions of Jazz: The First Century*. New York: Oxford University
    Press, 1998.
Gioa, Ted. *The History of Jazz*. New York: Oxford University Press, 1997.
Murray, Albert. *The Omni-Americans*. New York: Outerbridge & Dienstfrey (dis-
    tributed by E. P. Dutton), 1970.
Rose, Tricia. *Black Noise: Rap Music and Black Culture in Contemporary America*.
    Hanover, N.H.: Wesleyan University Press, 1994.

We also direct readers' attention to an excellent recorded series on the history, aesthetics and sociology of African American music that first aired on National Public Radio:

Reagon, Bernice Johnson, compiler. *Wade in the Water*. Vol. I, African American
    Spirituals: The Concert Tradition. Vol. II, African American Congregational
    Singing. Vol. III, African American Gospel: The Pioneering Composers. Vol.
    IV, African American Community Gospel. Washington, D.C.: Smithsonian
    Institution/Folkways Recordings, Compact Disc No. SF 40072, SF 40073,
    SF 40074, SF 40075, 1994.

F. J.
A. C. J.

Index

Contributors

PETER R. ASCHOFF, a cultural anthropologist, has taught anthropology and African American Studies at the University of Mississippi since 1986. His professional interest is in African American expressive culture, especially the blues. He has been a featured participant in four National Endowment for the Humanities–funded symposia on the blues and also in the annual Southern Studies Teachers Institute sponsored by the Center for the Study of Southern Culture. He is the storyline creator and principal historical consultant and writer for the Delta Blues Museum's exhibition hall relocation and expansion project in Clarksdale, Mississippi. He has produced a series of thirteen one-hour blues programs for National Public Radio, "Hello Blues . . . How You Feel Today?" He is a regular contributor to *Living Blues*. Mr. Aschoff also teaches Music and Culture in the Caribbean for the University of Southern Mississippi's Caribbean Studies Program in Jamaica.

LEONARD L. BROWN, an ethnomusicologist and specialist in multicultural education, is an Associate Professor in the Music and African American Studies departments at Northeastern University. He also serves as principal consulting ethnomusicologist and cultural historian to the American Jazz Museum in Kansas City where he developed and directs the Kansas City Institute for Jazz Performance and History. Additionally, he is the developer and organizer of the annual Charlie Parker Symposium at the American Jazz Museum. Dr. Brown is also a professional saxophonist, composer and arranger. During thirty years of performance, including with his group "Joyful Noise," he has appeared with many outstanding artists such as Alice Coltrane, Pharoah Saunders, George Russell, Bill Barron, Yusef Lateef, Alan Dawson and Ed Blackwell. He is the co-founder in 1977 and producer of the annual John Coltrane Memorial Concert in Boston.

ARTHUR C. JONES (Co-Editor) is Senior Clinical Professor of Psychology at the University of Denver and founder and Chair of *The Spirituals Project*, a Denver-based nonprofit agency concerned with keeping alive the rich legacy of sacred songs created and first sung by enslaved Africans in the eighteenth and nineteenth centuries. Most of his scholarship over the last ten years has been concerned with the cultural and psychological impact of the black spirituals. His book *Wade in the Water: The Wisdom of the Spirituals* received a First Book Award from the Catholic Press Association of America. An experienced singer, Professor Jones has performed lecture-concert programs on black spirituals nationwide, and has appeared as a featured soloist in opera, oratorio and recital programs. Under his direction, *The Spirituals Project* is developing a documentary program on black spirituals for public television.

FERDINAND JONES (Co-Editor) is Professor Emeritus of Psychology and the retired director of Psychological Services at Brown University. His study of jazz in African American culture combines a life-long love of the music with his observations from clinical practice. This scholarship represents his efforts to identify and articulate the psychological resources that enhance individuals' abilities to surmount internal and circumstantial obstacles to their development. Professor Jones researched jazz in culture as a Visiting Scholar at the Schomburg Center for Research in Black Culture in 1987. He taught jazz and its cultural context as a Visiting Professor at the University of Dar Es Salaam in Tanzania in 1993. He is a past president of the American Orthopsychiatric Association. He lectures extensively on jazz improvisation and African American adaptive styles. In addition to writing on the subject in his retirement he has also been a Visiting Professor at the Rhode Island School of Design, Oberlin College, the University of Cape Town, and Sarah Lawrence College.

MICHAEL S. HARPER is the author of nine books of poetry: *Songlines in Michaeltree*; *Honorable Amendments*; *Dear John, Dear Coltrane*; *History is Your Own Heartbeat*; *Song: I Want a Witness*; *Debridgement*; *Nightmare Becomes Responsibility*; *Images of Kin*; and *Healing Songs for the Inner Ear*. He has twice been nominated for the National Book Award and has been cited or given awards by the National Institute of Arts and Letters, the National Endowment for the Arts, and the Guggenheim Foundation. He is a Professor at Brown University.

CHERYL L. KEYES is an Assistant Professor of Ethnomusicology at the University of California, Los Angeles where she teaches core courses in ethnomusicology, popular music, African American music, and gender-related music issues. She has conducted extensive research on rap music in Mali (West Africa), London, New York City, Detroit, and Los Angeles. Her writings on this subject appear in *Ethnomusicology, Journal of American Folklore*, and in a forthcoming book tentatively titled, *Beats, Rhymes, and Street Science: Rap Music as a Phenomenon of Consciousness*. Professor Keyes has been cited as one of the country's most creative scholars of contemporary indigenous music.

WILLIAM C. LOWE is an Associate Professor of African American Studies, Education and Music at Northeastern University. In a parallel career he is also a composer and a performer on tuba and bass trombone. He has performed and recorded with countless celebrated artists including Sam Rivers, Dizzy Gillespie, Eartha Kitt, Clark Terry, Thad Jones/Mel Lewis, Slide Hampton, and Bill Barron as well as with various Broadway and symphonic orchestras. He is the co-producer and a featured soloist at the annual John Coltrane Memorial Concert in Boston. He is the co-leader of the Bill Lowe/Philippe Crettien Quintet. His opera, "Reb's Last Funeral: Resolution of Invisible Whips," received commissioning support from the Connecticut Commission for the Arts and Northeastern University. He has also taught at Wesleyan University, Yale University, and the City University of New York. His present research activities at Yale University involve contemporary science fiction writing, African American intellectual history, New World Aesthetics and popular culture theory.

ANGELA M. S. NELSON is Associate Professor of Popular Culture at Bowling Green State University. She received her Ph.D. from Bowling Green in Cultural Studies, and has been a student and collaborator of the ethnomusicologist Jon Michael Spencer. In addition to her scholarship dealing with black urban and contemporary gospel music, she has written on a wide variety of topics, ranging from the issue of black women in television situation comedies to the theology of hip hop. She is also the editor of the 1999 volume *"This is How We Flow": Rhythm in Black Cultures*. Beyond her work as a scholar of black music and black popular culture, Professor Nelson is also an accomplished singer. Her public performances have included programs of European classical music as well as recitals of spirituals, gospel music and black art songs.

MICHAEL G. WHITE is a Professor of Spanish and African American music at Xavier University in New Orleans. He is a jazz scholar, historian, clarinetist and band leader. He is a member of a New Orleans musical family that includes many artists who were active contributors to jazz in its earliest days. From his position as an authority on early jazz history, Dr. White seeks to promote a holistic approach to it, emphasizing the relatedness of the traditional music of New Orleans to all jazz and American music forms. He has been literally instrumental in bringing the vibrancy of traditional New Orleans jazz to national and international attention through the performances and recordings of his Original Liberty Jazz Band of New Orleans. He has also performed and recorded with innumerable other bands in the United States and abroad. He is most proud of his associations with over two dozen authentic jazz players born between 1896 and 1910. Dr. White is active in the program development of the Lincoln Center Jazz program in New York City. He lectures and writes extensively on jazz history and jazz musicians, and he has himself been the subject in over 400 periodicals worldwide.